ROYAL HISTORICAL SOCIETY
STUDIES IN HISTORY
SERIES
No. 32

FAITH BY STATUTE

Parliament and the Settlement of Religion, 1559

Recent volumes published in this series include

26   Julian S. Corbett, 1854-1922: Historian of British   *D. M. Schurman*
     Maritime Policy from Drake to Jellicoe

27   The Pilgrimage of Grace in the Lake Counties,   *S. M. Harrison*
     1536-1537

28   Money, Prices and Politics in Fifteenth-   *Angus MacKay*
     Century Castile

29   The Judicial Bench in England 1727-1875:   *Daniel Duman*
     The Reshaping of a Professional Elite

30   Estate Management in Eighteenth-Century England: *J. R. Wordie*
     The Building of the Leveson-Gower Fortune

31   Merchant Shipping and War: A Study of   *Martin Doughty*
     Defence Planning in Twentieth-Century Britain

For a complete list of the series please see pp.246-7

FAITH BY STATUTE

Parliament and the Settlement of Religion 1559

Norman L. Jones

LONDON: Royal Historical Society
NEW JERSEY: Humanities Press Inc
1982

The Society records its gratitude to the following, whose generosity made possible the initiation of this series: The British Academy; The Pilgrim Trust; The Twenty-Seven Foundation; The United States Embassy bicentennial funds; The Wolfson Trust; several private donors.

British Library Cataloguing in Publication Data

Jones, Norman L.
Faith by statute: Parliament and the Settlement of Religion 1559.
(Royal Historical Society Studies in history series; no. 32).
1. England and Wales. *Parliament*
2. Church of England — History
I. Title   II. Series
283'.42   BX5071

First published in Great Britain in 1982 by Swift Printers (Publishing) Ltd, London EC1
for The Royal Historical Society
and in the U.S.A. by Humanities Press Inc., Atlantic Highlands, NJ 07716

Printed in England by Swift Printers Ltd. London EC1

PREFACE

'Hasn't the Elizabethan Settlement been done?' I heard that reaction to the subject of this book many times while writing it, and each time I had to explain that it has been done but its history is not settled. The creation of the Anglican Church by Act of Parliament in 1559 occupies a strategic hill in English history that has been climbed by many historians on their way to other places, but few have stayed to admire the view. Oddly, no one has made a detailed, non-apologetic study of the Parliament that played midwife to Elizabeth's settlement of religion. This book is an attempt to correct that defficiency. It grew out of my 1977 Cambridge doctoral dissertation which, enlarged, revised, and rewritten, was awarded the Archbishop Cranmer Prize in Ecclesiastical History by Cambridge University in 1978.

Because the Settlement has been dealt with by so many I, like Bernard of Chartres, am conscious of standing on the shoulders of giants — scholars of the stature of Maitland and Pollard. In particular I am aware of the scholarly debt I owe the groundbreaking works of Professor Sir J.E. Neale. Although I often disagree with his interpretations, his writings have been a valuable guide to the Elizabethan Parliaments, and the questions he asked have stood before me as a fascinating challenge.

In a much deeper, more personal sense I wish to thank Professor G.R. Elton for his advice, inspiration, and friendship. He supervised my dissertation, read and improved the present work, and has been ever generous with his time and knowledge. His wife Sheila has also freely shared her wide knowledge of Parliamentary history with me, as well as her warm hospitality.

I am very aware of those in my personal history who have helped me along the way: my parents, who fed and encouraged a young bookworm; T.H. McDonald, who taught me what it meant to be an historian; and Carl Christensen, Boyd Hill, James Jankowski, and Stephen Fischer-Galati, who turned me into one. I have also appreciated the advice and gentle criticism provided by Wallace McCaffrey, Mrs. D.M. Owen, Patrick Collinson, and David Loades; the enthusiasm of my fellows in the Tudor Seminar at Cambridge; and the rapid typing of Sherry McCloud.

Since this book was completed and sent to the printer Winthrop S. Hudson's *The Cambridge Connection and the Elizabethan Settlement of 1559* (Durham, North Carolina, 1980) has appeared. Though

Professor Hudson and I have at times discussed the issues with which we both deal we reached our conclusions independently.

Another work which has appeared since this book went to the printers is T.E. Hartley's edition of *Proceeding in the Parliaments of Elizabeth I: I, 1558-1581*, published by Leicester University Press. Since this volume makes available many of the original documents in a reliable printed form it supercedes some of the sources I cited. Because Hartley collated the various texts my quotations sometimes vary from the texts as he prints them, however I have found no cases in which the variations have forced me to change my arguments. Indeed, the one document he prints which I missed in my research, Montague's speech on the supremacy bill, confirms many of the suppositions I made about that bill's content.

This book is dedicated to my best friend, Carolyn Rhodes-Jones, who is a fine historian and a wonderful wife.

Norman L. Jones

CONTENTS

List of Abbreviations   viii

Introduction   1

1   The Opening of the Reign   5

2   Preparing for the Change in Religion   31

3   The Membership of Parliament   61

4   Parliament Before Easter   83

5   The New Strategy for Reform   112

6   Parliament After Easter   138

7   Appropriation of Ecclesiastical Revenue, 1559   160

8   The Parliament of 1563   169

Conclusion   186

Appendices

A: Members of the House of Commons by County, 1559   190

Bibliography   215

Index   234

ABBREVIATIONS

APC	=	Acts of the Privy Council of England
ASV	=	Archivio Segreto Vaticano, Rome
B.L.	=	British Library, London
Cal. Pat. Rolls	=	*The Calendar of Patent Rolls*
Corp. London R.O.	=	Corporation of London Record Office, London
C.C.C.C.	=	Corpus Christi College, Cambridge
CSP For.	=	*Calendar of State Papers, Foreign Series, of the Reign of Elizabeth*
CSP Rome	=	*Calendar of State Papers, Relating to English Affairs, Preserved Principally at Rome, in the Vatican Archives and Library.* J.M. Rigg (ed.)
CSP Span.	=	*Calendar of Letters and State Papers Relating to English Affairs, Preserved Principally in the Archives of Simancas.* Martin S. Hume (ed.)
CSP Ven.	=	*Calendar of State Papers and Manuscripts, Relating to English Affairs, Existing in the Archives and Collections of Venice.* Rawdon Brown (ed.)
DNB	=	*Dictionary of National Biography*
EHR	=	*English Historical Review*
H.L.R.O.	=	House of Lords Record Office, London
HMC	=	Historical Manuscripts Commission
P.R.O.	=	Public Record Office, London
VCH	=	*Victoria County History*
ZL	=	*The Zurich Letters*

INTRODUCTION

The Elizabethan Settlement, the great middle way of the Anglican confession, has deeply coloured the historical mirror in which the English nation watches itself and is watched by its neighbours. This cultural myth has become so deeply rooted in the mentality of the English speaking world that historical research into the making of the Settlement has been at a near standstill since the friends and enemies of the Oxford Movement exhausted themselves at the dawn of the present century. When the research stimulated by the political and theological dispute ended historians, tired of the well-worn subject, abandoned it. Only one important contribution has been made since, and that came from a political historian. Professor Sir J.E. Neale, who knew Parliamentary history much better than he knew the religious history of Tudor England.

When the world began to lose interest in the arguments between Catholics and Anglicans, the historians took the story of the Settlement as it had been established over the previous 300 years and put it in the drawer where textbook outlines are kept. As written by some very able 19th century scholars, this version maintained that Elizabeth came to the throne in 1558 intending to regain the royal supremacy over the Church and unite the nation under a uniform order of worship based on the prayer book of 1552. In achieving this she was aided by a loyal, Protestant House of Commons in the Parliament of 1559. Opposing them stood the Marian bishops and their friends in the House of Lords. Fighting to wreck Elizabeth's intended religious reforms, these peers very nearly succeeded.

The list of scholars who accepted this scenario reads like a roll call of great English historians. John Foxe wrote it first, and Sanders and Camden joined him before the 16th century was out. Strype and Burnet documented the story, adding the weight of paper proof to the contentions of contemporaries. Over one hundred years later scholarly interest in the 16th century reawakened, and Froude made the first of a long series of new contributions to our knowledge of that century and its religious history. Henry Gee, H.N. Birt, R.H. Dixon, F.W. Maitland, and J.H. Pollen, to name only the more important, followed him and added their mites to the tale of how Elizabeth struggled with the Catholics in her first regnal year. In 1910 A.F. Pollard summarized the knowledge they had gained, but the story had changed very little since Foxe recorded it in the beginning.[1]

[1] For a more detailed account of the historiography of the Elizabethan Settlement see my dissertation: 'Faith By Statute: The Politics of Religion in the Parliament of 1559', (Cambridge University: 1977), 1-16.

Silence followed Pollard's 1910 publication. For the next forty years nothing new was said about the fashioning of the settlement of religion in 1559. The standard tale was repeated and believed until 1950, when J.E. Neale launched a startlingly new hypothesis about the Parliament that permanently established the Anglican Church. Neale dared to do the unthinkable: he argued that Elizabeth did not intend to ask for anything but the supremacy in 1559. Moreover, he moved the parliamentary battle over the form of the settlement out of the Lords, where tradition had placed it, into the Commons. There in St. Stephen's Chapel he saw, with the eyes of a cold warrior, a cadre of revolutionary Puritans leading the struggle to enact their ideological platform against the will of their conservative Queen.

Neale's scenario begins with the introduction of the government's first bill for the supremacy in early February. The content of this bill, he believed, was the same as that which, in the end, became the Act of Supremacy. When the Protestants in the Commons saw that the Queen did not intend to ask for a prayer book they introduced a bill for one which, Neale thought, was more radical than the 1552 book. Then, in a committee led by Sir Anthony Cooke, they joined the supremacy and the prayer book together, forming the second bill for supremacy. When it reached the Lords (who, Neale assumed, were subservient to the Queen) a committee of that House, acting on instructions from Elizabeth, removed the articles for uniformity of religion from the bill. Needless to say, that angered the Commons very much, but all they could do was launch a bill granting toleration for the Edwardian religion.

Elizabeth had intended to dissolve the Parliament on March 24, only two days after the Supremacy received its final approval. The international situation, however, intervened and saved the day for the Protestant religion. Fearing to declare her nation fully Protestant until a peace with France made her secure on her throne, Elizabeth, Neale conjectured, decided to proceed with the reform after hearing that a peace had been concluded at Cateau Cambrésis. Accordingly, she did not dissolve Parliament. Instead, a committee of divines was called into consultation to prepare a new prayer book. Elizabeth wanted the service of 1549; the divines and their friends in the Lower House wanted something more radical than the 1552 book, such as the book produced in exile at Frankfurt. In the end, thought Neale, they compromised on the 1552 Book of Common Prayer. It was a compromise that Elizabeth did not like, but politically she had no choice. The divines, whom she needed to run her new Church, would not cooperate unless she gave them what they wanted. The struggle between the Queen and the exiles ended in the writing of the Act of

Uniformity, with which neither party was happy. The stage was set, thought Neale, for the political conflict that racked the Parliaments of the reign. By teaching the Protestant radicals the political power of an organized group in Parliament, Elizabeth had unwittingly created the Puritan party.[2]

This theory succeeded in capturing the imagination of the historical profession and, although Neale himself insisted that it was pure hypothesis, it quickly became the standard interpretation. As Philip Hughes said of it, 'Rarely have we had such a chance to see how swiftly learned hypothesis can become a 'fact' of popular knowledge'.[3] In the years since 1950 various scholars have been disturbed by anomalies in Neale's theory. What bothered them the most was the simplicity of this new explanation. R.B. Wernham suspected that Neale's conclusions about the Puritan nature of the Commons failed to account for other stimuli which could have influenced the members' behaviour. 'Indeed', he wrote, 'nationalism and anti-clericalism, two of the strongest and most enduring passions of Tudor Englishmen, could perhaps account for many actions which appear at first sight to betray Puritan sympathies, particularly after the national humiliation and clerical excesses of Mary Tudor's reign.'[4] In the same vein, C.W. Dugmore noted that Neale had oversimplified the theological differences among the various reformers, and that his interpretation of the events in Parliament in 1559 was too subtle to be convincing.[5]

Although a few scholars have been disturbed by Neale's theory, no one has tested it by re-examining the Parliament of 1559. Consequently, it has become the stuff of textbooks and the background for many scholarly works.

The traditional history of the creation of the Elizabethan Settlement and the interpretations based on Neale's thought are separated by point of view, not by factual evidence. No important new documents that would alter the story have been uncovered since the late 19th century. However, the historians before Neale assumed that the conflict over the Settlement was between the Roman Catholics and godly Elizabeth. It did not occur to them to look for Protestant resistance to the Queen's will. Neale, approaching the problem with the knowledge of one who had witnessed the explosive birth of world

[2]J.E. Neale, 'The Elizabethan Acts of Supremacy and Uniformity', *EHR* (1950), 304-32.

[3]Philip E. Hughes, *The Reformation in England,* rev. ed. (London: 1963), III, 26n.

[4]See Wernham's review of Neale's *Elizabeth I and Her Parliaments* in *EHR* (1954), 632-6.

[5]Clifford W. Dugmore, *The Mass and the English Reformers* (London: 1958), 209.

communism, understood the power that a small, well-organized group could exert over a larger body. He saw the Puritans as such a group, using Parliament as a weapon in their struggle against their conservative Queen. This conflict became the unifying theme for his history of Elizabeth's Parliaments. There is little doubt that the Puritans did play an important opposition role in the middle years of the reign. However, as Neale admitted, Puritans can only be assumed to have been active in the sessions of 1559 and 1563. There is no concrete proof that they were organized and politically conscious in the early stages of the reign.

The old and new interpretations are not mutually exclusive, but no one has attempted to juxtapose them with the documents on which they lean. This study will do this. By a detailed reassessment of the origins of the Settlement, it will show that, while the traditional story is more plausible than Neale's, both interpretations are too simplistic. Like any historical event, the re-establishment of Protestantism in England was influenced by things which reached far beyond theological beliefs.

1

THE OPENING OF THE REIGN

'History', wrote C.V. Wedgwood in her biography of William the Silent, 'is lived forward but it is written in retrospect. We know the end before we consider the beginning and we can never wholly recapture what it was to know the beginning only'. The history of the Elizabethan Settlement has been a victim of this intellectual myopia. From the first to the last, its historians have been able only vaguely to discern it, lying like a barnacle-encrusted shipwreck at the bottom of an ocean of Puritans, seminary priests, Dissenters, Anglicans high and low, Anglo-Catholics, and other theological and political distillations. We can never know the beginning only, but it is salutary to consider what Elizabeth faced on November 17, 1558, the day she inherited the throne of England. If we can uncover the troubles and limitations she inherited from Mary and determine what she hoped to do about religion in those first days, we can better understand the history of the creation of the Elizabethan Settlement.

When Henry VIII's second daughter inherited the throne she received with it a perilously weak realm. Mary Tudor's disastrous Spanish marriage had led the kingdom into a war with France and Scotland that reached its nadir in the loss of Calais, and although peace negotiations were under way, the prospects for ending the war or recovering Calais were dim. The French were in Scotland, and nothing stood between them and England but the ill-defended fortress at Berwick. Moreover, the French had, in theory, a papal mandate to invade. The Pope had declared Elizabeth a bastard, leaving Mary Stuart, the Dauphiness of France and Queen of Scotland, as the legitimate, Catholic claimant to the kingdom. In the world of dynastic politics it would have been unnatural not to expect the French and the Scots to exert their claim to rule their enfeebled arch-enemy.[1]

England's chief defence against the French was her alliance with Spain, but Mary's death and Elizabeth's Protestantism raised the frightening possibility that Philip, freed from his English wife and zealous in the defence of Catholicism, might make a separate peace, abandoning Elizabeth to her fate. It is difficult to assess how real Elizabeth and Cecil thought this danger to be, but the Spanish

---

[1] For a succinct explanation of French claims and the joy in the French court at Mary's death, see *CSP Ven.*, VI, 1561-1562.

ambassador did his best to keep alive what fears they may have had.[2]

In the midst of the diplomatic web enveloping England sat Pope Paul IV, who had a natural hatred of schism and heresy and was violently anti-Spanish. Consequently, everyone expected the bolt of excommunication to fall on Elizabeth because she was both an heretic and an ally of Spain. The papacy could do little to interfere directly in England, but if the Pope absolved English Catholics of their obedience to the Crown he might light the fuse of a powder keg. The Pope's curse would also open England to invasion by crusading Catholic princes who would be morally bound to help reconquer the island for Mother Church.[3]

To whom could England turn for help if these things came to pass? If Catholic Europe turned against her, Elizabeth could muster support only from the Protestant princes of Germany and Scandinavia. It is, however, difficult to see how the German princes could have helped England in any meaningful way. The Duke of Württemberg bragged that if Elizabeth was threatened on account of her religion she could have 10 to 15,000 men from the Protestant princes. He also boasted that the Protestants could always raise 15,000 horse and 50,000 foot in a pinch — but he did not offer them to Elizabeth.[4] In order for the Germans to be of real help to England Elizabeth needed more than boasts; she needed a full offensive-defensive treaty. Only if the Lutheran princes were willing either to attack France or invade the Spanish Netherlands would they be really useful to the English. To make matters worse, the German Protestants were divided among themselves, squabbling over the truths of Lutheranism and Calvinism. Before Elizabeth could expect any help from them she would have to declare whether she subscribed to the Confession of Augsburg or the Tigurine Consensus. To do so, however, would have introduced the squabble into England, alienating part of the Protestants and exacerbating the national xenophobia. Prince Eric of Sweden, who was doing his utmost to marry Elizabeth even before Mary's death, could offer little but a backward Lutheran kingdom. No help could be expected from that quarter, even if Elizabeth had been willing to pay the price of marriage.

If the Spanish abandoned her, Elizabeth faced the prospect of having to confront a hostile world with little but the resources of her

---

[2]For instance, see Feria's letter to Philip on 14 December 1558, *CSP Span., Eliz.*, I, 9. However, it is striking to note that in none of the extant advice presented to Elizabeth and Cecil is this danger mentioned.

[3]B.L. Cotton Julius F. VI, fol. 167. P.R.O., SP 12/I/fols. 156-157.

[4]*CSP For.*, I, 112.

kingdom, and England was in deep trouble. Thanks to the war and mismanagement, the nation's economy was stricken. The coinage had suffered several debasements, the government was deeply in debt to foreign bankers, and the war had led to heavy taxation. At the same time, the conflict with France had damaged trade. Inflation was rampant, and 1558 had been a year filled with deadly pestilence. Writing in 1560, Sir Thomas Smith said of Mary's reign, 'I never saw England . . . weaker in strength, men, money and riches'.[5]

Mary's chosen method of restoring Catholicism and the losses of the war had combined to reduce the nation's morale to a very low point. This at least rebounded to Elizabeth's benefit. Because the blame for the troubles of the kingdom was heaped upon Mary and her Spanish friends, the new Queen could expect popular support.[6]

Elizabeth may have had the support of the generality, but in the hierarchical society of sixteenth-century England that did not guarantee to her the support of the nobility and the bishops. Some of the nobles and gentry, along with the London aldermen, could be counted upon to take her part, but among Mary's appointees and the great families of the North there were men who posed a threat. During Wyatt's rebellion many of them had been issued arms and armour, giving them the wherewithal to arm their followers if they decided to resist their new Queen.[7] Nor were the historical omens auspicious. If recent history was any indicator, Elizabeth could expect resistance, if not to her accession, then at least to a change in religion.

There is evidence that Elizabeth and her friends were very aware of this danger and that, as Mary's death grew imminent, they took steps to counter it. In the Hatfield Manuscripts there is a paper, written by one Thomas Markham in 1592, in which the Queen's attention was called to Markham's service to her in 1558. In the fall of that year he was at Berwick, in command of a company of 300 foot, when he received a letter from Elizabeth's cofferer, Sir Thomas Parry, asking him to repair quickly to Brockett Hall in Hertfordshire, a few miles from Hatfield House where Elizabeth was living. Markham was instructed to leave his men with captains he knew could be trusted to be in readiness to maintain Elizabeth's royal state, title, and dignity. This he did, and when he arrived he carried signed testimonies from the captains to the effect that they and their men stood ready to

[5] John Strype, *The Life of the Learned Sir Thomas Smith* (Oxford: 1820), 249. See also *CSP Span., Eliz.,* I, 3.

[6] *CSP Ven.,* VI, 1538. *CSP Span., Eliz.,* I. 3.

[7] P.R.O., SP 12/I/fols. 157-158. B.L., Cotton Julius F. VI, fols. 167-168.

8

spend their lives in Elizabeth's service.[8] Contemporary letters support Markham's testimony. Three weeks before Mary's death Elizabeth wrote from Brockett Hall to thank an unnamed individual for his readiness to support her.[9] Three other letters written to Parry seem to infer that Sir John Thynne was gathering support for Elizabeth in Wiltshire and was in close contact with the princess.[10] As it happened the new Queen did not need to fight for her throne so that we shall never know how extensive her preparations were, but she was prepared for trouble.

Aside from the fact that the bishops were armed, they were a major concern to Elizabeth and her advisers in November 1558 for two reasons. They were, for the most part, intellectually gifted men capable of forceful argument and in control of many of the nation's influential pulpits, but in addition, together with the Abbot of Westminster, they formed a significant portion of the House of Lords. If the Queen hoped to restore the supremacy and reform religion by constitutional means, these men had to be won over or removed. On her accession day Elizabeth could not know that death and disease would shrink the number of active bishops before Parliament met, and she must have assumed that she would have to deal with a more numerous episcopate.[11]

Elizabeth's personal intentions on the day of her accession are easier to guess. Writing in his *Annals* in 1612 John Hayward preserved men's thoughts at Elizabeth's accession: 'For the change in religion which then insued, and had alsoe happened not long before, was easily fore-seene by men of understanding, not onely by reason of the consciences of the Princes, formed in them by education, but alsoe out of their particular interests and endes'.[12] It did not take a man of great prescience to guess the course Elizabeth would take. Her personal history left her little choice.

Raised a Protestant in the household of Catherine Parr, Elizabeth had become the centre of Protestant hopes under Mary, and had some very good personal reasons for disliking her sister's Church.

[8]HMC, *Hatfield M.S.S.,* IV, 189.

[9]B.L., Cotton Vespasian F. III, fol. 27. The letter is dated 28 October 1558.

[10]I have not seen these letters myself. Sir J.E. Neale cites them as being at Longleat in the Thynne Papers, III, fols., 21, 23-24. He quotes them in his article 'The Accession of Queen Elizabeth I', *Essays in Elizabethan History* (New York: 1958), 49.

[11]Cardinal Pole, the Bishop of Rochester, the Bishop of Chichester, and Thomas Tresham, the Master of the Knights of St John in England all died shortly after Mary.

[12]John Hayward, *Annals of the First Four Years of Elizabeth's Reign,* J. Bruce, ed. (London: Camden Soc., VII, 1840), 4.

Bastardized by the Pope, Elizabeth's claim to the throne depended upon the will left by Henry VIII. If she continued the nation in its Roman allegiance, she would be admitting that her mother was a harlot and herself an illegitimate child in need of a papal dispensation to inherit her throne. Besides, in those cold days of early November 1558 her only sure friends were those very people whose support of her claim had imperilled her during Mary's reign. The genuine Protestants, the Edwardians out of favour, the people who associated Mary and her husband, Philip of Spain, with injustice and national disgrace, and the xenophobes and patriots who hated the Spanish Catholic domination had expectations that Elizabeth could not safely ignore. They were her loyal supporters, and she had to repay their loyalty.

Elizabeth the politician and Elizabeth the person can never be disentangled, but some things can be concluded about her preferences. In the matter of religion she was a Protestant. Although it is difficult to tell exactly what theology she preferred, it is obvious that she would not tolerate a Church independent from the state. The royal supremacy was at the very centre of both her political and religious ideals. Elizabeth gained a reputation for being a conservative in matters of church ceremony and decoration, if not dogma, but this only became obvious after the Parliament of 1559, when objections to 'scenic apparatus' and 'popish rags' became closely involved with criticism of the royal prerogative. It would seem that what so upset Elizabeth's episcopate was her broad application of the idea of adiaphora. She was as Protestant as Jewel, Grindal or Cox, but she was more tolerant than they towards popish (or Lutheran) behaviour. Camden described Elizabeth as being a very religious woman, praying daily, attending chapel on Sundays and holy days, and listening attentively to the Lenten sermons. 'But', he adds, 'concerning the Cross, the Blessed Virgin and the Saints, she had no contemptuous opinion, nor ever spoke of them but with reverence. . . .'[13] To say that she preferred a bit of colour in her religion and had a good opinion of the mother of Christ does not mean, however, that Elizabeth rejected the second Book of Common Prayer, or the theology espoused by the Swiss reformers. Vestments, a crucifix and candles did not make a Henrician. It is notable that none of the reformers accused her of being regressive when the words of institution were altered in 1559. The formula may have echoed the 1549 book, but it also brought the 1559 Book of Common Prayer into line with the latest Swiss theology.

[13]Camden, *Annals,* 17.

It is a senseless exercise, however, to attempt to separate Elizabeth's religion from her politics. In the 16th century no such distinctions can be made — especially for a princess like Elizabeth. Wallace MacCaffrey has suggested that Elizabeth's theo-political behaviour relates directly to her conception of the role of the Crown. According to MacCaffrey, the monarch had traditionally been the force in the kingdom which preserved and protected it from harmful change. Under Henry VIII, Edward VI and Mary, however, the monarchy's traditional role was reversed, and it became the aggressive leader of change. Elizabeth, MacCaffrey believes, attempted to return the throne to its former conservative and preservative role.[14] Once she had restored the Church to its former legally recognized Protestant standard Elizabeth would expend her energy in the attempt to prevent further disruptive changes. First, however, the Church had to be returned to its former state, as recognized by king, Parliament, and Convocation. This interpretation makes much of the 1559 Settlement easier to understand. If we may risk misusing the word, we may say that Elizabeth took a 'constitutional' position toward the change in religion. John Jewel explained the Queen's behaviour to Peter Martyr, telling him how the Queen had retained a harmless semblance of the mass in the royal chapel 'only from the circumstances of the times'. He added that 'this woman [Elizabeth] excellent as she is, and earnest in the cause of true religion, notwithstanding she desires a thorough change as soon as possible, cannot however be induced to effect such change without the sanction of law'.[15]

Although we know very little about what specific theology Elizabeth espoused when she acceded, we know a good deal about what people assumed, hoped or feared she would do in religion. The two questions foremost in the minds of everyone were 'whom will she marry?' and, 'what will she do about religion?' These two questions became one for many people, for it was generally assumed that whomever the Queen married would determine the extent to which religion would be altered.

The Roman Catholics were horrified by the accession of a Protestant and foresaw disaster for themselves and the country. Thomas Thirlby, Bishop of Ely, gloomily told one of Granvelle's secretaries that he had no friends among the new Queen's councillors and prophesied the fall of true religion in England. If that happened,

---

[14]This argument was outlined by Professor MacCaffrey in a paper read at the Anglo-American Historical Conference, held at the Institute of Historical Research, University of London, 11 July 1976.

[15]Jewel to Martyr, from London, 14 April 1559. *ZL*, I, 18.

thought, Spain would abandon the English to the French, who would swallow them.[16] Bishop White of Winchester made public his anxiety about the new regime when at Mary's funeral he preached a sermon in which he tried to stiffen the clergy's resistance to the return of heresy. Speaking less than a month after Elizabeth's accession, White compared the clergy to a watchdog and warned them that if, yielding to flattery or fear, they allowed the wolves of heresy to come unchallenged into England the blood of their people would be upon their hands.[17] Then, in a comparison which earned him a house arrest, he showed how Mary, who had restored religion, had been greater than Elizabeth (his text was 'Laudam mortuos magis quam viventes').[18] White concluded this incendiary sermon by urging his listeners to dedicate themselves ' . . . wholye to his [God's] service, remaining under his obedyence and with in the unitie of his churche with the which none can perishe neyther without it be saved'.[19]

The one hope to which the Catholics could cling was Elizabeth's future husband. If she married a Catholic all might be well. Philip of Spain had been aware of the necessity of a religiously sound marriage for her for a long time. Consequently, he sent the Count de Feria to England to propose marriage to Elizabeth on his behalf. The King believed that if he, or one of his Habsburg relatives, married the English Queen England would remain within the Roman Church.[20] The importance attached to this mission was simply expressed by the Jesuit Peter de Ribadeniera, a guest in Feria's home. Writing from London in early January he requested Father Lainez to pray for Feria;

> . . . porque tiene aqui un negocio entre manos que as muy importante, y del qual depende la conservacion de la fe y religion en este reyno; la qual comienca ya a vacilar, y temo que cayra si nuestro Senor milagrosamente no la sustena. . . .[21]

While the Catholics were praying for a miracle to save England from schism, the Protestants were proclaiming that Elizabeth's accession demonstrated God's love for his faithful children. God, according to John Hales, explained it to His people thus:

[16]Antoine Perrenot, cardinal Granvelle, *Papiers d'État,* ed. Charles Weiss (Paris: 1841-1852), V, 416. Le Secrétaire J. de Courtville a l'Eveque d'Arras, 22 January, 1559.

[17]B.L., Cotton Vespasian D. XVIII, fol. 97.

[18]*Ibid.,* fols. 102v-103v.

[19]*Ibid.,* fol. 105.

[20]*CSP Span., Eliz.,* I, 22. King Philip to Feria, 10 January 1559.

[21]Peter de Ribadeniera, *Epistolae aliaque Scripta Inedita. Monumenta Historica Societatis Jesu,* LVIII, 309.

12

> I have not only discovered mine, yours, and my land of England's enemies, and all the crafts, subtleties, and policies that have been, or may be used by them, or any like hereafter; but I have also taken away their head and captain, and destroyed a great number of them, that ye should not be troubled with them; and some of them have I left, that ye may make them spectacles and examples to the terror and fear of their posterity.[22]

When they were not putting words into God's mouth, the Protestants were acclaiming Elizabeth as England's Deborah, the pious judge in Israel who delivered her people from the oppression of the Canaanites. God chose Elizabeth to be His instrument — and as His instrument she was expected by the reformers to follow God, dedicating herself to following the example of King David and holy Deborah. England welcomed the new Deborah with joy, but because the Protestants conceived Elizabeth to be God's instrument they expected her to obey God's will as they understood it.[23]

All the Protestants were united in believing that Elizabeth should waste no time in casting out the Pope, but they were divided over the question of the type of Church that should replace Catholicism. Nor were they agreed upon what political role they, as interested parties, should play in the forthcoming alteration of religion.

By late 1558 English Protestantism had splintered into several different factions which reflected the general doctrinal divisions within continental Protestantism, but the greatest dispute was over the form of worship and church government proper for a reformed Church. Those who had fled from Mary's persecution had been split by the famous quarrel at Frankfurt, when those who believed the Edwardian second prayer book to be sufficiently pure for use managed to expel the party which believed that further sweeping changes should be made in the order of worship. Nor were they agreed on how a Church should be governed. This division between those who upheld the national Church of King Edward and the Calvinist faction led by John Knox continued through the time of Elizabeth's accession, but Knox's Genevan group had little positive political influence in 1558-1559.

Thanks to their shortsighted advocacy of regicide and their rejection of female rulers, John Knox and Christopher Goodman had brought Elizabeth's wrath down upon the Genevan congregation of English exiles. The woman who succeeded Mary did not appreciate

[22]Foxe, Acts, VIII, 675.

[23]Peter Martyr epitomized the joy and expectations of the Protestants in his congratulatory message to the Queen, 22 Dec. 1558. B.L., Add. 29549, fols. 12-14v.

their arguments that monarchy was reserved for men alone. She saw an even greater danger in their idea of a social contract between ruler and ruled. Few rulers could like the proposition that the people or the lesser magistrates had the right and duty to force their king to cease from sinning. As a consequence, Knox was barred from returning to England, and the members of his congregation were regarded with suspicion.

Before he discovered that he could not re-enter England, however, Knox tried to reunite the religious exiles so that they could present a common political front when they returned home. As M.M. Knappen observed, Knox seems to have been the only influential exile who understood their potential power as a religious lobby.[24] Realizing this, the Scotsman's congregation sent a letter to the English churches outside Geneva asking them to stick together in the days ahead:

> ... yet if we (whose sufferance and persecutions are certain signs of sound doctrine) hold fast together, it is certain that the enemies shall have less power; offences shall sooner be taken away; and religion best proceed and flourish.[25]

It went on to suggest that they give up their contention over superfluous ceremonies and other trifles, striving together to reach and practise the 'true knowledge of God's word which we have learned in this our banishment and by God's merciful providence seen in the best reformed churches'.[26]

This attempt to form a power block that could influence the restoration of Protestantism failed. Some of the exiles, like Thomas Lever's group at Aarau, embraced the plan, but the Frankfurt congregation rejected it. On January 3, 1559 the exiles in Frankfurt answered Knox's letter, explaining their expectations about England's readjustment of its worship and rejecting a political role for themselves. Rebuking the Genevans' presumption to meddle with the settlement of religion, they wrote:

> For ceremonies to contende (where it shall lye neither in your hands or oures to appoint what they shall be but in suche mennes wisedomes as shall be appointed to the devising off the same which shall be receyved by common consent off the parliament) it shalbe to small purpos. But we truste that bothe true religion will be restored, and that we shall not be burthened with

[24] M.M. Knappen, *Tudor Puritanism* (Chicago: 1965), 164.

[25] William Whittingham, *A Brief Discourse of the Troubles Begun at Frankfort, in the year 1554, About the Book of Common Prayer and Ceremonies* (London: 1846), 187.

[26] *Ibid.*

unprofitable ceremonies. And therefore as we purpos to submit oure selves to such orders as shall be established by authoritie, beings not of themselves wicked, so we would wish you willingly to do the same. For where as all the reformed churches differ amonge them selves in diverse ceremonies, and yet agree in the unitie of doctrine: we se no inconvenience if we use some ceremonies divers from them, so that we agree in the chiefe points of oure religion.[27]

This letter was signed by, among others, James Pilkington, the leader of the Frankfurt congregation; Henry Carowe, who has been identified as Lord Carey de Hunsdon; Henry Knolles, Alexander Nowell, and John Graye, possibly Lord Graye of Pyrgo.[28] The subscription of Pilkington to these principles is notable, since he was one among those named in the memorial called the 'Device for Alteration of Religion' for consultation about the revision of the Edwardian prayer book.[29] Lord John Graye of Pyrgo is also named in the 'Device' as a nobleman fit to be made privy to the plans for the change in religion.[30]

The split between Knox and those who were allowed into England may have been reinforced by their fear of impeachment for sharing Knox's political views. When the recently returned exiles delivered a statement of their faith to the Queen they expressly declared that the word of God did not condemn rule by a woman. They also denied that any subject had a right to commit regicide or rebel against the magistrate, 'man or woman, good governor or evill'.[31]

The exiles who had returned to England had experienced continental Protestantism, and all of them had moved, to a greater or lesser extent, away from the theology and ceremonies of Edward's second prayer book. Their brethren who had remained in England were without that experience. Indeed, theirs had in some ways been the opposite fate to that of the exiles. Many had found that the threat of the Smithfield fires had caused their ardour to abate and had taught them just how much compromise they could accept in their lives. Others, isolated by a hostile government from the continent and from each other, became increasingly individualistic in their thinking and moved away from positions they had once held to be the truth. Richard Hilles is an example of this. In a polite but firm letter to the

[27]*Ibid.*, 189.

[28]Christina Garrett, *The Marian Exiles* (Cambridge: 1969), 109.

[29]B.L., Cotton Julius F. VII, fol. 168v.

[30]*Ibid.*, fol. 169.

[31]C.C.C.C. 121, 159.

Zürich reformer Henry Bullinger, Hilles explained that his theological opinions had changed since Edward's reign, having, he said,
discovered that Bullinger and his friends erred contrary to the
consensus of the 'Holy Fathers'. The upshot of Hilles' reading was
that he had become a Lutheran and desired no further contact with
Bullinger.[32]

Further down the scale of Protestantism were those Englishmen
who were Henrician Catholics: they wished to see the Pope ejected
but the mass preserved. Christopher d'Assonleville knew of at least
one man near the Queen who felt this way. He reported to Philip that:

> J'ay sceu de quelc'un qui entend une partie des affaires, que son
> intention est se regler au faict de religion comme l'on faisoit hict
> ans devant la mort du Roy Henry, que lors l'anchienne religion
> s'observoit, saulf en ce qui concernoit la puissance du Pape et les
> choses en deppendentes.[33]

This attitude toward the old religion and the Pope was common among
the lay members of the House of Lords, and it greatly influenced their
voting in 1559.

In other cases prolonged exposure to Catholic propaganda must
have introduced self-doubt or strengthened Catholic sympathies
which had once shown signs of waning. The most striking examples
of this are certain clergy who had conformed under Henry and
Edward, but who refused to give up their Catholicism under Elizabeth.

For most of the English Protestants who stayed at home during
Mary's reign, the Protestantism they desired was conditioned by their
memories of religion under Edward, and they most likely expected a
reenactment of the old forms. That is not to say that they were united
in their vision of the sort of Church they wanted. A majority probably
assumed that the Queen would become the supreme head of an
episcopal Church, but there seems to have been discord over what
theological alignment that about-to-be-reinstated Church should
adopt. The evidence is very sparse, but what there is indicates that, at
least in London, people fell to quarrelling over this almost as soon as
they heard of Mary's death. John Jewel reported arguments about
ceremonies in which some people declared for Geneva and others for
Frankfurt. The Swiss reformers seem to have heard rumours that
made them fear that England would accept the Augsburg Confession
rather than Edward's reformation.[34]

[32]See his letter of 28 February 1559. *ZL,* II, 15.

[33]K. de Lettenhove, *Rélations Politiques,* I, 313.

[34]Rudolph Gualter to Queen Elizabeth, 16 January 1559, *ZL,* II, 5. *ZL,* I, 8. Strype, *Annals,* I, i, 76-77, 259. *ZL,* II, 15.

Theological matters aside, there were other stimuli which urged the gentry and nobility to interest themselves in the coming reversion of the English Church to Protestantism. Unlike Marian Catholicism, Henrician and Edwardian Anglicanism had been profitable to many of these men, and they hoped to benefit from a return to Protestantism. As the bills introduced in 1559 amply demonstrate, the royal government and the laity were anxious to resume control of church lands and revenues. Of course there were pious reasons for wishing to make these changes, but land, money and mens' livelihoods were involved in every case. This concern for their own affairs helps explain why the lords temporal who in 1559 used their votes to assert their faith in transubstantiation refused to oppose the supremacy. Casting out the Pope re-ensured the continued possession of church spoils and held out the satisfactory prospect of more spoils to come.

Another aspect of this self-interest was the hope for office and favour which gave such vigour to the nation's strong belief in and respect for authority. Englishmen had shown their malleability in the previous three reigns, bowing before the royal will like grass before the wind where religion was concerned. Aware of this, Elizabeth and her advisers were not too concerned about securing the support of most of the gentry. The 'Device for Alteration of Religion' reminded the Queen that she need have no fear of appointees who were slack in the cause of religion: 'Whom . . . their own safety and state shall cause to be vigilant, careful, and earnest for the conservation of her state and maintenance of this alteration.'[35]

It was a logical corollary that if some men sought to please the new regime in hopes of favour, some others would oppose it because it meant the loss of their places, honours and prestige. The 'Device' warned that the change of religion and its concomitant turnover in church and government offices would cause discontent among those who had held them in the late Queen's time. Bishops and clergy, it argued would see their own ruin in the change and would obstruct it. Laymen who had been appointed to their offices because they were papist, thinking themselves discredited and their actions on behalf of Catholicism in vain, would despise the alteration and would try to retain their faith.[36] After all, says the 'Device,' there is no man who does not love the time in which he flourished. A man will maintain and defend those laws and policies in which he had a part, 'for every man naturally loveth that which is his own work and creature'.[37]

[35] B.L., Cotton Julius F. VI, fol. 168.
[36] *Ibid.*, fol. 168.
[37] *Ibid.*

The people who might have opposed the new regime were, fortunately for Elizabeth, leaderless. The Catholics had lost their greatest leaders when Queen Mary, Cardinal Pole and several other chief ecclesiastics died. Of the bishops left alive most were too old or ill to be the active leaders of a popular opposition movement, even if they had been so inclined. Feria, the Spanish ambassador, tried to guide the Catholic resistance in Parliament, but he was too contemptuous of the English to be able either to attract them or retain their loyalty. The Protestants had no one but the Queen herself to look to for guidance. None of the exiles would be home before early January, and even they, returning penniless from long periods abroad, were in no position to build a following. Moreover, Elizabeth and Cecil took steps to see that they did not attract one. Their political role was to be limited to court preaching and what personal contact they had. Hence circumstances and royal sagacity, combined with Protestant disunity, saved the Queen from organized pressure by any strong religious interest group outside the government.

From within the government Elizabeth received good advice, if not pressure. The leaders of the Council were sagacious men, politically astute and committed to Protestantism. There is no written evidence which can be definitely attributed to William Cecil, Nicholas Bacon, or the Earl of Bedford to tell us what policies they thought the Queen ought to pursue. There are, however, four manuscripts which do make policy suggestions. One, a letter written by Sir Nicholas Throckmorton to the Queen before she even acceded, exists only in an imperfect copy.[38] Two others, Richard Goodrich's 'Divers Points of Religion Contrary to the Church of Rome' and Armagill Waad's 'Distresses of the Commonwealth with the Means to Remedy Them,' survive in their original form.[39] The fourth and most intriguing paper of advice, the anonymous 'Device for the Alteration of Religion,' survives, charred about the edges, in a 16th-century copy among the Cotton manuscripts.[40] These papers are of interest because they tell us a good deal about the problems which were worrying the politicians, and about the solutions they considered.

Throckmorton's letter to Elizabeth was discovered by J.E. Neale, who wondered why Throckmorton had written it.[41] This possibly foolhardy attempt to influence the Queen is filled with detailed suggestions for appointments and a speech which Throckmorton recommended

[38] C.C.C.C., 543, fols. 31 v-35 v.

[39] Waad: P.R.O. SP 12/I/fols. 147-154. Goodrich: *Ibid.*, fols. 156-158.

[40] B.L. Cotton Julius F. VI, fol. 167-169.

[41] J.E. Neale, 'Sir Nicholas Throckmorton's Advice to Queen Elizabeth', *EHR* 65 (1950), 91. I continue to cite Neale's accurate transcript of this manuscript.

18

the Queen make to Mary's Privy Council. It was not solicited by the Queen. Throckmorton, who was in London on Elizabeth's business on November 18, 1558,[42] excused himself for writing the letter, saying:

> The bruites which I heare consonant to some advertisementes, the place wher I am presentlie, so farr distant from your presence, the faithfull zeale which I owe to your Graces honor saftie and happie government, which is to succeed happilie through a discreete beginning, hath moved mee to tell your Grace my poore opinion either in the beginninge or before the beginning of your weightie and comberous charge. I doubt not of your gratious acceptation (wherof I have experiencede) because I meane well. I doe neither dispaire of a good sequell (god forbidd I should speake too arrogantly) if yt shall like your grace to putt in ure my younge and peradventure singuler devises.[43]

Neale overdramatized the nature of this letter in his notes on the published text. He wrote that the reader of Throckmorton's memorandum would be struck by its 'pervading sense of danger, calling for circumspection and even cunning in the opening moves of a new, revolutionary government. "To succeed happily through a discreet beginning": as the text of a "hot-gospeller" how significant!'[44] Nonetheless, Throckmorton's advice is the most complacent and least Protestant of any of the four extant policy papers. In fact, he failed to deal with the war and the religious climate, the real problems at the time. Moreover, one is struck by his bipartisan suggestions for appointments. To judge by his list, he did not expect the government to be particularly Protestant in its makeup. For the office of Lord Chancellor or Lord Keeper he listed Nicholas Heath, Archbishop of York and Mary's Chancellor; Dr. Wotton, Dean of Canterbury; Sir Anthony Cooke, who was still in exile in Strassburg; Richard Lord Riche, who stoutly defended Catholicism in the 1559 Parliament; and James Dyer, a judge of known conservative sentiments. 'And if a church man have the Great Seale then a man well learned in the lawes of the Realme,' wrote Throckmorton, should be Master of the Rolls.[45] How odd for a 'hot-gospeller' to suggest so many conservatives for high offices.

The letter has another peculiarity. Throckmorton seems to have believed that Elizabeth was politically naive and dependent upon his

[42]P.R.O., SP 12/I/fol. 7.
[43]Neale, 'Throckmorton's Advice', 93.
[44]*Ibid.*
[45]*Ibid.*, 95.

advice. For example, he told the Queen that she should appoint some new members to the Privy Council, 'but yt may please you to deferr the sweareing and nominateing of them until I may enforme you of some most necessary respectes'.[46] Throckmorton so often assumes this patronizing tone that he borders on committing *lèse majesté*. One wonders if this address accounts for Throckmorton's lack of any noticeable role in the government until he was sent as ambassador to France in May of 1559.[47] The Queen's delicate pride may not have survived his letter unbruised.

The letter must have been written some time in October or the early part of November, for, as its prologue says, it was written when its author was far from Elizabeth and was prompted by rumours of Mary's death; yet wè know that Throckmorton was with Elizabeth when her sister's decease was reported to her. According to a letter of his written from London to the new Queen on November 18, he had been despatched to that city on the 17th, the day Mary died, with commissions given him by Elizabeth for delivery to Norfolk, Bedford, Cobham, Admiral Lord Clinton and others.[48] His employment on the Queen's business may mean that she had liked his advice. Certainly she had tolerated it, for in the letter of the 18th he gives her some more suggestions and refers to his suit, made in address of advice, on behalf of his cousin.[49]

For all his brashness, Throckmorton concluded his memorandum with a very sensible observation. "It shall not bee meete," he wrote,

> that neither the old or new should wholely understand what you meane, but to use them as instrumentes to serve yourselfe with: for some bee meete to countenance your service and some meete to give advise and serve indeed.[50]

Whether or not Elizabeth took his suggestions seriously, she made only some of the appointments he had proposed.

Armigal Waad's 'Distresses of the Commonwealth and the Means to Remedy Them' is disappointing. In spite of its title, it is little more than a sketchy outline wastefully written on numerous sheets of paper. It sets out the nation's problems: the poverty of the Queen, the poverty of the nobility, the wealth of the meaner sort, the dearth of things, the divisions within the realm (class and religion), the wars, the

[46]*Ibid.*, 94.
[47]*CSP For.*, I, 236.
[48]P.R.O., SP 12/I/fols. 7-7v.
[49]*Ibid.*, and Neale, 'Throckmorton's Advice', 97.
[50]Neale, Throckmorton's Advice', 98.

want of justice. His solutions are equally sketchy and vague, written in beautiful, quotable Tudor prose but with little substance. The sum of his advice is caution in all things. Do nothing hastily, step carefully, and keep looking behind you, especially in the matter of religion.[51]

The 'Device for Alteration of Religion' and 'Divers Points of Religion Contrary to the Church of Rome' deserve much closer attention than do the others. These two flashes in the dark Tudor night brilliantly illuminate Elizabeth's religious intentions in the first months of her reign. Because of them we know with certainty that she meant to regain the supremacy over the Church in England and that she wished, as soon as it was politically safe to do so, to replace the Catholic mass with a service based on the Book of Common Prayer of 1552. Whether or not later decisions resulted from the suggestions put forward in these papers, they are of supreme importance.

These writings may have been linked in their origins. Their format suggests that both of them were written for a specific purpose, perhaps in answer to questions sent them by a third party. Neither manuscript has an introduction, and neither was given a title by its author. The copy we have of the 'Device' was entitled by the copyist: 'The Device for Alteration of Religion in the First Year of Queen Elizabeth.' The heading of Goodrich's paper was added by a clerk: 'Goodryck Divers points of religion contrary to the church of Rome.' Nor does either have an address or salutation. Both take up their subject as if the intended reader was already familiar with the question at hand — the change in religion which the government was desirous of accomplishing. Considering their subject and their specificity, it is almost unthinkable that they were not written in response to a request. No experienced politician or lawyer, such as the authors obviously were, would have voluntarily sent advice on how to alter religion to the Queen and her ministers without knowing that they wanted it. Moreover, the harmony of their recommendations makes it plain that both authors did know what Elizabeth wanted to do about religion. Their aim in writing was to suggest the most expedient means of achieving her end. Moreover, the 'Device' seems to have been in Cecil's possession. On the last folio of the British Library's copy appears a note which is almost certainly in his hand.

Richard Goodrich was a good man to consult about the proposed alteration of religion. An ancient of Grey's Inn and an attorney for both courts of Augmentation who had served on several Edwardian ecclesiastical commissions, he was qualified to combine advice with

[51]P.R.O., SP 12/I/fols. 147-154.

sound legal opinion. This he did when, sometime before December 6, 1558,[52] he sat down to apply legal and political precedents to the problems of proving that the Pope's curse was invalid in England, of providing anti-papal propaganda, of how and when the Pope's authority should be abolished, of how the Queen ought to treat the Protestants until their religion was legalized, of how to prevent trouble with the bishops, and of how diplomacy might be used to delay the Queen's excommunication.

He began by reciting Bracton's famous dictum: 'Ipse autem rex non debet esse sub homine sed sub Deo & sub lege, quae lex facit Regem, attribuat ergo Rex Legi quod Lex attribuit ei Viz. Dominationem et Potestatem.' Using this as a tool, he demonstrated that the Pope's power had never been exercised in England without the king's permission. Nor, he showed, had any bull of excommunication ever been allowable in the king's courts. Moreover, the Archbishop of Canterbury could call a Convocation and pronounce excommunication without any mention of the Pope, and had done so in Henry III's time. Ergo, the Pope's curse was of no value in the realm.

In spite of this, the realm had been grieved from time to time by the usurpations of the Pope and his clergy. Parliament had repeatedly fought this encroachment with statutes of praemunire and laws against alienation into mortmain. Proofs of this usurpation, he noted, were to be found in the Exchequer and the Tower, and among the records Lord Riche had gathered when he was solicitor to Henry VIII. These proofs would stir the nobility and the commons to defend the liberty of the realm against the Pope.

Because he thought it was dangerous to touch the authority of the Pope either wholly or in part, Goodrich counselled that cautious preparations be made before a schism was openly declared. The sad story of King John of England was ample proof that the clergy should be bridled, for unless they were humbled the restoration of the supremacy could not be safely attempted. It followed that all the principal prelates and Mary's chief counsellors should be committed to the Tower and excluded from the coronation pardon. Also, trustworthy men in each county needed to be assigned to seize the arms, armour and horses these Catholics possessed. In order to

---

[52]I date Goodrich's 'Divers Points' as before 6 December because it was on that day that the writs calling Parliament for 23 January were issued. Since Goodrich did not know when Parliament would meet when he wrote (nor at the Parliament if it be holden before or in Marche next, P.R.O., SP 12/I/fol. 157v), he must have written before the date of its meeting was made public by the writs.

22

prevent any word of this from reaching Rome, merchants should be stayed while letters were sent to the royal agent there. These letters would instruct the Queen's ambassador to deceive the Pope with reports that a great embassy would be sent to Rome in the coming summer. In the meantime the changes at home could be carried out.[53]

Until the country was secure nothing should be done against the Pope, not even if Parliament was held before or in March. If it was held before then only the heresy statutes of Henry IV and Henry V ought to be repealed. That way the bishops could no longer act *ex officio,* and quiet persons could live safely.

> In the mean tyme her Majesty, and all her Subiects may by licence off law use the Inglysh latynye and suffrages usyd in Kinge Henry's tyme, and besides her Majestie in her closett may use the Masse without lyfting upp above the Host accordyng to the ancient Canons and may also have at every masse some communicants with the Ministers to by usyd in both kinds.[54]

It would also be good to authorize learned and discreet ministers to preach the Gospel purely, without inveighing against any sects except Anabaptists and Arians. Homilies in English ought to be published, to be read in every church, treating of 'our Religion' plainly and simply, without raising controversial matters.[55]

Clearly, these measures, which would have begun the reintroduction of Protestantism, were meant to be an interim until the Queen thought it safe enough to make a thorough reform.

The 'Device for Alteration of Religion,' written by an unknown but highly placed individual sometime before Christmas, 1558[56] has been the axis around which most histories of the Elizabethan Settlement have turned. The story of its call for a committee of divines to meet at Sir Thomas Smith's house to prepare a new prayer book is

[53] *Ibid.*, fols. 156-158.

[54] *Ibid.*, fol. 157v.

[55] *Ibid.*

[56] It has been suggested by Dixon, *History,* 5, 22n. that the 'Device' was written by the committee 'For consideration for all things necessary for the Parliament' appointed by the Privy Council on 23 December which committee included Sir Thomas Smith and Richard Goodrich (*APC,* VII, 28). This, however, is not likely. When the 'Device' was written its author did not know of Elizabeth's refusal to witness the elevation of the Host on 25 December as is plain from his advice that the Queen might take communion as she pleased on high feasts (B.L., Cotton Julius F. VI, fol. 168v.). From this I deduce that the 'Device' was written before December 25, and probably before the committee could have taken any action.

well known. Interpretations of this document have centred around the question of whether or not the government carried out the scheme set forth in it. Camden, Strype, and a multitude of others assumed that the plan was followed; J.E. Neale denied it. None of them saw its true value, for the 'Device' is, like all policy papers, a suggested blueprint for future events, not an history of those events. It tells us not what the government did, but what it hoped to do in the early months of 1559.

The author of the 'Device' arranged his plan for altering religion into a series of questions and answers. When should the alteration first be attempted? At the next Parliament, if proper precautions have been taken. What dangers may ensue upon alteration? The Pope will excommunicate the Queen, placing the realm under an interdict, and the French will renew the war, invading through Scotland. The Irish may rebel, while the clergy and papists at home will make trouble. When the subsidy is granted there will be discontent, while many who would gladly have a break with Rome will complain that the alteration is but a 'cloaked papistry' and that the realm should embrace some other doctrine.

What remedy is there for these problems? Make peace with France, and the Scots will follow the French example. Rome can do nothing but curse and plot, but Berwick should be strengthened and some money spent in Ireland. Those men Queen Mary had advanced to office 'only or chiefly for being of the Popes religion' should be debased and discredited in their own counties. At the same time, the Queen's loyal servants should be placed in positions of authority and credit. Those bishops and clergy who are good papists must be treated by the clement Queen with more severity than is her want. She must 'seek as well by parliament, as by the just laws of England, in the praemunire, and other such penal laws' to force them to acknowledge their error and adhere to the alteration ('And by this means well handled, her majestys necessity of money may be somewhat relieved.').[57]

The threat presented by disgruntled papists, judges, and justices of the peace could best be met by following the lesson taught by Queen Mary. New justices, lieutenants and muster captains, somewhat younger and poorer than the Marian ones, ought to be appointed. These men should be ready to enforce sharp laws against unauthorized assemblies and to prevent tumults and illegal musters.[58]

[57]B.L., Cotton Julius F. VI, fols. 167v-168.
[58]*Ibid.*, fols. 168-168v.

24

Those who wanted religion altered but would take the change too far deserved to be treated brusquely. The author of the 'Device' hoped that 'straight laws upon the promulgation of the book [containing the alteration], and severe execution of the same at the first' would so repress them that only a few people would be hurt by them. 'And better it were that they should suffer, than her highness or commonwealth should shake, or be in danger. And to this they must well take heed that draw the book.'[59]

This is the most important passage in the 'Device,' for it encapsulates Elizabeth's and Cecil's attitude toward the reform: it must be done, but the change should not be so radical as to endanger the commonwealth. The theologians involved in drafting the book had to remember that England's political tranquillity was as much at stake in the change of religion as its spiritual salvation.

Finally the 'Device' gets to the central question: what changes should be made in religion? This question, it suggested, ought to be referred to such learned men as are meet to 'review the Book of Common Prayer, and order of ceremonies, and service in the Church.' Having done this, they should present a 'plat or book' containing the changes they desired to the Queen. When she had approved it, it should be submitted to Parliament for passage into law. The 'Device' suggests that of the divines Bill, Whitehead, Grindal, Parker, May, Cox and Pilkington were fit to be taken into consultation in the matter, and that after preparing their recommendations they ought to show them to other men of learning and gravity, who were apt for the purpose, 'as for that is necessary to be done before'. The Marquis of Northampton, the Earl of Bedford, the Earl of Pembroke, and John, Lord Graye ought to be made privy to these proceedings before they were opened to the whole Council.[60]

This portion of the 'Device' is interesting, for it indicates that its author probably expected the revision to be more extensive than were the changes made in the 1552 book in 1559. The divines were to review the prayer book (since no distinction is made between the 1549 and 1552 versions, it is highly probable that the 1552 edition was meant) and present Elizabeth with a book or schedule containing the proposed changes. Since the alterations made in 1559 were so few that they hardly required a 'plat or book' to explain them, we may take this passage as indicating several possibilities. Perhaps the divines met and decided that fewer changes were necessary than were

[59]*Ibid.*, fol. 168v.
[60]*Ibid.*, fols. 168v-169.

envisaged by the author of the 'Device.' Or perhaps it was decided
that the book needed so little revision that the committee never met
(thus explaining why there is no evidence of any meeting). Or perhaps
Elizabeth's conservatism exerted itself in limiting the number of
changes she allowed the committee to make. Finally, there is the slight
possibility that the committee prepared a revision which met so much
opposition in Parliament that it was withdrawn and replaced with the
slightly modified 1552 version.

The 'Device' conceived the restoration of true religion to be a
matter separate from the supremacy, to be introduced into Parliament
as an independent bill. And this, apparently, is what was to happen in
the Commons in February. A bill for the supremacy was introduced
and then, shortly afterwards, a bill to restore the Book of Common
Prayer was sent into the Lower House.

The 'Device' asks and answers one other question: what can the
Queen, for her conscience's sake, openly do about religion before the
alteration becomes law, and, if the change must tarry very long, what
religious order is fit for the realm in the meantime? The answer given,
though less specific than Goodrich's reply to this question, is
substantially the same. Things should remain as they are, except that
the Queen may receive communion as she pleases at high feasts
(which in fact she began to do at Christmas), there should be extra
chaplains at mass, and they should always communicate in both
kinds. Also, until the alteration it would be better if some devout form
of prayer or memory was said, rather than mass.[61]

Neither Goodrich's paper nor the 'Device' was followed in its
entirety, but it is striking how nevertheless the course of events tended
to follow their outline. Both, but especially Goodrich, foreshadowed
the steps the Queen took to alter worship before the passage of the
Act of Uniformity. A revised edition of Edward's second prayer book
was enacted by Parliament, as the 'Device' had suggested, and a
comparison of Cecil's notes from the first days of the reign with the
'Device' shows that he agreed with it on most points of foreign and
domestic policy.[62]

The greatest objections against accepting these treatises as
representative of Elizabeth's intentions have centred around the
chronology for the alteration suggested by Goodrich and the question
of whether or not the 'Device's' committee of divines ever met. For
our present purpose, however, neither of these complaints matters.

[61]*Ibid.,* fol. 168v.
[62]P.R.O., SP 12/I/fol. 3.

Plans may have been modified by events, but, as has been seen, a careful comparison of the two with the history they were intended to plan makes it clear that they do reflect Elizabeth's desires and concerns in her first month on the throne.

Not only Elizabeth's intentions and foreign entanglements moulded the Parliament of 1559. Many of its bills and debates had been roughed out by Mary's Parliaments. Elizabeth and others were reacting to their decisions and were bound by their precedents.

Though from the beginning of her reign Mary gave highest priority to restoring the old faith, she could not act without using her power as supreme head of the Church. Nor could she change religion without parliamentary sanction. In August, 1553 the new Queen reluctantly admitted to a papal emissary that, although she was a faithful daughter of the Church, '. . . it was necessary to repeal and annul by Act of Parliament many perverse laws made by those who ruled before her' before Catholicism could be restored.[63] On the other hand, Reginald Pole, who returned from Rome to lead the restoration, had little use for Parliaments and less for popular sentiment. He insisted that Mary '. . . must compel her subjects . . . to honour God and punish the disobedient in virtue of the authority she had received from God'.[64] In the end, political realities forced Mary to rely on Parliament more than God, no matter how much in her heart she agreed with Pole.

Although she realized that she needed Parliament's permission to change England's religion, Mary did not understand the gulf that separated Englishmen from the Pope. Twenty years of anti-papal propaganda had had its intended effect on the English, and although few of them were doctrinal Protestants, most of them supported the royal supremacy and were loath to see it surrendered. It was deeply embedded in English law and minds, enjoying the support of the many nobles and gentry who now owned the property of the former monasteries and chantries. Moreover, the Crown had been using the first fruits and tenths collected from the Church to finance itself, reducing the tax burden imposed on the laity. As Mary would learn, the chief men of the English nation were not too concerned about theological niceties, but they knew that reunion with Rome would threaten their purses.

Although it required a Parliament to repeal the statutes that made the supremacy legal, Mary wilfully broke the law in her return to Rome. This was especially true in the matter of episcopal deprivations

[63]*CSP Ven.*, V, 429.

[64]*CSP Span.*, XI. 419. D.M. Loades, *Oxford Martyrs* (London: 1970), 109.

and appointments. At first she acted as if the use of the royal supremacy to deprive a bishop was illegal, reinstating men removed by Edward. Later, however, she reversed herself and deprived seven Protestant bishops by royal commission. She replaced those deprived by using royal *congés d'élire* — after secretly obtaining their confirmation from the papal legate and thus breaking the law of praemunire.[65] In the Parliament of 1559 her use and misuse of the supremacy would come back to haunt some of her appointees.

The parliamentary campaign to dismantle the Reformation began in the first session of Mary's first Parliament with the repeal of the Henrician and Edwardian Acts pertaining to felonies, treasons and praemunire. In the second session the government moved for the repeal of all the Edwardian religious legislation. To her chagrin, Mary found that a large number of the Commons were opposed to her programme. After 'marvellous dispute' the bill passed, decreeing that divine service should be performed as in the last year of Henry VIII. Parliament would not, however, rescind the royal supremacy and Mary had to disguise it with an ambiguous 'etc.' in her title.[66]

Before the second Parliament of the reign the kingdom was shaken by Wyatt's rebellion. Filled with hatred of the Spanish and hoping to prevent Philip of Spain from marrying their Queen, Wyatt's men marched on London, aided by the City's trained bands which had deserted to their cause. London failed to revolt, Wyatt was defeated, and the government took uneven retribution. Unable or unwilling to admit that the Spanish marriage had caused the uprising, Mary blamed it on the Protestants and sharply increased her efforts to suppress them.

Not wishing to seem disloyal, the members of the Parliament that met shortly after the revolt consented to the Spanish marriage, albeit grudgingly, but they refused to reenact the anti-Lollard statutes and the Act of Six Articles. Their intransigence, however, was not the result of Protestant scruples; rather, it was caused by the power struggle between Lord Paget and Bishop Gardiner. They had already split the Council, and Paget, leading the lay peers, fought Gardiner in Parliament by opposing his attempt to get the old laws reenacted.[67]

The battle between the two councillors disturbed the next Parliament, too. In this, the first session held under Philip and Mary, the Parliament was willing to restore Catholicism, but it was not willing to

[65]Loades, *Martyrs,* 115-117.

[66]A.G. Dickens, *The English Reformation* (New York: 1974), 260.

[67]*Ibid.,* 263.

return the secularized ecclesiastical property to the Church. The aristocracy adhered to the royal supremacy because it guaranteed their ownership of the formerly ecclesiastical lands. Paget represented and led this group in the Lords, and they refused to sanction the Roman connection until they were certain that their property rights would be assured.

The terror of confiscation conjured up by Paget continued to haunt the kingdom, and it soon became apparent that unless property rights were guaranteed Parliament would never agree to renew Roman authority in England. Mary, by herself, could not promise this. Only the Pope could bindingly renounce the Church's claim to the land. This Julius III was reluctant to do. Allowing a nation to appropriate the Church's property without penalty would set a potentially disastrous precedent. By the summer of 1554, however, he was finally convinced of the necessity of the concession and instructed Cardinal Pole to act accordingly.

The upshot of this was the passage of the 'Acte Repealing all Statutes Articles and Provisions made against the See Apostolick of Rome Since the XXth yere of King Henry theight, and also for the stablishment of all Spyrytuall and Ecclesiasticall Possessions and Herediamentes conveyed to the Layetye'.[68] The religious sections of this bill caused little discord, but the members insisted that Pole's dispensation be inserted in it, giving it the force of statute. Furthermore, the Act guaranteed that the titles to ecclesiastical lands were valid and made cases concerning them triable only in the royal courts. It was the price Mary's restored Catholic Church had to pay for admission to the realm.

The Act, however, did not settle men's minds. The Queen and the Cardinal refused to conceed that either their consciences or the Pope's could be bound by an Act of Parliament:

> ... the Legate having first of all endeavoured by several ways to recover as much as he could for the churches; at length, being unable to do otherwise, in order not to impede the completion of so important a work, and for the public welfare and quiet of England, condescended in such a way to the retention of this property that everybody might very easily perceive that his dispensation was a mere permission *ob duritiam cordis illorum*, as in this despensation he never would consent to add the clause *'quod absque aliquo conscientiae scrupulo possent huiusmodi bona retinere,'* although he was several times urged strongly to

[68] 1 & 2 Phil. & Mar. c. 8.

insert it; and this he did to leave in their minds a goad which in the course of time might move them to make some fitting and due acknowledgement. . . .[69]

Because of these terms, there was nothing to prevent a future Pope from revoking the dispensation, and misgivings about this were reinforced in 1555 when Pope Paul IV was elected. One of his first acts was to issue a bull denouncing the alienation of ecclesiastical property. Although Pole, after considerable exertion, had persuaded Paul to exempt England from the bull, news of it helped to convince the English aristocracy that 'only a return to a protestant and national church could provide a definitive answer to the problem.'[70]

No matter what the laymen thought of returning their property to the Church, Mary felt that it was sinful to retain ecclesiastical lands and incomes in the Crown's hands. Accordingly, she attempted to renounce them. Her pious intent was not appreciated by her Council, some of whom argued that 'what by the consent of Parliament had been assigned to the Crown could not be renounced by the Queen without the Parliament's consent'.[71] Not only a legal principle was at stake. Included in the items to be surrendered by the Crown were the first fruits and tenths paid by incumbents. These monies were an important part of the Crown revenue which it could ill afford to lose.

Understandably, when Parliament met in October 1555 its members were not anxious to tax themselves to meet the Crown's expenses when Mary was trying to give away such a lucrative source of revenue. 'The opponents say that so long as her Majesty is in debt she should retain, and not despoil herself as she has done of the sort of ecclesiastical revenue lately alienated by her from the Crown.'[72] After a great uproar the subsidy and the return of first fruits and tenths to the Churches passed, but the Lower House defeated an attempt by the government to force the religious and political exiles to return or forfeit their property.

In the years following the 1555 session there was little significant legislation affecting religion and the Church, but the stage had been set for the Parliament of 1559. Elizabeth's first Parliament was devoted primarily to reversing the Marian Acts dealing with ecclesiastical lands, laws and government.

[69]*CSP Ven.*, VI, 10.
[70]Loades, *Martyrs,* 146.
[71]*CSP Ven.*, VI, 154.
[72]*Ibid.*, VI, 229.

When 'England's Deborah' picked up the sceptre that had fallen from Mary's cold hand she had every intention of deserving her nickname. Presented by history with several problems and possible solutions, she chose to restore the supremacy over the English Church to the Crown and to return her nation's religion to the form established by law under Edward VI. Acting without attention to precedent and careful political preparations, however, would be folly, as she and her advisers knew. They had to take into account the kingdom's weaknesses, its foreign and domestic enemies, and the desires of its supporters, all the while remembering that their surest strength lay In God's favour. 'So that the dangers be foreseen, and remedies therefore provided', wrote the author of the 'Device,' the change in religion should be made at the next Parliament. 'For the sooner that religion is restored, God is the more glorified, and as we trust will be more merciful unto us, and better save and defend her highness from all dangers.'[73]

[73]B.L., Cotton Julius F. VI, fol. 167.

2

PREPARING FOR THE CHANGE IN RELIGION

A reform of religion was the purpose of the Queen of England and her intimate counsellors. As soon as affairs permitted the supremacy would be re-established and religion would be altered. First, however, the nation needed to be prepared, the reins of government firmly placed in the royal hands and the royal will supported by trusty servants. It was essential, too, to prevent civil disturbances and check religious enthusiasm lest the government's authority be undermined. Meanwhile, diplomatic preparations were needed before the alteration reversed England's diplomatic orientation, and preparations had to be made for a Parliament to relieve the Queen's poverty and enact the religious reforms.

Elizabeth, with the aid of William Cecil (or perhaps Cecil, by the authority of Elizabeth), set about resolving the problems she faced and attaining the end she desired from her first day on the throne. The notes that Cecil loved to scribble to himself tell us that within three days of the accession he had taken firm control of the government and was consolidating the new Queen's power.

Conyers Read believed that Cecil had begun playing his role as Elizabeth's principal secretary even before Mary died, and he may have been right.[1] Mary's Chancellor, Archbishop Heath, foreseeing who would count in the new government, called Cecil to him three or four days before Mary's death to confer with him about the state of the realm and matters of religion.[2] Certainly, by the time of Mary's demise on November 17 Cecil had taken up his leading role. That day he scribbled the first of the memoranda that are so familiar to historians of Elizabeth's reign. His concerns were mostly with the usual transition procedures, but he added a further note, in a different ink: 'To consider the condition of ye prechar at Pawles Cross that no occasion be gyven to hym to stirr any dispute towchying the governance of ye realme.'[3] This indicates that Cecil did not trust Bishop Bonner, who would normally have made that appointment, to find a preacher who was not hostile to Elizabeth.

Two notes, written on November 18, tell us that the supremacy was very much on the secretary's mind. The first serves notice that

[1] Conyers Read, *Mr Secretary Cecil and Queen Elizabeth* (London: 1965), 122.
[2] B.L., Cotton Vespasian F. XIII, fol. 287.
[3] P.R.O., SP 12/I/ fol. 3.

Elizabeth was not going to accept the royal style as truncated by Mary when she gave up the supremacy. Just as Mary had 'etceterated' herself to avoid mentioning the royal headship of the Church until it could be repealed, so now Elizabeth would add the abbreviation to her title to show her dislike of that repeal. Cecil wrote: 'A commission to make out wrytts for ye parlement — towching etc. in ye style of wrytte.' The second note says simply 'Mr Chytwoods case'.[4] Richard Chetwood and his wife Agnes had appealed to the Court of Rome against a sentence passed on them by the consistory court at St. Paul's; Cecil's note tells us that, on the second day of Elizabeth's reign, he was already thinking about stopping this appeal to the Pope and helping his friend Chetwood out of an awkward position. On December 1 the Council wrote to the English ambassador at Rome and ordered him to forbear using his authority to solicit or procure anything in Chetwood's case.[5] The suit eventually found its way into the Act of Supremacy as a proviso.[6]

Omnicompetent as he was, Cecil had to work with and through the Privy Council to make his scribblings into political realities. Generally speaking, the twenty men who entered Elizabeth's Council in the first days were of three sorts: political appointees, professional civil servants, and men who were intimate counsellors. The political appointees were Lords Arundel and Clinton, the Earl of Pembroke, the Earl of Derby, and the Earl of Shrewsbury. These men had all served Queen Mary as members of her Privy Council, and Elizabeth kept them because she needed their political strength on her side. All of them were landed magnates with important connections. Pembroke was one of the richest men in England; Clinton was a successful naval commander who had served Edward and Mary as Lord Admiral; Shrewsbury was Lord President of the North and Lieutenant of seven northern counties, where he had huge estates; Derby held a similar position west of the Pennines.[7]

The civil servants were all men of long experience. William Paulet, Marquis of Winchester, had been Lord Treasurer since 1550 and had proved malleable enough to suit all masters. He was, however, a man of intelligence and ability who had acquired a reputation as a financial expert. John Mason and Nicholas Wotton

[4]P.R.O., SP 12/I/ fol. 5.

[5]*APC,* VII, 11.

[6]1 Eliz. I, c. 1.

[7]Wallace MacCaffrey, *The Shaping of the Elizabethan Regime* (London: 1968), 30-32.

were both career diplomats who had served the monarchy since Henry VIII's time. William Petre had had a long government career.[8]

The retention of these Marian councillors by Elizabeth tells little about the kind of administration she was establishing other than that she understood the value of experience and the necessity of political support. The list of Marian councillors she dropped and the new men she appointed told the world that change was at hand. 'The kingdom,' wrote the Count de Feria in a fit of hyperbole, 'is entirely in the hands of young folks, heretics, and traitors, and the Queen does not favour a single man whom Her Majesty, who is now in heaven, would have received'.[9] Feria was exaggerating, but it is true that Elizabeth had destroyed the Marian power structure and replaced it with one of her own devising. With the exception of the respected Archbishop Heath, who was retained until early January, the most Catholic and ardent Marians disappeared from the Council when Mary died. Lord Hasting of Loughborough, Viscount Montague, Lord Riche, and, most importantly, Lord Paget were dismissed. Paget had been the kingpin of Mary's Council, and his dismissal — which may have been necessitated by his illness — caused the collapse of the Marian system.[10] These rejected lords, with the exception of Paget who was too ill to attend, stood with the bishops against the change of religion when it was debated in the House of Lords.

The new councillors were not young. Nor were they traitors to anything except Feria's ideals. Heretics they were, but their heresy was of a political kind — which is not to say that it was not resolute. All of them were close friends or relatives of either Elizabeth or Cecil. Sir William Cecil himself heads the list of intimates, and he became the engine of policy in the government. Francis Russell, second Earl of Bedford, was the most outspoken Protestant peer in the realm, and he controlled a large portion of the West Country. William Parr, Marquis of Northampton, was a brother of Catherine Parr and had been attainted for his support of Jane Grey. Elizabeth took her cousin, Sir Richard Sackville, into the Council, along with her longtime steward, Sir Thomas Parry. Lord Howard of Effingham, made Lord Chamberlain, was a special friend of the new Queen. Although Mary had raised Howard to the peerage and made him a member of her Council, he had staunchly supported Elizabeth when she was under suspicion after Wyatt's rebellion. Sir Edward Rogers, who had been a gentleman of the Privy Chamber under Edward, became Elizabeth's Comptroller of the Household. Sir Ambrose Cave, a friend of Cecil's,

[8]Ibid., 32.
[9]CSP Span., Eliz., I, 7. 14 December 1558.
[10]MacCaffrey, Shaping, 30.

was made Chancellor of the Duchy of Lancaster. Sir Nicholas Bacon, Cecil's brother-in-law and a highly capable attorney of the Court of Wards, became Lord Keeper. Elizabeth's last appointment to her Privy Council was another of her cousins, Sir Francis Knollys. Knollys was the most ardent Protestant on the Council, having spent part of Mary's reign in exile in Strassburg.[11] His swearing in on January 14 completed the new Council.[12]

Of these men only Bedford and Knollys were outspoken Protestants. The rest had conformed under Mary, as Elizabeth herself had done. However, all of them, with the exception of Winchester, preferred Protestantism for political if not spiritual reasons.[13] Most of this group had served in Edward's government and fallen from favour under Mary. Cecil himself exemplifies them. After serving in various positions under Edward he made his peace with Mary and seems to have hoped for some preferment, but he remained in contact with his Protestant friends and relatives on the continent, defending their property rights in Parliament — noting smugly in his diary that although he had run some risk in coming to their defence, it was better to obey God than men.[14] Read, who attributes Cecil's defence of the exiles' rights to political opportunism as much as to religious feeling, notes that Cecil's Protestantism began to warm up after it became obvious that Mary would never have a child and that Elizabeth was the legal successor. Cecil, it is argued, well knew that Elizabeth was a Protestant and accordingly aligned himself with the party of the future.[15] Whatever the motives of Cecil and his friends — he knew them all — they carried with them the Edwardian tradition, and in many ways Elizabeth's policy at the beginning of her reign echoed that tradition.

Before Elizabeth had been a month on the throne her reconstructed Council began to dismantle the commissions of religion established by Mary to ferret out Protestants. The first move was made on December 18, 1558, when the councillors directed letters to William Saye, Robert Warmington and William Babeham, the registrars attendant upon the commissioners. They were ordered to

> make a particular and perfect note of all suche matters as have
> been called before the Bishop of London, Sir Roger Cholmeley
> and other Commissyoners appointed to call before them
> certein persons of this realme, and to signifye withall what

[11] Ibid., 33-34.
[12] APC, VII, 43.
[13] MacCaffrey, Shaping, 38.
[14] Read, Cecil, 110.
[15] Ibid., 111-112.

judgementes passed against them, and what fynes were cessed and levyed of them and to whome the same was payed; and in the meane tyme they are commaunded, as they wyll aunswer for the contrary, to kepe this matter close to themselfes.[16]

Armed with the results of this secret survey, the Council summoned Edmund Bonner, Bishop of London, to Westminster on January 3. He was ordered to deliver to the Vicechamberlain all the commissions made to him and others for the examination of heresies and disorders in the Church in the time of Queen Mary. They thus deprived him of his power as head of the commission and ended the investigation of heresy.[17]

In the meantime, gentlemen in various parts of the country were ordered to examine prisoners jailed by the bishops' officers and to release those detained without legal cause. On the last day of December such an order was despatched to Lord Mountjoy, Sir William Kelleway and Sir John Zouche, who were to examine those imprisoned at Salisbury.[18] On January 14 John Teys and William Cardinall in Essex received instructions to release the prisoners being held on suspicion of heresy in Colchester Castle. They were to make the prisoners post bonds to guarantee that they would be quiet and appear if summoned.[19]

Thus although the Council was seeing to it that prisoners were released and all further prosecutions stopped, they were not acting extralegally. The accused were still being bound for good behaviour and appearance, but it was the end of the persecutions. The laws against heresy were allowed to stand unused until Parliament abolished them in May of 1559.

The hard pressed Crown did not miss a chance to make a profit descend to it from the commissions. On January 11 the proctors of the Court of Arches were ordered to pay over to the Treasurer of the Chamber all sums remaining in their hands which had been levied on people examined for heresy and other misdemeanours.[20]

Keeping the religious and civil peace was among Elizabeth's foremost concerns. She demonstrated this in her accession proclamation, which ordered her subjects to 'keepe them selves in our peace, and not to attempt uppon any pretence the breache alteration or

[16] *APC.*, VII, 22-23.
[17] *APC*, VII, 36.
[18] *APC*, VII. 34-35.
[19] *APC*, VII, 44.
[20] *APC*, VII, 43.

change of any order or usage presently established within our realme'.[21] Cecil, as we have seen, repeated her concern when he noted that a preacher should be picked for Paul's Cross, ' . . . that no occasion be gyven by hym to stirr any dispute towchying the governance of ye realm'.[22] Their precautions, however, were of little avail. True, the proclamation encouraged some Catholics to believe that she would not change religion, but Cecil's choice of a preacher alarmed them. When Dr. Bill, the Queen's Almoner and a known heretic, preached the first sermon of the reign from Paul's Cross he told the world by his presence that a new religious order was coming to England. Noting that change was in the wind, some Catholics of strong conviction spoke out against it.

Bishop Christopherson of Chichester may have been the first to sound the warning. Edmund Sandys, writing from Strassburg on December 20, told Henry Bullinger that Christopherson had preached at Paul's Cross on November 27, vehemently refuting everything Bill had said and calling on the crowd not to believe his doctrine, the invention of heretics. The Queen, greatly displeased by this, had ordered the Bishop to prison.[23] Sandys' report is uncoroborated, which is odd, for the Catholic diplomats would have been quick to report such an incident — although they failed to notice Christopherson's death and burial a month later.[24] Sandys said that his information came from a letter he had received out of England, and the rest of what he reports is fairly accurate. Whatever happened, it is not likely that the Bishop was actually imprisoned. Nor is it likely that he would have been allowed to preach at Paul's Cross, unless the government was entirely ignorant of his sympathies. However, it is doubtful that Sandys' informant fabricated the whole story, so it is probable that Christopherson did air his opinions somewhere and somehow.

His colleague, Bishop White of Winchester, took the chance offered by Mary's funeral sermon to speak out against the changes he feared. He did not, as John Jewel reported, preach that it would be meritorious to kill the exiles on their return,[25] but he did say some rough things about the Protestants and Elizabeth. White's oration, delivered on December 13, caused his arrest for sedition and resulted in his house arrest until January 19.[26]

[21]Oxford, Arch. Bodl., G.c.6 (1).

[22]P.R.O., SP 12/I/ fol. 3.

[23]ZL, I, 4.

[24]ZL, I, 6. It may be that a letter of Feria's is missing.

[25]ZL, I, 7.

[26]Ibid. and APC, VII, 45.

These two bishops were the most exalted disturbers of the religious peace, but they were not alone. We know very little about public reaction to the expected change, but some cases of discontent were egregious enough to come to the attention of the Privy Council. It is difficult to determine what percentage of the reports of lewd words the Council received had to do with religion, but many certainly were connected with it. The first religious disturbance dealt with by the Council is noted in the Act Book on December 9. That day the councillors asked Lord Riche to investigate a supplication sent by a parson in Essex, who complained of a disorder committed in his church by Thomas Pike. Riche was to punish Pike — who, given the shire in which he lived, was probably a Protestant — according to the quality of his offence.[27] December 15 found the Council investigating lewd words spoken by John Shory, sexton of the cathedral church of Chichester.[28] Incidents of this sort, which occurred with increasing regularity in the new year, were not isolated. That reliable Italian reporter, Il Schifanoya, testified that by December 31 many disputes and controversies had taken place.[29]

The Protestants were impatient because the Queen had not immediately abolished Catholicism, and a mob of them caused the greatest known breach of the peace. On Christmas morning a crowd, led by two preachers (whom Il Schifanoya described as a mechanic and a cobbler), broke into the Italian church of St. Augustine in London. Once in, the preachers occupied the pulpit and commenced reading and preaching to the crowd, 'uttering a thousand ribaldries concerning the reign of . . . Queen Mary and of the Cardinal, and vituperating the people for the errors they had committed in believing their former teachers'. This performance was repeated again in the afternoon, and yet again on the following day.[30] Sir Nicholas Throckmorton was a member of the mob.[31]

The authorities reacted oddly to these disturbances. An Italian complained to the Marquis of Winchester who lived nearby, but, although he was a member of the Council, 'he only shrugged his shoulders and begged them not to refer the matter to him'.[32] The Italian then carried his complaint to the Lord Mayor, who avoided the issue and referred him to the Privy Council. The councillors

[27] *APC*, VII, 17.
[28] *APC*, VII, 19.
[29] *CSP Ven.*, VII, 2.
[30] *Ibid.*
[31] *CSP Span., Eliz.*, I, 17.
[32] *Ibid.*

promised him that they would summon the people involved and make enquiries.[33]

This sounds natural enough, although one wonders at Winchester's and the Lord Mayor's reluctance to take any action against so manifest a disturbance of the peace. Interestingly, there is no evidence that the Council ever conducted their promised investigation. In cases of this kind they normally initiated an inquiry by ordering persons known to have been involved to be taken up for questioning; an order for imprisonment often followed. The Act Book of the Council bears no trace of any such action concerning the riot at St. Augustine's church. Neither do the records of the City of London. One is led to suspect that Winchester and the Lord Mayor avoided acting because they knew that the Council preferred that no direct action be taken against the Protestants.

Instead, a royal proclamation prohibiting unlicensed preaching was sent to the Lord Mayor on December 28.[34] Intended to protect the religious peace, it read:

> The Queen's Majesty, understanding that there be certain persons having in times past the office of ministry in the Church which now do purpose to use their former office in preaching and ministry, and partly have attempted the same, assembling specially in the city of London in sundry places great number of people; whereupon riseth amongst the common sort not only unfruitful dispute in matters of religion, but also contention and occasion to break common quiet: Hath therefore . . . thought it necessary to charge and command, like as hereby her highness doth charge and command, all manner of her subjects, as well those that be called to the ministry in the Church as all others, that they do forbear to preach or teach or to give audience to any manner of doctrine or preaching other than to the Gospels and Epistles, commonly called the Gospel and the Epistle of the day, and to the Ten Commandments in the vulgar tongue without exposition (or addition of any manner, sense, or meaning) to be applied or added; or to use any other manner of public prayer, rite or ceremony in the Church but that which is already used and by law received, or the common litany used at this present in her majesty's own chapel, and the Lord's Prayer, and the Creed in English, until consultation may be had by parliament, by her majesty, and her three estates of this realm for the better conciliation and accord of such causes as at this present are moved in matters and ceremonies of religion, the true advancement whereof, to the due honor of Almighty God, the increase of

[33]*Ibid.*

[34]*APC*, VII, 31. Corp. London R.O., Journals, XVII, fol. 103v.

virtue and godliness with universal charity, and concord
amongst her people, her majesty most desireth and meaneth
effectually by all manner of means possible to procure and to
restore to this her realm. . . .[35]

Those who disobeyed this decree would be punished both for the
offence itself and for being disobedient subjects.[36] In the meantime,
Richard Jugge hurriedly printed *The letanye, used in the Quenes
Maiesties chappel* so that the Protestants could use the newly
legalized forms.[37]

This proclamation, designed to quieten the Protestants and
promise reform, at once stopped preaching and signalled that,
although the Queen would keep the peace, she would tolerate certain
Protestant practices. Moreover, it explicity offered hope of further
and greater changes when Parliament met. Read in the City on
December 30, it gave the government an effective weapon against all
preachers who disagreed with government policy, and it would be
used to suppress clerical dissent while the transition went forward.
Since all exposition was forbidden, no Catholic or reformer could use
holy writ to challenge the Queen's writ. Deprived of this function, the
preachers lost much of their political influence.

The Council used its new weapon against preachers of both
persuasions during the next few months, but the Catholics, not
surprisingly, received more careful attention. The incidence of
charges of illegal preaching and lewd words bears a definite relation
to the activities of the Parliament, offences becoming increasingly
frequent as it became apparent that Catholicism was going to be
discarded. The first major breach committed by a Catholic occurred
in early February. It was reported to the Council that Dr. Nicholas
Harpsfield, Archdeacon of Canterbury and a famous Catholic, had
been stirring the people to sedition. Moreover, '. . . it is also reported
by some of the servauntes of the Colledge in Christe Church in
Cantourbury that Religion could not nor should not be altered, and
that one man of the Colledge hath well nere one hundreth harnesses'.[38]
This must have frightened the Council, for it confirmed some of their
worst fears. A seditious preacher with an armed following was
threatening revolt in defence of the Catholic faith. Acting quickly,

[35] Paul L. Hughes and James F. Larkin, eds. *Tudor Royal Proclamations* (New Haven: 1969), II, 102-3.

[36] *Ibid.*, II, 103.

[37] *The Letanye, used in the Quenes Maiesties chappel, 1559* (London: R. Jugge, [1559]).

[38] *APC*, VII, 54.

they ordered two aldermen of Canterbury to examine those involved and to commit those who were culpable to prison. The investigators were also enjoined to discover what armour was in the college, how much of it had been issued, to whom, and for what purpose.[39]

In the weeks that followed other arrests were made. John Murren, chaplain to the Bishop of London, was committed to the Fleet for preaching contrary to the Queen's order.[40] In late February a canon of Lichfield was ordered to appear before the Council to answer charges of lewd preaching and misdemeanor. He was eventually bound in 100 marks to guarantee his good behaviour.[41] On March 6 the councillors dealt with two more cases of preaching in Canterbury, committed on the first Sunday in Lent. The same day the Lords thanked the mayor and aldermen of Bristol for arresting a Spanish priest who had been saying unseemly things about the Queen.[42] Shortly thereafter letters were sent to the sheriffs of Devon and Cornwall complaining that certain men in those counties were preaching, contrary to the proclamation. Each sheriff was asked to 'call suche of the Justyces unto him as he knoweth to be servyceable to her Hieghnes' and confer with them about apprehending and jailing the culprits.[43] The Lords seemed unsure of the loyalty of the justices in these areas where Edward's prayer book of 1549 had caused a rebellion.

Il Schifanoya accused 'persons in authority' of molesting Catholics. In a letter written on February 6 he told the tale of two Doctors of Laws who were hailed before the Council and charged with speaking against the current state of religion. Both of them, he says, defended themselves bravely. Dr. John Story, a civilian who sat in Parliament for a borough in Wiltshire, is quoted by Il Schifanoya as telling the Council:

> you need not interrogate me about these matters, as I know better than any of you both the canon laws and those of this kingdom; let my accusers appear and prove what I have said, for I certainly said nothing at which you could reasonably take offence; but should her Majesty will otherwise, I do not refuse to die for the Church.[44]

If this story is accurate, and Il Schifanoya's usually are, it shows the Council attempting to silence an outspoken Catholic.

[39] Ibid.
[40] APC, VII, 59.
[41] APC, VII, 60, 64, 71, 87.
[42] APC, VII, 63.
[43] APC, VII, 66.
[44] CSP Ven., VII, 26-27.

Compared with the Catholics, the Protestants got off lightly. Only three identifiably Protestant preachers were arrested between January and June of 1559. The first person charged with disobeying the proclamation against preaching was Thomas Parrys, who does not seem to have been a minister at all. He was sent to one of the Compters of London because he permitted, contrary to the proclamation, assemblies of people at Worcester Place, of which he had charge.[45] It is odd that Parrys was committed for allowing assemblies, while the preacher, if he was some other person, was allowed to go unmolested. In mid-April the sheriff of Essex, the bailiffs of Colchester, and justices in that area were asked to apprehend the preachers Dodman and Pulleyn and send them to the Council for examination.[46] Strong Protestants, these two are the only returned exiles known to have run foul of the government during the first half of 1559. There is no evidence in the Acts of the Privy Council to indicate that either of them was punished.

While it is not known what offence Dodman and Pulleyn committed, it must have been flagrant to cause their arrest. Other men were preaching while the authorities looked the other way. Thomas Lever described the underground activities of the Protestant preachers in the days before the alteration became legal. In August, 1559, when it was safe to write of their disobedience, he told Bullinger how some preachers, 'considering that the silence imposed for a long and uncertain period was not agreeable to the command and earnest injunction of Paul . . . preached the gospel in certain parish churches'. Lever himself went to Coventry to minister the gospel. In London the Protestant congregation came out of hiding and began to meet openly.

> But as their godly mode of worship was condemned by the laws of the realm, the magistrates, though they connived at their frequent assembling in private houses, would not allow them, notwithstanding, to occupy the parish churches. In consequence of which, large numbers flocked to them not in the churches, but in private houses.[47]

Not only were the Protestants able to circumvent the ban on preaching, they were permitted to preach to the court. Richard Hilles told Bullinger on February 28:

> With respect to religion, silence has been imposed upon the Catholic preachers (as they are called) by a royal proclamation, and sufficient liberty is allowed to the gospellers, to preach three

[45] *Ibid.*, VII, 32.
[46] *Ibid.*, VII, 87-88.
[47] *ZL*, II, 29-30.

42

times a week during this Lent before the queen herself, and to
prove their doctrine from the holy scriptures.[48]

Hilles' statement underlines the relationship between the government
and the Protestant preachers, exile and otherwise. The preachers
were convinced enough of the Queen's good intentions not to be
forced into civil disobedience in the name of their faith. Allowed to
preach and expound the Gospel at court, they were reaching the
most important audience in the realm, and, impatient though they
were for the completion of the reform by Parliament, they were willing
to wait because they knew that reform would come.

Though the intellectual leaders of the reformed party were content
to await the change, the enthusiastic men in the pews were not.
Iconoclasm, which broke the peace as surely as it broke statues, posed
a recurrent problem. After an inconoclastic riot in Bow Church the
Council complained to Sir Thomas Lee, the Lord Mayor, that they
thought it odd that he had not taken any steps to redress the crime. Lee
was reminded 'of thexhortacion made by the Quenes Majestie unto
him on Candlemas day laste [February 2]' and commanded him to
use the best means possible to find the wrongdoers.[49] Il Schifanoya
tells how the windows of churches were broken and their ornaments
carried off, as happened on February 4 when the tabernacle was
stolen from St. Augustine's Church. The thieves remained
unpunished.[50] He also relates how, on Ascension Day, a printer's
apprentice snatched a crucifix from its bearer's hands during a
procession and smashed it to bits. The bystanders allowed him to do
this and to escape unmolested. In another case men with drawn
swords prevented a procession from leaving a church, threatening to
kill the clerics if they tried.[51]

The Council itself was ambivalent about punishing inconoclasts.
It felt that disobedience and riot were not to be tolerated, but that
inconoclasm was not evil in itself. Witness the case of a sailor, a
shoemaker, and a butcher of Dover who were each bound in the sum
of £20 after committing sacrilege in their parish church. The Council
ordered each of them

> ... to declare openly in the churche in the tyme of servyce that he
> did very yll and without order to pluck downe the Images of that
> churche *before any lawe dyd aucthorise him so to doo.*[52]

[48]*ZL*, II, 16-17.
[49]*APC*, VII, 77.
[50]*CSP Ven.*, VII, 27.
[51]*Ibid.*, VII, 84.
[52]My italics, *APC,* VII, 88.

Other forms of anti-Catholic activity were not banned, and London indulged its appetite greedily. Il Schifanoya was deeply offended by the plays and printed propaganda prepared by the heretics who, he told the Venetian ambassador in Brussels,

> are clever, locquacious, and fervent, both in preaching, and in composing and printing squibs and lampoons, or ballads, as they entitle them, which are sold publicly, of so horrible and abominable a description that I wonder their authors do not perish by the act of God. I thought of sending you a copy, but repented, not wishing to sow evil seed in your country.[53]

In another letter he complained of the plays deriding the Catholic faith, the Church, the clergy, and religion in general that were daily performed in the taverns.[54]

In this the Londoners were following the royal example. On Twelfth Night a mask was performed at court in which the dancers represented crows disguised as cardinals, asses as bishops, and wolves as abbots. Popes, priests, summoners, vergers, and monks clad in velvet and satin joined in the dance.[55] In early January there was a masquerade of monks in the streets of the city, and a statue of St. Thomas was stoned and beheaded, the stucco figure of a little girl being left on the saint's severed neck.[56]

That such activities were permitted hinted at where the Queen intended to lead the nation; Elizabeth's personal religious behaviour did more than hint. Until Christmas no one was certain what she would do. After that holiday no one doubted that the reform would return to England.

It is difficult to ascertain when Elizabeth began changing the ceremonies used in her private chapel. A rumour was abroad that the Queen was using an English litany, after the manner of King Edward, as early as December 17.[57] That rumour is unsubstantiated, but it is a fact that she chose the holiest day in the Christian calendar to deny the truth of transubstantiation. Just before she went to mass on Christmas morning Elizabeth sent for the Bishop of Carlisle, who was to officiate

[53] *CSP Ven.,* VII, 53, 19 March 1559.

[54] *Ibid.,* VII, 27; 80-81.

[55] *Ibid.,* VII, 11. E.K. Chambers, *The Elizabethan Stage* (Oxford: 1923), I, 155-156. The expenses incurred by the Office of the Revels for making cardinals' hats, priests' caps, and other accoutrements of this masque are printed in Albert Feuillerat, ed., *Documents Relating to the Office of the Revels in the Time of Queen Elizabeth* (Louvain: 1908), 80.

[56] *CSP Ven.,* VII, 11.

[57] *Ibid.,* VII, 1.

and told him not to elevate the Host for adoration. Righteously indignant, Oglethorpe refused, telling her that she was mistress of his body but not of his conscience.[58] Apparently she was not ready to deal with such recalcitrance, for the bishop did perform her Christmas mass. The Queen heard it until the Gospel had been read. Then, when she should have offered, she dramatically rose and returned to her privy chambers. It was, as one witness said, 'strange on to dyvers'.[59] It was also a blatant affirmation of her stand in matters of the faith.

Feria and Il Schifanoya agree that, by Christmas Tide, at least part of the service in the chapel royal was in English. Feria wrote on December 29:

> A litany has been printed which used to be sung in the time of King Edward, in which no saints at all are mentioned, and she hears mass in this way, although they tell me that the chaplains who perform it are some of them married, and others doubtful.[60]

This report is confirmed by the existence of an English litany and suffrages printed in 1558, after Elizabeth's accession. This particular one may have been published by Protestants without the licence of the Crown, but immediately after the proclamation of December 27 legalized the 'common litany' used in the Queen's chapel another English litany was published. Issued 'according to the tenor of the proclamation,' it gave the realm a partially reformed service.[61] It is interesting to note that neither of these litanies was taken from the still outlawed Edwardian prayer books. Instead they came from either the 1547 or 1545 Primer, in keeping with Goodrich's legal opinion that, until religion was altered, 'her Majesty, and all her Subiects may by licence off law use the Inglish Latynye and suffrages usyd in Kinge Henry's tyme'.[62]

The anti-Catholic nature of the accession revels is nowhere more apparent than in the pageant staged for Elizabeth on January 14, the day before the coronation.[63] Presented by the city of London, it demonstrated the city's expectations and underlined the royal policy. The planning for it began in early December, when the Common

[58] *CSP Span., Eliz.,* I, 17.

[59] HMC, *7th Report,* Appendix, 614. Sir William Fitzwilliam to Mr More, 26 December 1558.

[60] *CSP Ven.,* VII, 2.

[61] William Keatinge Clay, ed., *Liturgies and Occasional Forms of Prayer Set Forth in the Reign of Queen Elizabeth* (Cambridge: 1847), 1-8, 9-22.

[62] P.R.O., SP 12/I/fol. 157v.

[63] Sidney Anglo, *Spectacle Pageant and Early Tudor Policy* (Oxford: 1969), 345.

Council of the City appointed forty-four persons to committees to prepare the various stations of the procession. Four men were employed to devise the displays, and a schoolmaster was hired to express their devisings in English and Latin.[64] With the government's approval they set up five displays emphasizing their joy at the coming of godly Elizabeth. As she processed through the city the Queen encountered each presentation. In Cornhill she found an arch bearing an extravagant inscription declaring that religion, hereto misunderstood and misdirected, would hereafter proceed on a better course. This was represented by a seated queen, surrounded by labelled figures. On one side stood the shades of the past: ignorance, superstition, hypocrisy, vainglory, simulation, rebellion and idolatry. On the other side was the future: pure religion, just government, intelligence, wisdom, prudence, fear of God. A poem affixed to the arch said, in part, 'Vana superstitio et crassae ignorantiae fontes, Pressae sub pura religione jacent'.[65] In Soper Lane another arch depicted Elizabeth as possessed of all eight beatitudes. The arch in Cheapside illustrated the decayed state into which England had fallen under Mary and juxtaposed the nation's bright future under Eliza. Here she was presented with an English Bible, which she clasped in her arms and embraced passionately.[66] The orator of this arch reminded her that the Bible was the sure guide of the good commonwealth. The last arch represented Deborah consulting with her estates about the good governance of Israel — an obvious depiction of Protestant Elizabeth and her Parliament.[67]

As far as we know, none of these displays directly attacked the Pope or mentioned the supremacy. Superstition, ignorance, and idolatry — Catholicism — were the ills and Elizabeth was the cure: 'Salve, igitur dicas, immo de pectore summo, Elizabeth, Regni non dubitanda salus! Virgo venit, veniuntque opes.'[68]

The coronation ceremony ought to have been an even better indication of royal religious policy. Unfortunately, we are not sure what changes Elizabeth made in the traditional forms of the mass and coronation. This question became the subject of heated debate during 1907 and 1908. C. G. Bayne maintained that Elizabeth withdrew from the mass during the consecration of the elements, rather than

[64] *Ibid.*, 346. Corp. London R.O., Repertories, XIV, fols. 97v-99v.
[65] *CSP Ven.*, VII, 13-14.
[66] *Ibid.*, VII, 15.
[67] Anglo, *Pageant, 347-53 gives a detailed description.*
[68] *CSP Ven.*, VII, 16.

watch Bishop Oglethorpe elevate the Host.[69] H.A. Wilson rebutted Bayne's view and argued convincingly that Elizabeth had witnessed the elevation. He concluded that she thought a valid coronation was worth a popish mass.[70] The final word in this dispute was spoken by Il Schifanoya, through the mouth of G.L. Ross who contributed a short note on the subject. Quoting the original Italian of Il Schifanoya's letter concerning the coronation, he demonstrated that Rawdon Brown's translation in the Venetian State Papers was inaccurate. The Italian makes it clear, if we can accept him as a witness, that the Dean of Elizabeth's chapel performed the mass because none of the bishops would either celebrate without elevating the Host, or consecrate the elements in English. The Epistle and the Evangel were also given in English, after they had been sung in Latin.[71] Il Schifanoya's statement is supported by the apparent refusal of Archbishop Heath and the other bishops, with the exception of Oglethorpe of Carlisle, to officiate. The fact that only Oglethorpe, a very junior bishop, was willing to take part suggests that there was indeed something wrong with the coronation service.

By the time of her coronation, then, Elizabeth had changed the service in her chapel enough for it to evoke the doctrine and ceremony prescribed in the Book of Common Prayer. Not only was the litany, first Englished by her father in 1544, being said in the vernacular along with the creed and the Paternoster, but the consecration of the elements was also being performed in English, an innovation of 1549. Moreover, her refusal to offer at the Christmas mass and her refusal to permit the elevation of the Host, demonstrating her repudiation of the doctrine of transubstantiation, had, as had the 1549 prayer book, cut the living heart out of the body of Catholic worship, leaving only an elegantly dressed corpse. Elizabeth had now carried religious change as far as Goodrich and the 'Device' had said was permitted without parliamentary sanction, with one possible exception. We do not know if she began to receive communion *sub utraque specie* before Easter.

---

[69] C.G. Bayne, 'The Coronation of Queen Elizabeth', *EHR* (1907), 658-64.

[70] H.A. Wilson, 'The Coronation of Queen Elizabeth', *EHR* (1908), 89-90.

[71] G.L. Ross, 'Il Schifanoya's Account of the Coronation of Queen Elizabeth', *EHR* (1908), 533-34. Ross quotes Il Schifanoya: 'et fu dalli cantori cominciata la Messa, et Cantata dal decano della sua Capella suo capellano, non havendo voluto gli vescovi celebrare senza levare il Corpo di Christo, ne consecrare l'hostia con le parole Englesi, come fece quel buon homo, et fu detto l'Epistola et l'Evangelo in Englese doppo li cantati in latino'. Compare this with *CSP Ven.,* VII, 24-25.

The Queen now had a fully Protestant service in her chapel: her religious conscience could be at ease when she attended services there. Next these changes needed to be enacted by Parliament, so that the consciences of all her subjects could rest easy.

While the attention of the world was focused on the ceremonies and carousing that came with Christmas and the coronation, the members of Her Majesty's Privy Council were busy preparing for Parliament. The writs calling it had been issued on December 6, but it was not until the 23rd of the month that the Council appointed a committee 'For Consideration of all thinges necessary for the Parlyamente'. This large and unwieldy committee was composed of lawyers: the Lord Keeper, the judges, the serjeants, Mr. Attorney, Mr. Solicitor, Sir Thomas Smith, and Richard Goodrich.[72] Sadly, the Act Book does not indicate what the Council meant by 'all thinges necessary'. Judging from the committee's composition, it probably was entrusted with the physical organization of the Parliament and with advising the Crown about projected legislation. It is possible that its members devised such bills as the one continuing certain expiring acts, but they did not draft the important legislation. Other committees were doing that. Five men were appointed 'To consider the state of the Customes and what is mete to be reformed therin privately and what in a Parliament'.[73] From this committee came two bills concerning the enforcement of the new customs duties. Another group was asked to find out what lands and other things had been granted away by Queen Mary.[74] The results of this committee's activities became visible in and out of Parliament during the next few months. There is, on the other hand, no certain proof that any committee worked on the religious legislation of 1559. The 'Device' called for one, and we know that advice was solicited, but if it met it left no traces. There remain only the 1559 prayer book and the other acts to prove that someone revised the prayer book and drafted the legislation. Only one feeble hint suggests that learned divines were called into consultation.

This hint is found among Matthew Parker's correspondence. There, a series of letters show that Cecil and Bacon were very anxious to talk with Parker, one of the divines named in the 'Device,' about something of importance. Bacon wrote the first message to Parker, who was probably still in his refuge somewhere in East Anglia, on December 9, but was now asked to repair to London, where Bacon or

[72] APC, VII, 28.
[73] P.R.O., SP 12/I/fol. 127.
[74] P.R.O., SP 12/I/fol. 126.

Cecil would inform him of certain matters concerning himself.[75] Parker, sensing that he was about to be appointed to some onerous post, excused himself from coming and asked that he be given some prebend and left to enjoy his life in Cambridge.[76] He followed this letter with another to Bacon, offering to meet him in Newmarket; he did not want to visit London.[77] By late December the Queen was impatient with his reluctance to come to the City, and Cecil despatched an abrupt note on the 30th:

> After my hearty commendations. The Queen's highness minding presently to use your service in certain matters of importance, hath willed me so to signify unto you, to the end you should . . . make your indelayed repair hither unto London; at which your coming up I shall declare unto you her Majesty's further pleasure, and the occasion why you are sent for; and hereof praying you therefore in no wise to fail, I bid you well to fare.[78]

On January 4th Bacon wrote in a similar sense. He assured the reluctant divine that he would do everything he could to secure for him his prebend and Cambridge retirement, but he must come to London. 'I have been willed to haste your coming up,' he wrote.[79]

Parker, soon to be Archbishop-elect of Canterbury, gave in and went to London some time in January.[80] It is not known how long he stayed, although he preached twice before the Queen during Lent, and it is unclear why he was summoned at this time. Perhaps it was simply to offer him the archbishopric, or perhaps it was to consult him about the coming change in religion; in all probability it was to do both. Back in Cambridge by March 1, Parker admitted that he had been offered, and had not yet accepted, the see of Canterbury while he was in London.[81] It is unlikely that the man chosen to be the principal cleric in the realm was not asked if he could accept the coming alteration.

The Act of Uniformity and Parker's visit to London do not prove that the 'Device' was obeyed, although its explanation is probably as good as any we shall ever have of how the revision came about. For lack of concrete evidence, however, its champions (including this author) can resort only to negative proofs. There is not good reason for

[75] Matthew Parker, *Correspondence,* John Bruce, ed. (Cambridge: 1853), 49.

[76] *Ibid.,* 50-51.

[77] *Ibid.,* 52.

[78] *Ibid.,* 53.

[79] *Ibid.*

[80] P.R.O., SP 12/III/fol. 12, and Parker, *Correspondence,* 57.

[81] Parker, *Correspondence,* 57-62.

thinking that the committee did not meet. All of the clerics named in the 'Device,' with the possible exception of James Pilkington, were in London and available for consultation by February. Henry (Machym, London's chronicling undertaker, recorded that they were the Queen's preachers during Lent. Richard Cox preached at court on Ash Wednesday, the day before the bill for supremacy was introduced in the Lower House — which was especially adjourned to hear the sermon.[82] Matthew Parker spoke on February 10th, David Whitehead on the 15th, and Edmund Grindal on the 23rd.[83] Neither William Bill nor William May had ever left England, and Bill had been selected by Cecil to deliver the first sermon of the new reign at Paul's Cross. It is not known when Pilkington returned to England, but his absence would not have prevented the other six from preparing the revision. It may therefore be more than a coincidence that the ministers chosen to preach during Lent were the very men named in the 'Device.'

It has been assumed by some scholars that Edmund Guest was included in the committee to revise the prayer book because of an undated letter found by William Cecil among his papers and sent to Matthew Parker. The letter — it is not clear if it was addressed to Cecil — is a defence of changes made in a service book which had been recently prepared and which had been submitted to Parliament for confirmation. Strype was the first to link Guest's letter to the committee of the 'Device,' a mistake which has been perpetuated by many scholars, in spite of the anomalies the letter contains. Dixon, for instance, accepted Strype's evaluation of it, even though his footnotes show that he realized the inconsistencies between the prayer book of 1559 and the book of which Guest wrote.[84] Henry Gee subjected the epistle to a rigorous critique and demonstrated that it belonged to 1552, not 1559.[85] In spite of J.E. Neale's restoration of Guest's letter to an important place in the 1559 story,[86] Gee's analysis still awaits a cogent theological challenge.[87] We may leave Guest out of the 1559 proceedings.

[82]Henry Machyn, *Diary,* J.G. Nichols, ed. (London: 1848), 189. H.L.R.O., Commons MS. Journals, I, fol. 188.

[83]Machyn, *Diary,* 189-90.

[84]Dixon, *History,* V, 101-102.

[85]Gee, *Prayer-Book,* 225.

[86]Neale, 'Supremacy and Uniformity', 327-29.

[87]Winthrop Hudson has supported Gee's case in an unpublished paper which he was kind enough to show me.

The parliamentary strategy decided upon by Cecil before the beginning of the session, as traceable through the 'Device' and the events in Parliament, was simple. Separate bills for the return of first fruits and tenths to the Crown, the revival of the royal supremacy over the Church, and the establishment of religious uniformity based upon a prayer book were to be introduced at the beginning of the session. Once the schism with Rome had been revived the government could introduce bills to recover the revenues Queen Mary had given to the Church out of the Crown's possessions. Presumably, all of these objectives could have been accomplished before Easter if the bishops had not proved recalcitrant, and if the Commons had not been swamped with private bills.

By the time the government introduced its supremacy bill into the Commons it must have felt fairly secure at home. No major resistance had materialized; the Protestants, though impatient, were quiet; and the leading Catholics were working loyally in and with the government. Cecil and Elizabeth had been extraordinarily lucky, if we look at the situation from their point of view. They had feared much worse than had occurred. For reasons beyond their control, though probably not beyond their understanding, they were blessed in their foreign relations, too. During the crucial months of early 1559 they managed to maintain the Spanish alliance that was the keystone of England's security. Thanks largely to Philip II, Elizabeth was able to obtain an honourable treaty with the French and Scots, and she was saved from the excommunication she deserved and expected. Elizabeth based her foreign policy on a gamble. Calculating that the Spanish were so afraid of an England dominated by France that they would not dare abandon her, she demonstrated to the world that she was a free and independent princess and that England was no longer bound to the Spanish king.

Her gamble was a well-informed one. Her diplomats correctly argued that Philip would not leave England at the mercy of its enemy across the Channel.[88] Undoubtedly, Philip did fear a French conquest of England. A policy paper, written for the King of Spain and the Low Countries in May or June of 1559, put the problem succinctly: 'If England were lost, it cannot convincingly be denied, though some would dispute it, that these lands of Flanders themselves would be in imminent danger. And the loss of England, within a short space of

---

[88] P.R.O., SP 70/I/fol. 4v, and Wotton to Cecil, 9 January 1559 in *CSP For.,* I, 83.

time, is considered certain for many reasons.'[89] Count Feria had pounded home the lesson that England would fall at the first French onslaught, and this belief made the ruin of the Spanish Netherlands seem imminent unless England was propped up by Spanish power. Hence, the English and the Spanish realized that a continuation of their old friendship was important for their mutual well-being.[90] Philip and Elizabeth therefore worked hard to reassure one another of their amity. Philip's first thought was to retain England as an ally by the simple expedient of marrying Elizabeth. For her part, Elizabeth informed Philip of her desire to preserve 'brotherhood, friendship, and perpetual alliance' between their kingdoms, which she wished to confirm by renewing the treaties between their nations. Philip replied in kind. Elizabeth also freely admitted that the French were trying to secure a separate peace with England, and she insisted that the English would agree to nothing without Philip's full knowledge and consent. The Spanish King answered by thanking her and saying that he would safeguard English interests in the negotiations about to reopen at Cateau Cambrésis.[91]

That is where matters stood when the negotiators gathered at the half derelict château on February 10. Philip and Elizabeth were cultivating each other, the one in hope of a new marriage alliance, the other in hope of retaining Spanish support.

When the commissioners met they expected to complete a treaty very quickly. The negotiations had been adjourned in mid-November in order that the English might confer with their new Queen, and at their parting the diplomats generally agreed that only Calais stood in the way of peace. The French insisted that the city was theirs; the English and Spanish maintained that it should be returned to the English Crown from whom it had been captured. This issue prevented the French and Spanish from concluding a treaty, even though they had resolved their differences.[92] When they reconvened in February

[89] Simancas E° 137, fols. 95-97 as quoted in Fernand Braudel, *The Mediterranean and the Mediterranean World in the Age of Philip II,* Sian Reynolds, trans. (London: 1973), II, 947-48. Manuel F. Alvarez has written: 'Durante todo ese tiempo [1559-1587] Felipe II y sus consejeros habian vivido obsesionados por la posible integracion de un poderoso bloque contario: Francia-Escocia-Inglaterra. Se temia que Maria Estuardo uniese a Escocia con Inglaterra, en particular, clero esto, cuando era la Reine consorte de Francia. Era la epoca in que Felipe II se cree mar. En otras palabras, susistia la imagen de una Francia sempiterna enemiga, fuente mayor de todos los quebraderos de cabeza para la monarquia Catolica.' *Politica Mundial de Carlos V y Felipe II* (Madrid: 1966), 257. See also R. Trevor Davies, *The Golden Age of Spain 1501-1621* (London: 1964), 131-32.

[90] *CSP Span., Eliz.,* I, 13. *CSP For.,* I, 49.

[91] *CSP For.,* I, 49-50. *CSP Span., Eliz.,* I, 21.

[92] P.R.O., 31/3/23/fol. 258v. (Baschet Transcripts from the French archives). *CSP Span., Eliz.,* I, 14; 21.

everyone was anxious to know if Elizabeth would be more amenable to surrendering her claim to Calais than Mary had been.

She was not. The new Queen demanded the return of the city, insisted that Scotland (which was not at war with Spain) be included in the peace, and asked for indemnities.[93] She did this even though the Spanish tried to make her see that if neither she nor the French would give up Calais she must fight for it — and neither she nor Philip could afford to renew the war.[94] When the French met with the English on February 11 they were treated to a speech, in bad French, by the Lord Chamberlain of England. The 'spectators of the farce,' as a French witness called his colleagues and himself, listened as Howard repeated the formula they had heard so often: the English and Spanish would not act separately because of the treaties between them, and they would not agree to any treaty which did not restore Calais to England.[95]

The deadlock over Calais continued for a month, as the diplomats of France and Spain gnashed their teeth in frustration. 'Nostre négociation demeure suspendre et accrochée . . . sur les affaires des Anglois,' wrote the future Cardinal Granvelle to the Count of Meghes.[96] Various attempts were made to break the deadlock, including a suggestion that a yet unborn daughter of the Dauphin should marry a son of the yet unmarried Elizabeth, with Calais going as dower to the groom. The diplomats were clearly getting desperate. Matters were further complicated by the necessity of referring each new proposal to the Queen for her decision. One such proposal, that Elizabeth's title to Calais be submitted to arbiters who would decide whether it belonged to her or the Queen of Scots,[97] brought a wrathful reply from London. Elizabeth was furious, and her Council admonished the commissioners that no treaty that cast doubt on her title to the throne would ever be accepted.[98]

Gradually the two sides wore each other out, and a face-saving solution was finally found.[99] On March 11 the French met the Spaniards in the apartments of the Duchess of Lorraine with a new

[93] *CSP For.*, I, 10.

[94] *CSP For.*, I, 10. *CSP Span., Eliz.*, I, 14-15; 27-28. Granvelle, *Papiers d'Etat*, V, 484.

[95] P.R.O., 31/3/24/fol. 9.

[96] Granvelle, *Papiers d'Etat*, V, 486.

[97] P.R.O., 31/3/24/fol. 18v. P.R.O., SP 70/II/fol. 113.

[98] *CSP For.*, I, 164-165.

[99] Braudel, *Mediterranean*, II, 945-46.

proposal from Henry II. The King insisted that the city of Calais was rightfully his, but he was content to return it to the English at the end of eight years. He also agreed to include Scotland in the treaty and to dismantle the fortress of Ayemouth on the English frontier. The Spanish did not believe that the English would accept this proposition, but they did, and it became the basis of the treaty.[100] Once the Gordian knot of Calais had been cut it took only two weeks for the French and Spanish to conclude a treaty between themselves. Elizabeth and Cecil had won their gamble, and Calais remained technically English. Even though the French never gave it back, it could not be said that Elizabeth had surrendered it.

Elizabeth's amity with Philip paid a singular dividend when it saved her from excommunication. Pope Paul IV knew by mid-January that Elizabeth was not going to remain a loyal daughter of the Roman Church, and the French had been trying to start the machinery of excommunication since December.[101] In the normal course of things, the bull should have been issued by the spring of 1559. The Spanish, however, seeing the greed of the French for the English throne, threw themselves into the breach. Fearing French control of the British Isles and hoping that Elizabeth could be persuaded to keep the faith and marry him, Philip ordered his representatives in the Curia to forestall any hostile moves by the Holy See.[102] His plea to the Pope was couched in terms of piety: England was full of good Catholics and, if the Queen was excommunicated or an interdict decreed, their situation would become intolerable.[103] Philip's ploy,

---

[100]Granvelle, *Papiers d'Etat,* V, 526-29, 531-32. *CSP For.,* I, 171. Alphonse de Ruble, the historian of the treaty, maintained that the arrangement of the Spanish and French marriage forced England to come to terms, but the English documents do not support his argument. Nor do the Spanish. In spite of his contract with the King of France's daughter, Philip remained a staunch supporter of England. Moreover, there is no evidence that Elizabeth heard of Philip's engagement until long after she had given her ambassadors the instructions which allowed them to agree with the French terms. See Ruble's *Le Traité de Cateau-Cambrésis* (Paris: 1889), 25-7.

[101]*CSP Ven.,* VI, 1568.

[102]*CSP For.,* I, 53-54. *CSP Span., Eliz.,* I, 17. See especially Philip's letter to Feria, 10 January 1559 in *CSP Span., Eliz.,* I, 22.

[103]Father Ribadeneira, writing from the residence of the Spanish ambassador in London, sent Father Lainez in Rome a letter which neatly demonstrates the Spanish method of preventing Elizabeth's excommunication: 'IHS. Estando este reyno como esta, se ha de tener mucho advertencia por parte de su santidad de no hazer ninguna demonstracion contra el ni contra la reyna; porque donde agora la mayor parte, con mucho, es Catholica, seria facil cosa que se turbasse de maera que no lo fuesse, do agora esta el negocio en peligro, que se perdisse de suerte que no habiesse esperanca de remedio, como hasta este punto lo ay; in fin non est addendum oleum igni. Y scrivo esto de mio a V.P., porque ce lo que importa, para que si alla se hablare algo, sepa V.P. do que por aca passa y aiude in lo que juzgare conviene in Domino.' Ribadeneira, *Epistolae,* LVIII, 313-14.

aided perhaps by Paul's illness, worked. England would not be cut off from Rome for another 11 years.

The Privy Council of England, in spite of Goodrich's advice to the contrary, was acting on the assumption that a Protestant Queen desired no contact with Paul IV. Sir Edward Carne, the English ambassador sent to Rome by Queen Mary, was recalled on February first, 'in consyderacion there is no furder cause why he shuld make any furder abode there'.[104] The Pope prevented Carne from leaving Rome, [105] but England had no further relations with the papacy. Only the Spanish lobbyists in the Curia diverted the wrath of the successor of St. Peter.

While the negotiations at Cateau Cambrésis and the indecision of the papacy kept England's enemies at bay, the Council was working hard to strengthen the frontier with Scotland. If peace was not concluded a French invasion could be expected in the north, and, even if a treaty was signed, the Queen of Scots' claim to the English throne gave the French a perfect pretext for breaking it. It was therefore imperative that defensive measures be taken. The 'Device' foretold the policy that Cecil and his fellows were to adopt toward Scotland:

> Scotland will follow France for peace. But there may be practices to help forward their divisions, and especially to augment the hope of them, who inclineth them to good religion. For certainty, to fortify Berwick, and to employ demilances and horsemen for safety of the frontiers.[106]

They followed these suggestions to the letter. Scotland's religious divisions were exploited by Cecil, to England's benefit, culminating in the alliance with the Lords of the Congregation and the expulsion of the French from Scotland. In the meantime, the English prepared to resist an invasion in the North.

Time was on their side. Elizabeth had acceded in mid-winter, and no major offensives could be expected before spring. The Council began by surveying the forces available in the marches of the border, their supplies and their fortifications. Lord Eure at Berwick and the Earl of Northumberland were ordered to conduct surprise musters to ensure that the number of men appointed to remain on the border was actually there.[107] Thomas Gower, Master of the Ordnance in the North, sent a report detailing the artillery, powder, shot and weapons

[104]*APC,* VII, 50.
[105]*CSP For.,* I, 193.
[106]B.L., Cotton Julius F. VI, fol. 167v.
[107]*CSP For.,* I, 16.

in his charge[108] and various other officials wrote to the Council, expatiating on the strengths and strategic importance of Berwick, Norham and Wark.[109] On December 20 a proclamation ordered all captains and soldiers posted to the frontier who were absent from their duties to return.[110] Sir James Crofte, Sir Richard Lee and Sir John Brande, among others, helped the Council assess the military situation by arguing for an increase in the garrison at Berwick and for the rapid completion of the new fortificiations there.[111] In response to their urgings, 500 labourers were raised in the counties of Nottingham, Derby, Gloucester, Worcester, Suffolk and Norfolk, to be sent north for the Queen's service at Berwick.[112] Another 1400 were called for to be at Berwick by March 1st.[113]

Scottish raids lent urgency to these activities. On January 6th the Earl of Northumberland informed the Privy Council of a raid and pleaded for reinforcements. The enemy was increasing his forces on the frontier, and 'except the thing be speedily repaired, so as one force be to countervail the other', he wrote, 'ye shall in short time have the borders utterly destroyed'.[114] Less than a week later another 1,000 men were ordered North.[115] Meanwhile, Thomas Gresham was busy gathering munitions in Flanders. By early March he had purchased 50,000 weight of gunpowder, 20,000 weight of saltpeter, hundreds of corslets, several thousand daggs, matches and bowstaves, and he had warrant to purchase twice as many.[116] In order to pay for these supplies, Gresham suggested manipulating the exchange value of the foreign currencies received by the Merchant Adventurers. He proposed that setting the £ sterling at 22s. 6d. Flemish would make the Queen a good profit.[117]

All these preparations for the summer campaign were being rushed until early March, when they slowed appreciably. By the end of that month, the Council had begun reducing the forces in the North in order to abridge the Queen's expenses. The reason for this sudden change is that a truce had been concluded with the Scots.

[108]*Ibid.*, I, 15.
[109]*Ibid.*, I, 15; 58.
[110]*Ibid.*, I, 37.
[111]*Ibid.*, I, 57; 58.
[112]*Ibid,* I, 91, 96.
[113]*Ibid.*, I, 152.
[114]*Ibid.*, I, 77-78.
[115]*Ibid.*, I, 89-90.
[116]*Ibid.*, I, 152-153.
[117]*Ibid.*, I, 153-154.

The overture for a ceasefire came from north of the border. Sir Henry Percy conferred with the Duke of Chatellerault, the 'Governor of Scotland', in early January and discovered that he was opposed to both the war with England and the French presence in Scotland. The Duke promised Percy that he would forewarn the English if the French attempted to force an invasion. He also said that if the English invaded Scotland the Scots would help them destroy the French, and that if a truce was made between the English and the Scots the French would be unable to break it. Percy, having urged upon Chatellerault the idea that the Scots and English should join together against the Catholic French for 'the maintenance of the Word of God', departed to write an account of his interview to Parry and Cecil.[118] By January 24 he had instructions to arrange a truce:[119] promptly seizing upon this overture, Elizabeth ordered her wardens in the Marches to negotiate.[120] The result was a two-months cessation of arms, beginning on March 6.[121] The ceasefire was superseded by the peace of Cateau Cambrésis, but neither the truce nor the peace allowed Cecil to relax. He was determined to dislodge the French and cast them out of Scotland.

While England sought time to prepare for the expected war in the north, moves were set afoot to restore the friendly relations Henry VIII and Edward VI had enjoyed with the Protestant princes of Germany. A month after her accession Elizabeth commissioned Christopher Mundt, Henry's and Edward's agent in Germany, to serve her in the same capacity. Instructed to go to the Diet scheduled to meet at Augsburg in January, he was to revive and maintain amity with all the princes and states that had borne good will toward her father and brother.[122] In practice this meant that Mundt declared to these princes Elizabeth's preference for the 'true and right doctrine and religion'.[123] Beyond this, Mundt had nothing specific to offer the Germans, but it was sufficient to win their friendship. Good relations with the northern Germans were important to Elizabeth, for it was from that region that England obtained her military supplies. Amity with the Lutherans would open the ports of Hamburg and Bremen to

[118] Whether or not he was acting on instructions, Percy was, in January, carrying out the policy of the 'Device', by cultivating religious dissent in Scotland in order to defend England. *CSP For.*, I, 99.

[119] *CSP For.*, I, 100.

[120] *Ibid.*, I, 120.

[121] *Ibid.*, I, 170.

[122] *Ibid.*, I, 39.

[123] *Ibid.*, I, 102.

English ships, guaranteeing a flow of munitions even if the Spanish stopped their exportation from Flanders.[124]

At the same time, Sir Henry Killigrew was entrusted with a more important mission to the Germans. His instructions are not extant, but the correspondence shows that he was sounding the Lutheran princes about a military alliance. In early December Killigrew was in contact with Paul Vergerio, a councillor of the Duke of Württemberg, and it was through Vergerio that Killigrew proposed an offensive and defensive alliance.[125] The Duke replied on February 1. He said that Elizabeth could expect the Protestant princes to aid her 'with their counsels and their help' — which included 10 or 15,000 men — but that she could not expect to obtain an offensive and defensive league concerning non-religious matters. If she wanted a religious alliance, she could have it by accepting the Confession of Augsburg. That was the point to be settled. If she accepted the Confession she would gain the princes' support, and Philip and the Emperor Ferdinand would tolerate her just as they did the Lutherans in Germany.[126]

A letter on the same subject, addressed to Killigrew and Cecil, reached London from Heidelberg on February 15. It came from Vitus Polantus, a servant of the Count Palatine Otto Henry who, as the letter announced, had just died. However, said Polantus, the new elector, Frederick, would most probably yield to the Queen's wishes. Part of this letter is burnt, but enough remains to tell us that Duke Richard, Frederick's brother, would levy and lead the troops of Germany if the plan was approved.[127] The plan in question was undoubtedly a Protestant league. The Count Palatine was, as Mundt often reiterated, the leading Protestant prince in Germany.[128] However, perhaps because Elizabeth never accepted the Confession, or perhaps because of the divisions among the Lutherans, the alliance never materialized.

In discussing Elizabeth's diplomacy toward the Lutherans it is germane to consider her attitude toward the Confession of Augsburg. She often intimated that England would embrace it, or that she liked it, and some historians have assumed that this indicated her intention

[124]G.D. Ramasay, *The City of London in International Politics at the Accession of Elizabeth Tudor* (Manchester: 1975), 220-1.

[125]*CSP For.*, I, 32. This letter from Vergerio is dated 14 December. Another, which is not in the Calendar of Foreign State Papers, dated 28 December, is at B.L., Add. 35830, fols. 37-38. The letter's Italian is nearly illegible, but in it Vergerio does say that the events in England had strengthened the ardour of the German Protestants. He also reports that his Duke and the Duke of Cleves are discussing a league.

[126]*CSP For.*, I, 111-113.

[127]*Ibid.*, I, 134-135.

[128]*Ibid.*, I, 149; 173.

either to accept it, or to re-establish the prayer book of 1549, which could be reconciled to it.[129] This argument is invalidated, however, when the chronology and sources of her statements about the Confession are examined. Without exception, Elizabeth's references to it were made in diplomatic contexts, and several of these adulatory sentences were spoken after it was clear that England would not accept it. For instance, on April 29, 1559, the day after the bill for uniformity in religion was passed by Parliament, Elizabeth told Feria that she wished the 'Augustanean' Confession to be maintained in her realm. Pressed by the Spaniard, she finally admitted that it would not be the Confession, 'but something else like it'.[130] By that time she knew perfectly well that the prayer book of 1552 would be maintained in her kingdom. Another loose reference to the Confession of Augsburg occurs in the instructions, given by Elizabeth and Cecil to Armagil Waad on April 15. Ordered to visit the Duke of Holstein, Waad was to discover if he embraced the 'Confession of Augusta'. If he did, Waad was to declare to him that Elizabeth also accepted the religion set forth in the Confession, and to suggest that 'some further intelligence for the maintenance of the said Confession' be arranged between the Duke and England.[131] Waad's instructions were written three days before the bill for uniformity was introduced in the Lower House, and it is doubtful that Elizabeth had any illusions about her allegiance to the Confession by then. However, as late as 1568, she was still claiming that England agreed with the Lutheran creed.

This political smokescreen was useful. Disguising whatever was happening to religion in England as the Augsburg Confession gained Elizabeth support from the Lutherans who could, if they would do nothing else, shelter her diplomatically. The ruse also helped befuddle the Catholics, for the Augsburg Confession, although it was undeniably heretical, had been recognized by the Empire as the lawful doctrine in part of Germany. This recognition gave the Confession a legal standing with which Charles V's successors could ill afford to tamper. They might of necessity allow English Lutheranism to go un-challenged. The hope that Elizabeth would become a Lutheran unquestionably gained her friends among the German Protestants. Hopes for her hand persuaded Protestants and Catholics alike to humour her. It has often been said that she exploited their matrimonial

[129]Neale, 'Supremacy and Uniformity', 317-18.

[130]CSP Span., Eliz., I, 61-62.

[131]CSP For., I, 218.

aspirations like a master diplomat, but that is not exactly correct. It is fair to say that Elizabeth learned the value of her hand in diplomacy, but in the early months of her reign she was intent only on not marrying. Completely honest with her suitors, Elizabeth could not convince them that she was serious about remaining a virgin.

The young Queen's eligibility and determined virginity were an unexpected piece of good fortune for England. It was not something which anyone had foreseen, with the possible exception of Elizabeth herself. Men assumed that Elizabeth, being but a frail woman, would marry, and, once married, would be governed by her husband. In the way of dynastic politics, the Queen's marriage was, as Thomas Challoner phrased it, the 'cardo nostri negotii'.[132] The question foremost in men's minds in and out of England was 'whom will she marry', not 'will she marry?' A number of potential consorts appeared in the diplomatic gossip. Some thought she would marry an Englishman: Sir William Pickering, or perhaps the Earl of Arundel. Lord Robert Dudley did not emerge as a favourite until May. Others surveyed the field of eligible foreign princes and speculated on which of them Elizabeth would choose. King Philip was the prime contender. The Archduke Ferdinand or his brother Charles were preferred by some, while Duke Adolphus, (brother of the King of Denmark), the King of Sweden and the Duke of Holstein were mentioned but had little popular backing. Parliament petitioned Elizabeth to marry and was gently rebuffed.[133]

Elizabeth's determination to avoid matrimony baffled and frustrated the Spanish ambassador who proved unable to comprehend the idea that she would not marry. Sent by Philip to propose marriage on his behalf, or, failing that, on the behalf of the Archduke, Feria tried to lure her into marriage by playing on her emotions.[134] When he finally breached the subject, however, Elizabeth declared flatly that she did not want a husband.[135] Frustrated but still hopeful, Feria blamed her dislike of marriage on the devil and the heretics who surrounded her.[136] Never understanding her intransigence, he 'would have no answer that was not a very good one'.[137] It was not until March 19,

---

[132]*Ibid.*, I, 65.

[133]H.L.R.O., Commons MS. Journals, I, fol. 187v.

[134]*CSP Span., Eliz.,* I, 9.

[135]*Ibid.*, I, 35.

[136]*Ibid.*, I, 31; 37.

[137]*Ibid.*, I, 28.

when a bill for the supremacy had passed both houses of Parliament, that Elizabeth was able to convince him that she did not want Philip for a husband. On that day she told the pious Feria pointblank that she was an heretic, and that she knew Philip would never marry her because of it.[138] The extent of Feria's self-delusion is shown by the rumours he sparked off in the Spanish Court from where a Venetian reported that Feria's letters spoke of a 'favourable intention' toward marriage with Philip having been communicated to him by the Queen.[139] Feria's confusion (one gets the impression that Elizabeth delighted in toying with him) earned England a bonus. So long as Philip, and the rest of the world, believed that Elizabeth would marry him, the hopes of Catholics all over Europe were kept alive long after it should have been obvious that she was determined to lead England into schism.

Good fortune and astute policy had, by March 1559, made England as ready as it could be for the alteration of religion. Abroad, the Spanish alliance remained intact and a peace with the French was all but signed. In Rome, the anger of Paul IV was being restrained by the Spanish, keeping English Catholics uncertain about how to react to Elizabeth's heresy and allowing them to serve her happily. At home, the kingdom was fairly quiet and the Council was making certain that it remained so as the Queen ejected Catholicism from her chapel and offered the Protestants the prospect of a parliamentary rejection of the Pope's religion. Confusing the opposition while she consolidated her power, Elizabeth was prepared to keep the country under her firm control when the alteration became public. She had taken the cautious but firm steps to make ready for the destruction of Catholicism that her advisers had recommended in her first month of rule.

The Queen and her Council were doing what they could in preparation for the change in religion. It remained for the Parliament to transform the royal desires into laws of the realm.

[138] *Ibid.*, I, 37; 40.
[139] *CSP Ven.*, VII, 21.

3

THE MEMBERSHIP OF PARLIAMENT

The religious orientation of Elizabeth's first Parliament has been disputed almost from the day it rose. Nicholas Sanders charged, in both his *De Visibili Monarchia* and his *De Schismate*, that the government had packed the House of Commons with men who were sympathetic to reform. Camden borrowed the story and passed it into the mainstream of English history. Lingard and Dixon assumed that Cecil had rigged the election, while Maitland, Birt and Pollen accepted the charge of packing with caution, but believed it. This hoary myth was finally debunked by C.G. Bayne in 1908, in the first truly historical analysis of the membership.[1]

J.E. Neale, who was the last to speak on the subject, agreed with Bayne that the members were not chosen by higher authority. On the contrary, Neale argued, they were freely elected and acted like it. Where all the witnesses and scholars before him had believed that Elizabeth planned reform and manipulated Parliament to achieve it, Neale asserted that the Queen, who desired a very conservative settlement, was forced by the Commons to compromise with them and accept the 'Elizabethan Settlement'.[2] Any study of the Parliament of 1559 must now begin with Neale's thesis that a radically Protestant House of Commons, led by returned 'Puritan' exiles from within and without, was able to seize the initiative from the government. Moreover, the membership and behaviour of the House of Lords must be considered. Professor Neale assumed that the lay peers would never touch a government bill without instructions to do so, and that the Lords could be used by the Crown as a weapon against a 'runaway' House of Commons.

Although this is, to the best of the author's knowledge, the first study of the Parliament of 1559 since the History of Parliament Trust discovered the complete list of members of the Lower House, the membership of the Commons will not be considered in detail here.[3]

---

[1]C.G. Bayne, 'The First House of Commons of Queen Elizabeth', *EHR* (1908), 455-76, 643-82. Bayne's article includes an excellant summary of the historiography of this question.

[2]Neale, 'Supremacy and Uniformity'.

[3]The sources for the names of the members of the Commons in 1559 are three: Browne Willis, *Notitia Parliamentia*, 3 vols. (London: 1730) is the oldest and least reliable. The returns, which are in the P.R.O., were edited and published in the Parliamentary Papers, pt. 1 (1878), 400-402. This list is good, as far as it goes, although it sometimes varies from the list recently found in an Exchequer roll in the P.R.O., E 371/402, fols. 1 ff. See Appendix I for the list of Commons members.

62

The History of Parliament Trust will soon publish their volumes on the sixteenth century which will supersede any biographical contributions that could be made. Instead, more basic questions will be asked about the religious divisions in the Houses of Parliament and the government's ability to control members.

Some generalizations can be made about this House of Commons. First, as has been said, the House was not selected or elected by the government, and with a few exceptions the election was regular. The membership was a mixture of old Parliament hands and fresh faces. According to Bayne, of 388 members identified by him approximately 170 had prior parliamentary experience. About 105 of these sat in the previous Parliament, and at least 56 had been members of the House during the reigns of Henry VIII and Edward VI. Moreover, Bayne demonstrated that the percentages of old and new parliamentarians sitting in 1559 were normal for the mid-sixteenth century.[4]

Socially, the members of the Commons were what one might expect. Country gentry, corporation officials, merchants and lawyers accounted for over seventy percent. Most of the rest were members of the official class, such as privy councillors, courtiers and government officials.[5] Of course, the official element carried more weight than its numbers would indicate, since, as Wallace MacCaffrey has said, power in Parliament was not reckoned by heads but by influence.[6]

The Crown made no concerted effort to direct the elections of members, but it would be asking too much to expect sixteenth-century gentlemen of influence not to exert their powers of patronage. Some of the more obvious instances involve Cecil, who must have arranged for the election of Sir Anthony Cook, still abroad at the time of his selection, to Sir Edward Waldegrave's Essex seat. For the same reason, Cecil's hand is to be seen in Sir Thomas Wrothe's election for Middlesex. Sir Francis Knollys, the returned exile member of the Council, certainly owed his seat to patronage exerted in his behalf, for he, too, got back to England only a fortnight before Parliament met. It is striking to note that these friends of the new Queen took the seats which had been occupied by leading Marian privy councillors. Lord Howard of Effingham attempted to secure places in Parliament for his two sons. He managed to carry the family borough in Surrey for one, but Sir William Fitzwilliams and Sir Thomas Cawarden, who held a

[4]Bayne, 'First House', 645.

[5]*Ibid.*, 681. Bayne's statistical breakdown was made before all the members were known. His figures are, however, generally correct.

[6]Wallace MacCaffrey, *The Shaping of the Elizabethan Regime* (London: 1968), 46-47.

grudge against the Howards, thwarted his attempt to get his eldest son elected for the county.[7] Lord Clinton nominated a man of his choice at Great Grimsby, and the Earl of Bedford did the same at Melcombe Regis.[8] In Lincoln City the common council accepted the Earl of Rutland's servant, Robert Farrar, to represent them, as he had done in 1552 and 1553.[9] At King's Lynn the Duke of Norfolk nominated Thomas Hogan, whom the burgesses of the town accepted.[10]

Two cases of gerrymandering occurred in 1559. The towns of Sudbury and Newton were sent writs to elect two members each to represent them at Westminster. Sudbury, evidently following instructions, returned two men who had no connections with it — Clement Throckmorton and Henry Fortescue who were both courtiers. Newton village, as rotten a borough as one could find, returned Sir George Howard, Elizabeth's first cousin once removed, and Richard Chetwood, scion of a Cheshire family and a friend of Cecil's.[11] A third borough, that of Clitheroe in the Duchy, was also enfranchised, but its two members were both local gentry. One of them, Walter Horton, was probably a member of the staunchly Catholic Houghton family that owned land in Clitheroe.[12]

The presence of the clients and friends of peers and councillors in the Parliament raises a question which directly relates to Neale's thesis. How many men who had been exiles for religious reasons had seats in Elizabeth's first Parliament? According to Neale, 'there was a vital core of at least twelve and probably sixteen returned exiles in the House: possibly more'.[13] He named only two, Cooke and Knollys. Shortly after Neale published this, Conyers Read commented that, in spite of Neale's assertion that at least a dozen sat, a comparison of the returns with Garrett's list of Marian exiles reveals only nine of them in Parliament.[14] Admittedly, Garrett's list is not always accurate and Read was using an incomplete roster of the members, but further research has done little to disprove his

[7]Bayne, 'First House', 467.

[8]*Ibid,* 468-69.

[9]J.W.F. Hill, *Tudor and Stuart Lincoln* (Cambridge: 1956), 69. Hill, following Willis, says Robert Monson held the other city seat, but the Exchequer list shows Anthony Thorrold, esq. occupying it. P.R.O., E 371/402/ fol. 6.

[10]Bayne, 'First House', 470.

[11]*Ibid.,* 479-80.

[12]*Ibid.,* 479.

[13]Neale, *Elizabeth I and her Parliaments,* I, 57.

[14]Conyers Read, *Mr Secretary Cecil and Queen Elizabeth* (London: 1965), 480, n. 29.

statement. The following men may have returned from exile to sit in Parliament: Sir Anthony Cooke, Richard Cooke, Thomas Crawley, Sir Henry Neville, John Bateman, Sir Edward Rogers, Sir Francis Knollys, Francis Walsingham, and Sir Thomas Wrothe. The names of John Ashley and Sir Nicholas Throckmorton can be added as folk who spent part of Mary's reign outside the country. Miss Norah Fuidge would add Gawain Carewe to the list, although Garret gives his name as Henry.[15]

This provides us with Neale's round dozen, but these statistics only demonstrate Churchill's third type of lie. Were they all exiles for religion's sake? It is difficult to tell, but Walsingham, Ashley and Neville did not visit the Protestant cities of refuge. Instead they spent their time in papist Padua studying the civil law. Wrothe spent much of his time in Padua as well. Young Walsingham went to France to polish his manners. Moreover, several of these 'godly exiles' came home and were pardoned by Mary. Throckmorton, Neville and possibly Ashley were back in England in 1557. Some of them had left for less than holy reasons, too. Several fled for treasonous activities that illustrate their opportunism but do not prove their faith. Neville, both Cookes, Ashley, Wrothe, Carewe, and perhaps Walsingham and Crawley left because of their political involvements. Neville and Cooke had both supported Jane Grey's claim to the throne, while Wrothe, Walsingham and Crawley were implicated in the Duke of Suffolk's rebellion. Besides these problems, there is the question of proper identification. The John Bateman who was admitted to the Geneva congregation in October of 1558 may be the same man who sat for Nottingham Borough, but again, he may not. The same can be said of Thomas Crawley of Essex — was he the man who sat for Aylesbury? If Sir Edward Rogers went to the continent it must have been for a very short visit; his presence in England is accounted for throughout Mary's reign.[16] That leaves eight men sitting in Parliament who were undoubtedly genuine Marian exiles.

[15] Christina Garrett, *The Marian Exiles* (Cambridge: 1938), Norah M. Fuidge, 'The Personnel of the House of Commons, 1563-1567' (M.A. thesis, University of London, 1950), 42.

[16] Sir Anthony Cooke: Garrett, *Exiles,* 124-126. Richard Cooke, *Ibid.,* 126. Marjorie McIntosh, the historian of the Cooke family, has characterized Richard Cooke as 'a man of great personal modesty and limited intelligence, devoted to hunting,' and noted that he joined his father 'at least briefly' in Strassburg while the rest of the family remained in England. McIntosh also draws attention to the fact that Sir Anthony did not act like a 'Tudor Puritan' in his later years, showing little concern for the quality of the clergy or for Christian charity. See 'Sir Anthony Cooke: Tudor Humanist, Educator, and Religious Reformer,' *Proceedings of the American Philosophical Society,* 119 (1975), 23n; 35; 243; 248-249. Sir Henry Neville: *Ibid.,* 235. John Bateman: *Ibid.,* 82. Bateman was an active member of Nottingham Borough and his

Because of their varieties of experience it is only fair to ask if the exiles all had the same religious outlook: would they form a united front in Parliament? Though all of them were Protestants, their theology varied. The Cookes went to Strassburg, Bateman to Geneva, and Walsingham and Neville to Padua. Certainly the latter two were not as smitten by the passion for the 'best reformed cities' common among the Puritans as were the former. All in all, the 'vital core' of exiles shrinks to four men: Anthony Cooke, Francis Knollys, Nicholas Throckmorton and Thomas Wrothe. These are the only ones who had the influence and might have shared the determination to force reform on the Queen. However, most of their influence stemmed directly from their close relations with Cecil and Elizabeth.

These four might have been enough to take the lead if the other members had been attuned to their plea, but there is no evidence that the Commons, containing as they did a clear Protestant majority, were interested in resisting a Protestant Queen. The determination of members' preferences in religion is doubly hard for this Parliament; we can only read their futures back into their pasts. The Puritans of 1563 and later may not have been proto-Puritans in 1559. The religious squabbles of later Parliaments arose out of the Queen's enforcement of the Settlement, but this stimulus was lacking at the meeting in her first year. With that caveat, let us find out how many 'Puritans' identifiable in the 1563 Parliament were present in 1559.

Norah Fuidge, whose research Neale used as a guide to religious radicals, listed 48 men as Puritans, 21 of whom were in the House of 1559.[17] These figures are, however, misleading because of the criteria used to define Puritans. Eleven of the names are those of our exiles, Puritans by virtue of their sojourns on the continent. The mere fact of the experience of exile does not, however, guarantee their opposition to the Settlement of 1559. Seven of the remaining ten are classed as Puritans because of their Marian activities. Two supported Jane

name appears often in the city records. See Bayne, 'First House', 669. Sir Edward Rogers: Garrett, *Exiles,* 57. Rogers's inclusion is a puzzle. He sat in Mary's first Parliament and was imprisoned in February 1554 for complicity in Wyatt's Rebellion. Released from the Tower in January 1555, and restored to his offices and possessions in April 1555, he was made a justice that year. He was a commissioner for the loan in 1557, and in the Parliament in 1558, during which year he was employed to levy men in Somersetshire. He had little time for a trip abroad. See Bayne, 'First House', 656. Sir Francis Knollys: *DNB* and Garrett, *Exiles.* Francis Walsingham: Conyers Read, *Mr. Secretary Walsingham* (Oxford: 1925), 17, 22-25. Read did not believe that Walsingham sat, but the Exchequer roll shows him as present. Sir Thomas Wrothe: James E. Oxley, *The Reformation in Essex to the Death of Mary* (Manchester: 1965), 180; *DNB;* Garrett, *Exiles.* John Ashley: Bayne, 'First House', 676; Fuidge, 'Commons 1563', 42. Sir Nicholas Throckmorton: *DNB.*

[17]Fuidge, 'Common 1563', 42.

Grey, one supported Wyatt and another Dudley, two had behaved in an anti-Catholic manner in Mary's Parliaments, and another lost his job as president of Magdalen College, Oxford because of his religion. By these criteria William Cecil himself must be called Puritan! Only two members of 1559 and 1563 ever provided evidence of a genuinely Puritan opposition to the Settlement: William Strickland supported Puritanism in his speeches in Parliament in 1571, and Robert Hopton signed a petition supporting Puritan ministers in 1567. However, the Exchequer Roll shows Ralph Hopton, not Robert, sitting in 1559, so that Miss Fuidge may have the wrong man. Sir Anthony Cooke she classes as a Puritan because of his 'record in the 1559 Parliament', an assumption that is based squarely upon Neale's interpretation of what may have happened there, not on concrete evidence. At any rate, even if we use her list it must still be reduced to at most six men who were clearly potential Puritans in 1559.

One obvious question touches the number included in Neale's so-called 'Puritan choir' who sat in 1559.[18] This chorus of 43 men was lampooned in 1566 in a pasquil, but most of them sat in 1563 as well. The author of the lampoon intimated that these 43 led the rest of the House of Commons:

> Here resteth us our quire
> as for the rest
> theye be at devotion
> and when theye be prest
> theye crye a good motion.[19]

The 'choir' is important because Neale argued that the radical clergy, having failed to get their way in Convocation in 1563, fell back on the 'irregular expedient of 1559' and agitated for their platform through sympathizers in Parliament:[20] these choristers would then be the men who supported the clergy and led the Parliament in 1563. Neale based his argument partially on Miss Fuidge's thesis and partially on his own analysis of the 1559 Parliament, so that one wants to know how many of the 'choir' came to Westminster in 1559. The answer is, at most 17 of the 43. The identification of the members in the pasquil is difficult since no first names are given, but seventeen men with the same surnames as those in the 'choir' appear on the Exchequer Roll. There are complications, however, such as sorting out which of the many Browns in the two

[18] Neale, *Elizabeth and her Parliaments*, I, 91-2.

[19] Cambridge University Library, Ff. V. 14, fol. 84v. The entire 'lewde pasquyle sette forthe by certen of the parlyament men 8. Eliz'. occupies fols. 81v-84v.

[20] Neale, *Elizabeth and her Parliaments*, I, 89-90.

Parliaments is 'Browne the Blasphemer' (a singular title for a Puritan). All things considered, perhaps one quarter of the 'choir' sat in 1559 — but there is no evidence that they were all Puritans or that they agreed on anything.

Westminster was thus graced by very few returned exiles and proto-Puritans in the January of Elizabeth's first regnal year. The numbers are bound to be inexact, and tell us little anyway, but not more than 20 or 25 of the nearly 400 members of the Commons can with any certainty be reckoned as radicals in religion. The evidence for their political activities in that year is even scanter than evidence for their presence. Moreover, the parts the known exiles played in Parliament could be better attributed to their membership on the Council or their close ties with the leaders of the government than to their opposition to Elizabeth's intentions. If they were in opposition, none of them recorded their dislike of Elizabeth's religious aims at the time.

There were few exiles inside Parliament; what of the influence of exiles outside Parliament? Neale assumed that the ministers who came home from the continent helped direct the resistance to the Queen. That is not correct, if we can believe the documentary traces they left behind. Neither the returned preachers nor their friends in Parliament ever recorded anything but trust in the Queen's pious desires. Their complaint lay with the speed, not the direction, of the change in religion. They did admit that there was resistance to reform, but they never ascribed it to Elizabeth. John Jewel, whose letters are a principal source for the period, neatly summarized all this when he wrote to Peter Martyr on March 20, 1559. The bishops, he said, were a great hindrance, and

> The queen . . . though she openly favours our cause, yet is wonderfully afraid of allowing any innovations: this is owing partly to her own friends, by whose advice everything is carried on, and partly to the influence of Count Feria, a Spaniard, and Philip's ambassador. She is however prudently, and firmly, and piously following up her purpose, though somewhat more slowly than we could wish.[21]

Sir Anthony Cooke, writing while he had the first bill for supremacy in his possession, told Martyr:

> We are now busy in parliament about expelling the tyranny of the pope, and restoring the royal authority, and re-establishing true religion. But we are moving far too slowly . . . The zeal of the queen is very great . . . but still the work is hitherto too much at a stand.[22]

[21] *ZL*, I, 10.
[22] *ZL*, II, 13-14.

Richard Cox, returned from Strassburg, echoed his sentiments. 'It was not without great difficulty,' he wrote, 'that our pious queen, with those about her who stood forth with alacrity on the side of truth, could obtain room for the sincere religion of Christ. The bishops . . . opposed it . . . '[23] Jewel agreed: 'We have a wise and religious queen, and one too who is favourably and propitiously disposed toward us.'[24] The exiles had faith in the goals of the Queen's advisers, too. Although they were impatient with delays, and although they bitterly resented the apostasy of some of their former friends, no criticism of Cecil, Bedford or Bacon survives from their pens. In fact, Bedford and Cecil are both noted as friends of reform.[25]

The exiles and their stay-at-home counterparts did not always agree with each other, either. Hungry and poor, the ministers had returned expecting to be given work. There was none, however, and their hope soon turned to bitterness. For instance, Dr. Edmund Sandys acidly old the archbishop-elect, Matthew Parker: 'Ye have rightly considered that these times are given to taking and not to giving, for ye have stretched out your hand further than all the rest. They never ask us in what state we stand, neither consider that we want; and yet in the time of our exile were we not so bare as we are now brought.'[26] Nor did the leading political lights among the exiles, Sir Anthony Cooke and Sir Thomas Wrothe, live up to the expectations of their fellow exiles.[27]

Finally, we must ask what sort of influence the returned ministers could in fact exert. If they affected the Commons in the manner suggested by Neale, the radical clerics must have been in London between February 9, when the bill for supremacy was introduced, and February 25, when it was passed. This was the crucial time when, according to Neale, some sort of radical prayer book was attached by the Commons to the bill for supremacy. Unfortunately for the theory, very few of those radicals were back by then. Thomas Bentham, Edmund Sandys, Edmund Grindal, Richard Cox and David Whitehead were there during February, but they are the only ones. John Jewel did not reach the city until mid-March. It is reasonable to object that those who were in London in February would have been enough to see the job through, but the fact that Grindal, Cox and Whitehead were busy preaching at court and appealing to the Parliament to act

[23] ZL, I, 27.

[24] ZL, I, 32-33. See also ZL, I, 17; CSP For., I, 160-61; Parker, Correspondence, 65.

[25] ZL, I, 34 and Parker, Correspondence, 66, respectively.

[26] Parker, Correspondence, 65.

[27] ZL, I, 53.

in the Queen's favour makes it doubtful that they would have opposed the royal bill at the same time. These three were also named in the 'Device' as men fit to be consulted about preparing a prayer book: if they helped draft it they probably did not attempt to defeat it.[28] In addition, the ministers who returned from exile were impoverished and had been away for a long time. Without the help of powerful friends they could not have established their influence as rapidly as they would have had to if, frustrated by the government, they succeeded in working their will through their sympathizers in Parliament.

It is much easier to count the number of Catholic sympathizers in the Commons than it is to estimate the influence of the exiles. Because they were on the losing side, the Catholics more quickly attracted government attention than did the Puritans. Twenty-one conservatives in religion can be positively identified in the House of Commons, and more will probably come to light when the History of Parliament Trust publishes its research.[29] These men were not all friends to the Pope, but they did prefer the Catholic mass. At least 7 later took the oath of supremacy in order to remain in office, but they cannot be construed as favourers of reform, and they probably voted against it. The most eminent Catholics sitting were Dr. John Story, John Carrell and Thomas Saunders. Story, who had been a Marian commissioner for religion, spoke in Parliament 'pro Pontificis Romani primatu insigni cum laude', and was pressured by the Council to keep his opinions to himself.[30] He was eventually executed for treason.[31] Carrell, attorney for the Duchy of Lancaster, came from a Catholic family, had refused to subscribe to the prayer book of 1549, and was a known conservative, although he was allowed to hold local commissions until his death in 1566.[32] The aged Thomas Saunders

---

[28] See the names of these men listed alphabetically in Garrett, *Exiles.*

[29] This estimate is based on the members whose religion I have been able to ascertain from the list in Fuidge, 'Commons 1563', 44; and from various other sources, especially Rodney Fisher's 1974 Cambridge Ph.D. Dissertation, 'The Inns of Court and the Reformation 1530-1580'. Both these authors depend heavily on the bishops' lists of 1564 and recusant lists. Besides the men named, the following are on Fuidge's list: William Barker, Sir George Blount, Henry Paget, Leonard Dacres, Simon Harecourt, Maurice ap Powell, William Lawrens, Christopher Monckerton, John Purvey, Thomas Stoughton, Simon Thelwall, William Ward, John Yonge (Young). Fisher adds: William Boyer (p. 236, n.l.), George Gascoigne (p. 105), Thomas Churche (p. 219, n.l.), Robert Wythe (p. 292). Josiah C. Wedgewood, *Staffordshire Parliamentary History*: 2 vols. (London: 1919), I, 354-5, adds: Edward Stafford (a nephew of Cardinal Pole); William Twynhyn. (This man may not have sat. He is not on any of the extant lists of members.)

[30] Rome, ASV, arm. LXIV, 28, fol. 272v and *CSP Ven*, VII, 26-27.

[31] Strype, *Annals*, I, i, 115.

[32] Fisher, 'Inns', 118.

70

was a vehement conservative who had been governor of the Inner Temple in 1557.[33]

This group was not large enough to have much voting power in a house whose attendance averaged perhaps 250. They were numerous enough, however, to cause obstruction, and we could expect them to do so. There is no explicit evidence which explains why the bill for supremacy was debated for three days,[34] but, as Neale has noted, some objections must have been raised against it. Neale maintained that the objectors were the Protestants who desired a more thorough reform than the bill contained. It is more logical, however, to suspect these Catholic members of vigorously protesting against the destruction of their religious freedom, just as their spiritual leaders did in the Upper House.[35] These gifted and experienced lawyers, with a dozen members at their backs, could easily have generated a great deal of debate.

Professor Neale ignored the presence of these conservatives when he tried to calculate 'the irreducible Puritan (*sic*) core in this Parliament of 1559'. Commenting on a division of the House in which ninety negative votes were counted against the bill granting the Crown the right to exchange the temporalities of vacant sees, he assumed that those opposed to the bill were Protestant zealots, the Puritan core. He himself, however, tells us in the same paragraph that the peers spiritual united against the bill in the Lords.[36] Once again, it is rather more logical to believe that the conservative members followed the bishops than it is to think that only 'Puritans' would oppose a bill which could strip the bishops of their princely estates and force them to enjoy apostolic poverty.

The vast majority of the men in the House of Commons are not readily classifiable according to their religion. They did not distinguish themselves by public acts of faith either before or after they met in 1559. Most of them were undoubtedly Protestant, but how devout they were is impossible to tell. Of course, the change in national theology debated *in primo* Elizabeth was influenced by secular interests to which most of the members were exposed.[37] For example, Francis Jobson had sat for Colchester in 1553, 1554 and 1555 before attending in 1559. He had been a receiver for the Court of Augmentations, had served on a commission for dissolution, and had

[33] *Ibid.*, 182, 287.
[34] H.L.R.O., Commons MS. Journals, I, fol. 189-189v.
[35] See below, pp. 90-91, 99-102.
[36] Neale, *Elizabeth I and her Parliaments,* I, 74.
[37] Read, *Cecil,* 127.

profited from Church lands under Edward.[38] Undoubtedly Protestant, Jobson exerted himself in 1559 to restore, to himself and others, lands Mary had taken from them and returned to the bishops. Walter Blount, another land profiteer, had probably first come to Parliament in 1523.[39] In 1559 his reforming zeal was stimulated by the same hopes that moved Jobson. Randolph Cholmely, recorder of London, was plainly a Protestant. A member of Edward's first Parliament, he was a commissioner for church goods in 1553. A bencher of Lincoln's Inn, Cholmely was promoted twice under Mary, and he was made a serjeant by Elizabeth. His religion seems to have been moderate. When he died in 1563 his will stipulated burial by the rites of the Church of England and that all his volumes of Erasmus should go to Sir William Chester.[40] A colleague of Cholmely's, George Bromeley of the Inner Temple, was to distinguish himself as a persecutor of recusants after Cecil obtained for him the post of attorney of the Duchy.[41]

Richard Kingsmill was an early suppprter of the Elizabethan Settlement, a friend of Bacon and Pilkington, and a client of Cecil and Bedford.[42] He played a very active role in the Parliament. Thomas Copley, on the other hand, deserted the Elizabethan church shortly after its establishment. A firm Protestant during Mary's reign, Copley had been imprisoned for his parliamentary speech favouring Elizabeth's succession. Having sat for Gatton (Surrey) in Elizabeth's first Parliament, Copley was soon off to the continent: he had become a convert to Catholicism in 1562 or 1563.[43] Dr. Robert Weston sat for Lichfield in 1558 and 1559, thanks to the influence of his brother Richard, Mary's solicitor general. Robert had been a member for Exeter in 1553, and he helped enforce the Settlement as dean of the Court of Arches from 1559 until 1567.[44] Sir Henry Gates' experiences under Mary were more unpleasant than Weston's. A close friend of the Duke of Northumberland and a gentleman of Edward's Privy Chamber, Gates was imprisoned and attainted for his support of Jane Grey. The Parliament restored him in blood in 1559, and he became a politician and an active member of the Council of the North under Elizabeth.[45] Another Edwardian who sat in 1559 was Walter

[38] Oxley, *Reformation in Essex,* 105-107.
[39] Wedgewood, *Staffs. Parliamentary History,* I, 355.
[40] Fisher, 'Inns', 174-5, 348.
[41] *Ibid.,* 203, 289-90.
[42] *Ibid.,* 176, 281, 348. P.R.O., SP 12/I/fol. 96.
[43] Fisher, 'Inns', 148, 150, 205-6.
[44] Wedgewood, *Staffs. Parliamentary History,* I, 355.
[45] Fuidge, 'Commons 1563', 140-1.

Haddon. An advocate of the Court of Arches and a member of Gray's Inn, Haddon had become a prominent religious reformer in the early fifties. Although he had conformed under Mary and sat in two of her Parliaments, he quickly aligned himself with the new regime.[46] In the first year of her reign Elizabeth granted him an annuity of £50 'for good counsel and attendance'.[47] Yet another group in the Commons is typified by Robert Bowyer, burgess for Chichester. A young member of the Middle Temple — perhaps no more than a barrister — Bowyer was a nonentity.[48]

These arguments, however, do not imply that there were no zealous Protestants other than exiles. There undoubtedly were radicals in the Lower House who had never left England. The real question is whether or not they formed a solid interest group which could effectively resist Elizabeth's policies. If they did, 1559 was a true *annus mirabilis* in Anglican history. By the middle of that year their unity, if it ever existed, would be shattered, and by 1563 the Marian exiles who had become bishops would block the militant programme for fuller reformation.[49] As we shall see, the radicals may have introduced some bills and amended others, but they did not dominate the Lower House any more than did their Catholic opponents.

What, therefore, we know of the members of the Commons does not indicate that major religious opposition to any proposal of Elizabeth's, as long as it was Protestant, could have been expected. Various interest groups would safeguard their own well-being, but none of them, with the exception of the ardent Catholics, would resist Elizabeth's plans for reforming the church.

The religious sympathies of the 77 men who had the right to speak in the House of Lords were generally more conservative than those of the Commons. The bishops, and the abbot of Westminster, were Roman Catholics; with a total of 17 they composed 22% of the total membership. The religion of the lay peers is less manifest, but 9 of them voted against the alteration of religion and two joined the bishops in voting in favour of the Pope. Besides the 9 who voted their convictions, fifteen other conservative members — men who preferred the mass but not necessarily the Pope — can easily be identified.[50]

[46] *Ibid.*, 154.

[47] *Cal. Pat. Rolls, Eliz.*, I, 111.

[48] Fisher, 'Inns', 155, n. 1.

[49] Haugaard, *Elizabeth and the English Reformation,* 210-11.

[50] Lords Temporal who voted against the Act of Uniformity: William Paulet, 1st Marquis of Winchester, Lord Treasurer; George Talbot, 6th Earl of Shrewbury;

The Protestant party in the Lords was not large. The Earl of Bedford and Lord Keeper Bacon were indisputably on the side of reform, and perhaps a dozen others shared their preference, although it is impossible to distinguish between religious ideals and political opportunism.[51] As for the rest of the members, their religious persuasions are as little known as their biographies, but we know that they did not resist the alteration of religion.

Statistically religion would have been represented in Elizabeth's first House of Lords as follows, if all those who could have voted had attended:

Peers Spiritual	17	22%
Peers Temporal who voted against alteration	9	12%
Religious Conservatives	15	19%
Known Protestants	14	18%
Unknown	22	29%
Total	77	100%

Thus, if everyone was present, 41 members (53%) could be expected to resist changes in doctrine, 14 (18%) would argue in favour of reform, and 22 (29%) would probably follow the party which offered the best advantages.

As usual, however, the numbers hide the true situation. Although 77 persons could have sat, the attendance never exceeded 45 on the

Anthony Browne, 1st Viscount Montague; Henry Parker, 9th Baron Morley; Edward Dudley, 4th Baron Dudley; Thomas Wharton, 1st Baron Wharton; Richard Riche, 1st Baron Riche; Edward Northe, 1st Baron Northe; Henry Stafford, 1st Baron Stafford. See E. Jeffries Davis, 'An Unpublished Manuscript of the Lords' Journal for April and May, 1559', *EHR* (1913), 538.

Peers who might have been expected to support the Catholic faith: Thomas Percy, 7th Earl of Northumberland; Edward Stanley, 3rd Earl of Derby; William Somerset. 3rd Earl of Worcester; Henry Clifford, 2nd Earl of Cumberland; John, Lord Lumeley; John, Lord Mordaunt of Turvey; Edward, Lord Hastings of Loughborough; Henry Fitzalan, 12th Earl of Arundel; William, Lord Paget; William, Lord Dacre of Gillisland and Greystoke; William, Lord Vaux; Edward, Lord Windsor. The assessments of these mens' religious opinions are based on the information provided about them in the *DNB*, V. Gibbs, ed., *The Complete Peerage* (London: St. Catherine Pr., 1913), and a 1567 list entitled 'Nomine et Fide Nobilium Anglorum' in the Archivio Segreto Vaticano, arm. LXIV, 28, fols. 373v-374. It has been printed in the *CSP Rome*, 265-266.

[51] Protestant Peers: Nicholas Bacon, Lord Keeper; William Parr, Marquis of Northampton; Henry Manners, 2nd Earl of Rutland; Thomas Radcliffe, Earl of Sussex; Francis Hastings, Earl of Huntingdon; Francis Russell, Earl of Bedford; William Herbert, Earl of Pembroke; Edward Seymour, Earl of Hertford; Edward Fiennes de Clinton, Lord Clinton and Saye; Henry Stanley, Lord Strange; William Grey, Lord Grey de Wilton; Henry Scrope, Lord Scrope de Bolton; Henry Hastings, Lord Hastings; John Sheffield, Lord Sheffield. The assessments of these mens' religious opinions are based on the information provided about them in the *DNB*, Gibbs, *Peerage*, and *ASV*, arm. LXIV. 28. Fols. 373v-374.

days for which records survive, and the average attendance was 36. If only about half the total membership was active, our figures must be revised if we wish to present a realistic picture of the Lords. The Journal of the House of Lords tells us that about 40 men actively participated in 1559, and it shows us that 18 of these 40 were opposed to the Act of Uniformity. Thus almost half of those who went daily to Parliament voted against the government's plan to change religion.

It is true for the Lords as well as the Commons that influence counted more than numbers, and in the Upper House the ecclesiastics had great persuasive powers. John Jewel explained their strength:

> The bishops are a great hindrance to us; for being, as you know, among the nobility and leading men in the Upper House, and having none there on our side to expose their artifices and confute their falsehoods, they reign as sole monarchs in the midst of ignorant and weak men, and easily overreach our little party, either by their numbers, or by their reputation for learning.[52]

The government opposed this intellectual superiority with other weapons. What its supporters lacked in learning was made up for by the prestige of the Queen's name, the favours in her granting, and men's reluctance to oppose authority. The economic argument was strongly on the Queen's side as well. Most of the laymen had benefited from the appropriation of church lands under Henry and Edward, and they had a financial interest in renewing the Queen's control of the Church.

Normally, the government had no trouble in obtaining what it desired from the Lords. Everything from a subsidy to the seizure of the monasteries passed with little opposition, but the abolition of the Catholic mass was another matter. The Act of Uniformity was accepted by the peers by only three votes. The debates over religion posed a difficult problem for the lords who took their faith seriously. Arguing points they were trained to dispute, the bishops must have swayed men who had been taught from their youth to see the episcopate as their religious leaders. Torn between the Queen's desire and the bishops' arguments, many followed the bishops; the bill for unformity might have been defeated if Bishops White and Watson had not been conveniently locked in the Tower.

Neale argued that the Queen controlled the Lords and used them to defeat the settlement of religion proposed by the Commons. To make his case he wrote:

[52] *ZL*, I, 10, 20 March 1559. Richard Cox told a correspondent that the bishops had opposed the change in Parliament; 'and because they had in that place but few who durst even open their mouths against them, they always appeared to gain the victory'. *ZL*, I, 27.

'The Queen,' declared Philip II's special ambassador, the Count de Feria, writing on February 20, 'has entire disposal of the upper chamber in a way never seen before in previous parliaments'; and while we need not, indeed must not, endorse all that Philip's envoys wrote in their recurrent moods of depression and elation, we should be extremely chary of assuming that any appreciable number of lay peers would go the length of rejecting or drastically amending a government bill. The assumption that they would not — which I regard as sound — becomes an important element in my argument.[53]

It is upon this rock that Neale's thesis founders. Intent on reading the history of later Parliaments back into 1559, he dismissed the opposition to the alteration as meaningless. Trusting his own 'feel' for the period, he forgot the peculiarity of the 1559 Parliament, which led him to accept statements like Feria's as usable evidence.

Here is what Feria said, restored to its context:

The queen has entire disposal of the upper chamber in a way never seen before in previous parliaments, as in this there are several who have hopes of getting her to marry them, and they are careful to please her in all things and persuade others to do the same, besides which there are a great number whom she has made barons to strengthen her party, and that accursed cardinal left twelve bishoprics to be filled which now will be given to as many ministers of Lucifer instead of being worthily bestowed.[54]

An examination of this letter makes it plain why Neale thought it necessary to issue a warning about the Spaniard's dependability. Among the lords only Arundel was considered as a potential bridegroom (Robert Dudley sat in the Commons). The 'great number' of barons created by Elizabeth amounts to five, two of whom, as we shall see, were not active in the Parliament. There were 11 bishoprics vacant, not twelve, and only eight of these were left empty by poor Pole. Nor were the vacancies filled with Protestants, as Feria had feared, until after the Parliament ended. In short, the grounds upon which Feria based his assertion are at best only partially correct. Moreover, by February 20 he had not yet had the benefit of seeing the Lords in action. The only bill touching religion that had been debated by them up until then was the one restoring the first fruits and tenths to the Crown, and this was not a good test of the members' religious feelings. When the test did come, it showed that the Upper Chamber offered unprecedented resistance to the royal will.

[53]Neale, 'Supremacy and Uniformity', 307.

[54]*CSP Span., Eliz.,* I, 32.

76

Although Elizabeth did not control the Lords, the Catholics and conservatives failed to unite on any but the central issue of the mass. The confusion and indecision of the English Catholics, caused by their uncertainty over what action their religion required them to take against Elizabeth's innovations, helped to neutralize them as a cogent political force. They only agreed that the Roman eucharist should be defended.

These troubles of the Catholic faithful were not always remembered by Catholic apologists in later days, and they puzzled over the question how the kingdom came to be lost to the faith.[55] The most acceptable explanation was that Elizabeth had used coercion to have her will with the Lords.[56] The Protestant apologists, on the other hand, took pride in pointing out that, in spite of all the papists could do in Parliament, truth had prevailed.[57] Because it has caused controversy, the possibility of coercion ought to be examined, especially since there is evidence which suggests that, consciously or unconsciously, the government did alter the political balance in the Lords in its own favour.

In November 1558 the House of Lords appeared to be well stocked with men who might oppose reform. In the first place, of the 28 peers spiritual entitled by law to attend Parliament 20 were alive. In a house whose attendance seldom exceeded 40, these churchmen represented a strong potential threat to religious legislation, if they were united. Moreover, many lords temporal could be expected to side with the clerics. Thus it was with good reason that Sir Nicholas Throckmorton recommended to Elizabeth in early November that she should consider 'making you a better partie in the Lordes howse of parliament'.[58] At that moment no one could know that death,

---

[55] Henry N. Birt, *The Elizabethan Religious Settlement* (London: 1907) commits this error. See Frere's review of it in *EHR*, (1908), 572.

[56] Sanders, *De Visibili Monarchia* (Louvain: 1571), 686.

[57] See Foxe, Acts, VIII, 693 and Bartholomew Clerke, *Fidelis Servi, subdito infideli responsio, una cum errorum et calumniarum quarundam examine quae continentur in septimo libro de visibili Ecclesiae Monarchia a Nicholas Sandero conscripta* (London: 1573), Sig. L iii. Clerke answers Sander's charge as follows: 'Mira mehercule narras: erant omnes (ut tute dices) Papae et Ecclesiae Romanae non ita multo ante reconciliati, neninem horum Regine potuit excludere, et tamen constantia Catholicorum tribus suffragiis superata est. Quid aliud potuisses dicere, si in summam illorum inconstantiam invectus esses? Episcopos omnes fuisse Catholicos (credo) non negabis: maiorem quoque nobilium partem, cum de Papa recipiendo regnante Maria nomina darent: et tamen eorum constantiam laudes, cum si constantes essent, in eadem sententia perstitissent regnante Elizabetha: Quodsi constanter ab illis factum esset, nunquam suffragiis superari potuissent.'

[58] Neale, 'Throckmorton's Advice', 95.

disease and old age were working for the government: 4 peers spiritual died, and two more were prevented from attending by ill health and old age.[59] Nature, however, is slow and erratic in its workings, and Cecil may have been tempted to take some steps to keep Catholics out of the House of Lords. Legally he could not interfere directly, but other, seemingly innocent things could be done which would strengthen the government's position. Whether he deliberately did them is an open question, but by accident or design things were done which adjusted the political balance in favour of the Protestants.

The only overt example of force used on a member of the episcopacy was the arrest of Bishop White following Mary's funeral. There is, however, no way of determining if his incarceration was intended to sway his behaviour in Parliament. He was released from prison in time to attend, and the government had made an enemy. Lord Keeper Bacon may have tried another tactic to keep bishops out of Parliament when he acted on the Queen's warrant to summon it. Two bishops were not sent writs. On December 28 David Pole, Bishop of Peterborough, wrote to Cecil: 'I herd say a parliament shalbe the next month but yet as hitherto I have received noo wrytt for the same.'[60] The Bishop of St. Asaph, Thomas Goldwell, who had shared Cardinal Pole's exile in Italy, was in London when he wrote to Cecil with a similar complaint.

> I would gladly have cumyne unto you myself at thys present, but that I ame informed that by reson of your contynuall occupaon in the affares of the queenes hyghness I shold not have commodyte to speke unto you. Wherfore I ame so bold as by wryttyng to desyer you to show me so much favor, that by your help I may have lycense to depart here consyderyng my [purse?] and that I ame not by the quenes hyghness wryt called to be present at the Parlament, for the whych I ame nothyng sory thogh in dede it semyth sumwhat strange unto me, for I ame styll byshop of S. Asaphe, the whych bishoprych I never dyd nor cowd resygn. And as byshop of S. Asaphe I was present and gave my voyce in the last parlament, thogh before my cummyng to london, wythout myn other knowledge or consent I was named to oxford, the whych byshoprych, yf I may otherwyse have the queens hyghness favor, I do never intend to accept.[61]

[59]Cardinal Pole died on the same day as Mary; the Bishop of Rochester on 20 November; Bishop Christopherson of Chichester in late December. Thomas Tresham, the Master of the Knights of St. John in England, died on 16 March 1559. (Machyn, *Diary*, 178, 184, 192). Tunstal of Durham and Pole of Peterborough were prevented from coming by physical debility.

[60]P.R.O., SP 12/I/fol. 105.

[61]P.R.O., SP 12/I/fol. 52.

It may be injudicious to discover a plot where there may be only clerical error, but, given later events, one cannot help wondering why these two were missed out. In Pole's case, the error may have been the fault of an inattentive scribe. At any rate, Pole's chiding letter prompted correction of the mistake, for he did receive a writ, and he appointed proxies to represent him in Westminster.

Bishop Goldwell's case is more complicated. Thoughts of plots aside, the most obvious explanation for his failure to receive a writ is that he had been nominated to Oxford. He may not have received his summons because he was considered by the Chancery to be between sees. However, he was never formally elected by the chapter at Oxford, nor did he ever assume the temporalities of that see. Moreover, he was still acting as Bishop of St. Asaph until he fled England in June, 1559.[62] Although there is no good legal reason for Goldwell's exclusion from Parliament, he neither attended nor sent proxies, staying in Wales until he left for Italy, where he represented St. Asaph in the Council of Trent.

Goldwell's lack of a writ may have been an accident — although the fact that the mistake was never rectified is suspicious — but the error was distinctly advantageous for the government. Of all the occupants of the episcopal bench, Goldwell was the least likely to accept any compromise over the supremacy or uniformity. One of Cardinal Pole's closest friends, he had been in exile during the reigns of Henry VIII and Edward. Even in an optimistic moment Cecil could not have hoped that Goldwell would consent to the supremacy, as he probably believed that bishops like Tunstal, who had done so before, would do.

Some of the bishops failed to attend for less sinister reasons. The ancient Bishop of Durham, Cuthbert Tunstal, apparently requested permission from the Queen to remain in his see during the Parliament. 'Having consideration of your great age, the shortness of the tyme, the long waye, and the season of the yere unmete for a man of your yeris to traverse in,' answered Elizabeth, 'we do well suppose how much we may be your good and gracious . . . by pirmitting you to tary

---

[62] Besides checking the more obvious sources, such as the *DNB* and the *Handbook of Chronology,* for the dates and details of Goldwell's episcopate, I also examined the *sede vacante* register for Oxford in the Chapter Library at Canterbury Cathedral (Reg. U 2, 'Sede Vacante', fols. 39v-40v.) See also David Crowley, 'Thomas Goldwell', *The Venerabile,* V (1930), 65. Facts about this period of Goldwell's life are difficult to establish. I examined the archives of the Venerable English College at Rome in hopes of finding new information about this man, who died there as master of that College. Unfortunately, any records he might have left were destroyed when Napoleon's men looted the building.

at home.'[63] This far the letter is quite straightforward, but the draft contains an interesting alteration: originally the Queen had requested Tunstal to appoint 'three of your brethren bishops' to take up his duties at the coronation. This however, was crossed out, and 'three mete persons' was substituted. Durham's place at the coronations of Edward and Mary was at the sovereign's left hand, and it has been argued that this change in the draft was deliberate since the Earl of Pembroke occupied that position at Elizabeth's crowning instead of a cleric.[64]

The Bishop of Bath, Gilbert Bourne, did not attend Parliament, either. Why he did not is a mystery which the bishopric's historian has not solved. He was able, and it seems unlikely that his duties as President of the Council of Wales kept him away, although he was with the Council at Ludlow until mid-March.[65]

The government could do little to keep the bishops away, but it did directly influence the lay peers by keeping some of them out of London on government business, and by creating new barons. Whether this was done with the purpose of making a better party in the Lords is impossible to tell. That it did affect the balance of power between the conservatives and the reformers is unquestionable. Just before her coronation Elizabeth created or recreated five peers, all of whom had Protestant sympathies. William Parr, brother of Catherine Parr, a prominent Edwardian, and a member of Elizabeth's Privy Council, was restored to his old title of Marquis of Northampton.[66] Parr had been a close supporter of Somerset, whose son, Edward Seymour, was recreated Earl of Hertford at the same time.[67] Thomas Howard, Elizabeth's cousin, was created Viscount Howard of Bindon.[68] Lord St. John of Bletso and Lord Cary de Hunsdon were also created on January 13, 1559.[69] These five could be expected to support the government in Parliament, but not all of them did their duty. St. John sent his proxy and did not attend. Viscount Howard stayed in London until Easter, but he did not sit in the House after the holiday.

[63] P.R.O., SP 12/I/fol. 86.

[64] *Ibid.*, and Charles Sturge, *Cuthbert Tunstal, Churchman, Scholar, Statesman, Administrator* (London: 1938), 316-17.

[65] Phyllis M. Hembry, *The Bishops of Bath and Wells, 1540-1640, Social and Economic Problems* (London: 1938), 98-9.

[66] *DNB.*

[67] *Ibid.*

[68] Gibbs, *Peerage,* VI, 583-4.

[69] *Ibid.*, II, 652.

Several Catholic peers were absent from Parliament because of their official duties. For instance, Thomas Percy, Earl of Northumberland and the devoutly Catholic Warden of the East and Middle Marches, intended to come south to attend.[70] The Council, however, instructed him that it was the Queen's wish that he should remain in the North.[71] Lord Dacre of Gillsland, a staunch Catholic who had resisted the passage of the Edwardian books of common prayer, was reaffirmed Lord Warden of the West Marches and was sent to his post a few days before Parliament began.[72] Thomas Thirlby, Bishop of Ely, was away until mid-April attending the negotiations at Cateau Cambrésis, returning in time to vote against the Act of Uniformity. The peace negotiations also kept the Earl of Arundel out of London.

The absence of these men was largely due to their positions in Mary's government. As important servants of the Crown holding prestigious posts, they remained on the job. The new regime also needed men to serve, and some Protestant peers were absent because they were seeing to the Queen's business. Lord Howard of Effingham was in France during February and March, attending the treaty negotiations.[73] The captain of Berwick, Lord Eure, requested permission to attend the Parliament, but he was told to remain in Berwick until the Queen's pleasure was signified to him.[74] Eure missed the sittings in January and February, but he did arrive in time to take part in the crucial debate over the supremacy in mid-March.

There were many other reasons why lords did not come when summoned. William Paget, Mary's chief adviser, was too ill to travel to Westminster, and old age and infirmity probably kept Lord Mordaunt, an adamant Catholic, at home.[75] No doubt several others had similar excuses. The Earl of Cumberland was a recluse who seldom left his northern retreat.[76] Lords Latimer and Wentworth were both in prison during the session. Latimer had been jailed for a debt owed to Queen Mary, and Wentworth was awaiting trial on treason

[70] CSP For,. I. 78.

[71] Ibid., I, 90.

[72] Cal. Pat. Rolls, Eliz., I, 37, 45. CSP For., I, 90.

[73] DNB.

[74] CSP For., I, 73. APC, VII, 15.

[75] DNB.

[76] Ibid.

charges connected with his command of Calais.[77] In all, thirty five peers missed all or part of the Parliament.[78]

These absentees, thirty four of whom sent proxies, necessitate a note on procedure in the House of Lords. It is not certain how proxies were used in the mid-sixteenth century, but it is very unlikely that they were used on a regular basis. If they had been, the government would have had complete control of the Upper House, and religious legislation could have been passed with ease, since Bedford and Clinton held fifteen proxies between them. As Dom Henry Birt has pointed out, many of the lords bestowed their proxies upon men whose religion differed from their own, perhaps as a form of fence sitting, giving the government party a healthy majority of the proxies.[79]

In the absence of proof that there was any attempt to marshall Protestants and exclude Catholics, the possibility of a plot to improve the government's party in the Lords must be discounted, at least for the days before Parliament met. As we shall see, there may be some truth in the charge later on. The safest conjecture about Elizabeth's view of the House of Lords is similar to Neale's image of them. Judging by the realm's former experience, the Queen could assume that at least part of the episcopate and all of the peers temporal would follow the royal lead. The discovery that she had misjudged the strength of a sacramental Catholic faith and determination among her Lords would force her to change her parliamentary tactics in March.

The Parliament of 1559 was a freely elected and legally assembled body which contained men of all opinions. The House of Commons was predominately Protestant, but there were few there who were such ardent reformers that they would oppose a Protestant Queen. Membership in the Lower House was also enjoyed by a small group of Catholics who were led by experienced parliamentarians. A tiny bunch of returned exiles shared the benches with the rest, but there is no proof that they led their fellows in fighting to force the Queen to compromise on the prayer book of 1552. Their close association with the leaders of the Privy Council makes it even more unlikely. The

[77]Latimer: *APC*, VII, 57. Wentworth: *APC*, VII, 91.

[78]Based on the list of proxies given in the Lords'*Journal*, H.L.R.O., Original Journals, IV, fol. 1-1v.

[79]Birt, *Elizabethan Religious Settlement*, 50-3. I am indebted to Dr Michael Graves of the University of Auckland for sharing his knowledge of procedure in the House of Lords with me.

82

House of Lords had as many conservatives as it had members who were conformable to the royal policy in religion. Nearly all the laymen in that House voted to accept the supremacy, but enough joined the bishops in fighting the uniformity to ensure that the government had great difficulty obtaining its passage.

In examining the composition of the Parliament that assembled in January of Elizabeth's first year, it has become obvious that the logical place in which to expect opposition to governmental policies of religious reform was in the Lords, not in the Commons. On this the sources agree. This is what John Foxe, himself an exile for religion and a 'Puritan,' wrote about the Parliament:

> About this time, at the beginning of the flourishing reign of queen Elizabeth, was a parliament summoned and holden at Westminster, wherein was much debating about matters touching religion, and great study on both parties employed, the one to retain still, the other to impugn, the doctrine and faction which before, in queen Mary's time, had been established. But especially here is to be noted, that though there lacked no industry on the papists' side, to hold fast that which they most cruelly from time to time had studied, and by all means practised to come by; yet, notwithstanding, such was the providence of God at that time, that for lack of the other bishops, whom the Lord had taken away by death a little before, the residue that there were left, could do the less; and in very deed, God be praised therefor, did nothing at all, in effect: although yet notwithstanding there lacked in them neither the will nor labour to do what they could, if their cruel ability there might have served.[80]

That is the true story of the passage of the Elizabethan Settlement in the Parliament of 1559.

[80]Foxe, *Acts,* VIII, 693.

4

PARLIAMENT BEFORE EASTER

I

The writs for Elizabeth's first Parliament had directed the members to assemble on 23 January, but when they arrived at Westminster they discovered that their Queen was indisposed and had prorogued the gathering until the 25th.[1] On that day the members of the Lower House went to the abbey to await Her Majesty's attendance at the mass of the Holy Ghost, as was the custom. The tradition, however, was broken that morning, for the mass had already been sung at an early hour. As the royal procession approached the abbey the monks marched out with lighted tapers, incense and holy water to meet it. Elizabeth rebuffed them, crying 'Away with these torches, we see very well,' and as her choristers sang the litany in English she took her place under her canopy at the high altar. The sermon that morning was preached by Richard Cox, who had recently returned from exile in Frankfurt. Forecasting the religious changes about to be debated in Parliament, he began by lambasting the monks and arguing that they ought to be punished for their part in the heresy persecutions. Then, praising Elizabeth, he explained that God had made her Queen so that she could abolish past evils and exhorted her to destroy idolatry and monkery in England. Finally, after listening for an hour and a half, his audience repaired to the House of Lords to hear Lord Keeper Bacon speak on behalf of the Queen.[2]

Declaring Her Majesty's reasons for calling Parliament, Bacon spoke of the need for 'well making of laws, for the according, and uniting of these people of the Realm into a uniform order of religion'.[3] Expatiating on this theme, he talked of how the policies of every good commonwealth were buttressed by the proper worship of God, and of how faith and religion ought to be the stable base of every government. Wherefore, he admonished, it was the Queen's desire that

---

[1] H.L.R.O., Lords MS. Journals, IV, 2; H.L.R.O., Commons MS. Journals, I, fol. 186.

[2] *CSP Ven.*, VII, 22-23.

[3] Simonds D'Ewes, *The Journals of all the Parliaments during the Reign of Queen Elizabeth* (London: 1682), 11. *CSP Ven.*, VII, 23. *CSP Span, Eliz.*, I, 25.

84

> in this consultation, you with all humbleness, singleness
> and pureness of mind, confirm your selves together, using your
> whole endeavour and diligence, by Laws and Ordinances to
> Establish that, which by your Learning and Wisdom shall be
> thought most Meet for the well performing of this godly purpose
> . . . And like as in Council all contention should be eschewed,
> even so by Council provision should be made that no Con-
> tentions, Contumelious, nor opprobrious words, as Heretick,
> Schismatick, Papist and such like names, being Nurses of such
> Seditious Factions and Sects, be used . . .[4]

Having enjoined harmony, he went on to mention the sort of
settlement the Queen envisaged.

> Again, as in proceeding herein great and wary Consider-
> ation is to be had, that nothing be advised or done, which any
> way in continuance of time were likely to breed, or nourish any
> kind of Idolatry, or Superstitution; so, on the others side, heed is
> to be taken, that by no Licentious or loose handling, any manner
> of occasion be given, whereby any contempt, or irreverent
> behaviour towards God and Godly things, or any spice of
> irreligion might creep in, or be conceived; the Examples of
> fearful punishments that have followed these four extremities, I
> mean Idolatry, Superstition, Contempt, and Ireligion in all Ages
> and Times are more in number than I can declare. . . . And yet are
> they not so many, or better known than by the continual budding
> benefits and blessings of God to those that have forsaken those
> extremities, and embraced their Contraries.[5]

   Speaking for his mistress, Bacon had outlined the government's
intentions toward English religion. Translated from the vernacular,
his words indicate that Roman Catholic worship — idolatry and
superstition — was to be abolished and replaced with uniform order of
religion. The phrase 'uniform order of religion' could only mean one
thing to his listeners: a prayer book enforced, as the previous two had
been, by an Act of Uniformity. It is to the point that the supremacy
was not specifically referred to in the speech. It must have been
assumed that if Parliament was willing to reform religion it would
again recognize the Queen's supremacy over the Church in England.
Bacon coupled the abolition of superstition with a warning against
irreverent behaviour. It is likely that this was aimed directly at the
enthusiastic Protestants who had been committing iconoclasm and
other acts of contempt against the Church and against authority.

   After his speech the members of the Lower House went to their
chamber in St. Stephen's Chapel to elect a Speaker. As usual, the

[4] D'Ewes, *Journals,* 12.
[5] *Ibid.*

government had already selected its candidate, Sir Thomas Gargrave. Nominated by the Treasurer of the Queen's Household, he was elected with 'one voyce'.[6] The following Saturday, 28 January, the Queen attended another ceremonial sitting of the Upper House where the new Speaker was presented to her. As custom dictated, Gargrave made his disabling speech and then, after being reassured of his fitness and confirmed by the Queen, he proceeded to orate on the decay of the realm and to petition for the ancient liberties of the House.[7] After listening to the Lord Keeper's reply, Gargrave and the other members retreated to St. Stephen's Chapel and read the first bill of the Parliament, touching the felling of trees in forests.[8]

With the session officially begun, the Commons got down to serious business on 30 January. That morning someone raised the legal question of Mary's rejection of the supremacy. As a consequence, Thomas Parry, treasurer of the Household, and twenty-three others were appointed to a special committee,

> to treate together for a convenyent subsydye and also for the valydytye aswell of the parlyaments lately had as this parliament lackyng in the writte of sommons Supremum Caput.[9]

This group worked quickly, and on 3 February the bill for a subsidy was read. On the same day John Carrell reported on the committee's behalf that the lack of the words 'Supremum Caput' did not invalidate the writs for any Parliament.[10] The appointment of a special committee to consider the subsidy was not unusual, it had been done in Marian Parliaments, but behind the Commons' inquiry into the missing title was a question of law with far reaching consequences.

When Queen Mary dropped 'Supremum Caput Ecclesiae Anglicanae' from her style and replaced it with 'etc'. the justices and serjeants at Serjeants Inn had been concerned about the abbreviation. Discussing, apparently, the writs for Mary's first Parliament, some voiced grave doubts that they were valid without the supremacy formula since it had been annexed to the royal title by the statutes of 26 and 35 Henry VIII.[11] Those who thought the writs were valid

---

[6]H.L.R.O., Commons MS. Journals, I, fol. 186. J.E. Neale, *The Elizabethan House of Commons* (Harmondsworth: 1963), 341-3.

[7]H.L.R.O., Commons MS. Journals, I, fol. 186v.

[8]*Ibid.*

[9]*Ibid.*

[10]*Ibid.*, I, fol. 187.

[11]26 Hen. VIII, c. 13; 35 Hen. VIII, c. 1.

argued that the Henrician statutes only forbade alteration of the style in an affirmative sense, not in a negative one. Hence, although the Queen could not add to the style, she was not bound always to write it in full. Moreover, the words were an addition to the style, not a part of the Queen's name. When a vote was taken eight men said they believed the writ was valid and five alleged the contrary. Six of the men present at this debate were later on the committee to consider all things necessary for the Parliament of 1559. Another was John Carrell, who delivered the decision of the parliamentary committee.[12] Carrell was markedly conservative in religion, but in the debate at Serjeants Inn he had maintained that the writs of summons were invalid without the supremacy formula. The vote taken at the Inn was not an official ruling, and the 'etceteration' of the style continued to bother the legal profession — so much so that when the supremacy was repealed a special retroactive clause was inserted in the bill, guaranteeing the legality of instruments which bore the abridged style.[13] Technically this clause resolved the problem, but not everyone was willing to accept the rejection of the supremacy as a legal act. A larger principle was at stake.

When the bill returning first fruits to the Church was debated in 1555, members of the Council and of Parliament argued that the Queen could not legally diminish the inheritance of her successor. Mary had an obligation to uphold the laws and customs of the realm as she had received them: she had no right to give them away. The Dudley conspirators tried to justify themselves with similar arguments.

[12] Reported in William Dalison, *Les Reports de divers special cases Adjudge en le court de Comon Bank. . . .* (London: 1689), 14, pl. 4. James Dyer, *Ascun Novel Cases* (London: 1585), fol. 98. Edward Coke, *The Fourth Part of the Institutes of the Laws of England* (London: 1644), 344. I am indebted to Dr J.H. Baker for telling me of the mention of this case in Dalison's *Reports.* For a discussion of these unofficial legal debates at Serjeants Inns see Lewis W. Abbot, *Law Reporting In England, 1485-1585* (London: 1973), 180-181.

[13] 1 & 2 Phil. & Mar., c. 8, 19: 'And where your Highnes Sovereigne Lady since your comming to the Crowne of the Realme, of a good and Christen Conscience omitted to write the said Stile of Supremacye specified in onc Acte. . . of your late Father King Henry Theight, as well in Giftes Grantes letteres Patentes as in Commissions and other Writings; And also other have in their Writings done the same, as well in your time as before; And forasmuch as notwithstanding any Law made concering the said Stile of Supremacie, it was in the free choice Libertie and pleasure of the King of this Realme and of your Highnes whether ye would expres the same by aucthorite of this present Parliament, that all Grantes Writinges made in you our Sovereigne Ladies Name, or in the Names of yours Sovereigne Lorde and Ladye or any other, wherin the said Stile of Supremacye is omitted, is and shall be to alintentes and purposes as good and effectuall as if the same had bene therin expressed, and may bee deteined kept pleaded and alledged, without any danger paine penaltie or forfeiture to ensue to any person or persones or Bodye Polytyke, for or concerning the omission of the same Style or anye parte thereof, in any suche Writinges; and that no persone ne persones shalbe impeached molested or dampnified for or by reason of any suche omission.'

They claimed that Mary had, by intruding foreign authority into the realm, broken her coronation oath.[14]

Ponet developed this line of reasoning in his *Shorte Treatise of Politike Power* printed in 1556. Although the Queen had the crown by inheritance, he claimed, she could not do as she pleased with it, for 'she hathe it with an oathe, lawe and condicion to kepe and mayntane it, not to depart with it or diminishe it.'[15]

John Hales, in a sermon sent to Elizabeth shortly after her accession, linked these arguments to the lack of 'Supremum Caput' in the writs. Mary's third Parliament, which repealed the supremacy, was void and without authority, according to Hales, because the title of supreme head was omitted in the writs, contrary to the statute of 35 Henry VIII. 'Wherefore', he wrote,

> as a woman can bring forth no child without a man, so cannot those writs bring forth good and sure fruit, because this part of the title, which was ordained by parliament always to be used in the king's style, was left out. For greater error is in lack of form, than in lack of matter; and where the foundation is naught, then can nothing builded thereon be good. There is no law spiritual nor temporal (as they term them), nor any good reason, but allows these rules for infallible principles. And if any man will say, that it was in the free choice, liberty, and pleasure of the king of this realm, and the queen, whether they would express the said title in their style, or not — as that subtle serpent Gardiner . . . would have excused it, as appeareth by a piece of statute made in the eight chapter and two and twentieth leafe — it may be justly and truly answered, that they could not so do. For although every person may by law renounce his right in that which toucheth the commonwealth or a third person.
>
> And this title and style more touched the commonwealth and realm of England, than the king. For, as I said before, it was ordained for the conservation of the liberty of the whole realm, and to exclude the usurped authority of the bishop of Rome. And therefore no king nor queen alone could renounce such title: but it ought (if they would have it taken away) be taken away orderly and formally by act of parliament sufficiently called and summoned.[16]

John Aylmer offered a similar argument, claiming that no one could take away the title belonging to the king or queen, and that the Acts of Mary's Parliaments were not binding. Ergo, the reception of the

[14]Loades, *Oxford martyrs,* 243-5. *CSP Ven.,* VI, 154; 251.

[15]John Ponet, *A Shorte Treatise of Politike Power* (Strassburg: 1556), Sig. E ii (v).

[16]Foxe, *Acts,* VIII, 676-7. Foxe copied this from B.L., Harley, 419, fols. 145v-146.

Bishop of Rome was illegal.[17] Cecil, too, was concerned about the lack of the formula in the writs. On the second day of the reign he wrote a note to himself: 'A commission to make out wrytts for ye parlement — towching etc. in ye style of wrytte.'[18] The 'etc.' could stand only for one thing, and its presence indicated to the world that Elizabeth, like many others, believed that the supremacy belonged to her.

The parliamentary committee was created in order to answer these doubts and questions. If, as people were claiming, Mary's Parliaments were void because their writs were improperly drawn, then Elizabeth's writs were also improper and the actions of her Parliament would be void. Therefore it was important that the issue be settled before anything else was done. Coupled as it was with the subsidy and chaired by a privy councillor, the committee was probably created on a government motion intended to resolve the question and reassure the members.

The lords were occupied during the first weeks of February with returning the first fruits and tenths to the Crown and with the housekeeping bills necessary to begin the new reign, such as recognizing Elizabeth's right to the throne and passing the Commons' bill granting her tonnage and poundage.[19]

On Ash Wednesday the Commons adjourned to hear a sermon at court. Preached by Richard Cox, it prepared the minds of the knights and burgesses for the introduction of the bill for supremacy on the following day. Il Schifanoya sadly described the sermon, which proved to him that Catholicism in England was doomed:

> Of this I am more convinced by the sermon preached yesterday at court . . . [in which was] said so much evil of the Pope, of the bishops, of the prelates, of the regulars, of the Church, of the mass, and finally of our entire faith, in the presence of the Queen and of her Council, the rest of the congregation consisting of more than 5,000 persons, that I was much scandalized. . . . Consequently everything will go from bad to worse, and religion and the religious will be abolished.[20]

Thus addressed, the Commons gathered the next morning to hear

[17] John Aylmer, *An Harborrowe for Faithfull and Trewe Subjects, Against the Late Blowne blaste, Concerning the Government of Women* (1559), Sig. 0.

[18] P.R.O., SP 12/I/fol. 5.

[19] H.L.R.O., Lords MS. Journals IV 9-17. Eliz. I, c. 3; c. 5; c. 23; c. 20.

[20] *CSP Ven.*, VII, 30-31.

the first reading of the bill for supremacy. After it had been heard, the paper bill was entrusted to Cecil's father-in-law, Sir Anthony Cooke, presumably for articling.[21]

The following Saturday, 11 February, the House began a custom which continued throughout the reign. Before business commenced that day the members knelt while the clerk led them through the litany.[22] When they were back in their seats the clerk read a bill to confirm grants and leases made by deprived Edwardian bishops, the first of many bills which attempted to reverse the economic effects of the Marian reaction.[23]

Those who attended on the morning of 13 February were treated to the first reading of a bill for garbling feathers, the second of a bill to outlaw mechanization in the felt cap industry, and the second of the bill annexing the supremacy to the Crown. Obviously the supremacy aroused more interest than the felt business, and the clerk noted that the rest of the morning was spent in 'arguments upon the bill of Supremacy'.[24] The next day he had to repeat this entry.[25] The debate finally ended on the third day, and the bill was committed to Sir Anthony Cooke and Sir Francis Knollys, both of whom were returned exiles. The morning was completed with the first readings of two bills, one concerning the claims on the Bishop of Winchester's lands and the other 'for order of Servyce and mynysters in the churche'.[26] On Tuesday the 16th a bill called 'The boke for common prayer and mynystracion of sacraments' was read,[27] and on the 21st a new bill for the supremacy, which incorporated the bills for order of service and the book of common prayer, was introduced.

The story of the first bill for supremacy, its committal, and the emergence of a second bill for supremacy is the ultimate mystery of the Parliament of 1559. The contents of both the early supremacy bills are unknown, since they were later replaced by a third, and the reason for the unusually long debate on the first bill is equally obscure. Mystery surrounds the bills which would have produced a uniform order of service, too. Were they introduced, as Neale believed, by Protestants who found that Elizabeth's first

[21] H.L.R.O., Commons MS. Journals, I, fol. 188.
[22] Ibid., fol. 188v. Neale, Commons, 355.
[23] H.L.R.O., Commons MS. Journals, I, fol. 189.
[24] Ibid.
[25] Ibid., fol. 189v.
[26] Ibid.
[27] Ibid., fol. 190.

90

bill of supremacy contained too little reform? Or were they government bills? And why two bills? Neale did some brilliant work on these questions, and, although we cannot accept all that he said, he was right in arguing that the second bill for supremacy contained provisions for a prayer book as well as the supremacy.[28] Where Neale was mistaken was in ascribing the changes in the bill for supremacy to returned exiles, supported by inflamed Protestants, who rejected Elizabeth's planned interim policy and amended the bill to turn it into a complete reform package.

Henry Gee first noted that when the supremacy was introduced on 9 February it caused an unusually long debate, which he attributed to Catholics.[29] The evidence supports this conclusion. Count Feria reported that some members spoke strongly 'in favour of reason' and against the supremacy. Dr. Story defended the primacy of the pope and expressed his regret that Elizabeth had not been executed, as he had recommended to Queen Mary.[30] From a 'puritan' comes a comment on the matter which shows that he, Sir Anthony Cooke, one of the ring-leaders of Neale's conspiring radicals, was not opposed to the legislative plans of Cecil and Elizabeth. On 12 February Cooke had finished articling the bill for supremacy entrusted to him a few days before, and he still had it in his possession when, taking his leisure on Sunday, he wrote to Peter Martyr:

> We are now busy in parliament about expelling the tyranny of the pope, and restoring the royal authority, and re-establishing true religion. But we are moving far too slowly: nor are there lacking at this time Sanballots and Tobiases to hinder and obstruct the building of our walls. Wherefore we ought the more to think upon the exhortation, 'Pray without ceasing'. The zeal of the queen is very great, the activity of the nobility and people is also great; but still the work is hitherto too much at a stand. The advice 'Trust in God, and lean not to your own understanding,' is not sufficiently impressed on the minds of some parties; neither that saying, 'He taketh the wise in their own craftiness'. But the result of this meeting of parliament will, as far as I can judge confirm my hopes.[31]

[28]Neale, 'Supremacy and Uniformity', 317

[29]Gee, *Prayer-Book*, 81. Gee conveniently ignored the apparent introduction of two bills for uniformity, mentioning only one (he may have been right). See also Neale, 'Supremacy and Uniformity', 312.

[30]*CSP Span., Eliz.*, I, 33. See also ASV, arm. LXIV, 28, fol. 272v.

[31]*ZL*, II, 13-14. Cooke's purpose in writing was to tell Martyr that he and Cecil had seen Elizabeth weep when she read Martyr's letter.

There was opposition, then, but Cooke makes it clear that he was siding with the Queen, not opposing her. Papists, Lutherans like Richard Hilles,[32] or politiques who were more cautious than Cooke may have been the cause of his complaint.

Any or all of these groups, not to mention men who may have had legal reservations concerning the mechanics of the bill, could have contributed to the six or eight hours of argument it generated before it was committed to the group headed by Cooke and Knollys. Whoever the objectors were, the House must have thought their criticism valid enough to require a committee to resolve their complaints. Cooke's and Knollys' presence at the head of the committee militates against the idea that they were opposed to the terms of the bill, if the Commons' later procedure is any indication. Around the end of the century a tract on Commons procedure reported that 'fault hath beene found and motion made agaynst it that they above the chayre [Privy Councillors] have named all the committees', and noted that 'none may be named as a committee, that hath spoken agaynst the body of the bill'.[33] This is conjecture, however, for the committal procedure of bills was not yet standarized in Elizabeth's early years, and committees were rather informal. The clerk entrusted the bill to a member, whose name he noted in the Journal, and those who had objections or proposals coalesced around him.[34] The appearance of two names in the Journal on this occasion probably means that the bill was divided into two parts, Knollys and Cooke each receiving half.[35]

As the supremacy bill went into committee the first bill for a uniform order of service was introduced, to be followed the next day by what appears, in the printed edition of the Journal, to be another bill for a uniform service. There are three possible explanations for the appearance of these two entries. Two were suggested by Neale: either they were proposals made by the Puritans which would have revived the prayer book and ordinal of 1552, or they were actually part of the debate over the bill for supremacy and not really bills at all. Rather, they were readings of the Edwardian legislation which the Puritans wanted included in the

[32] ZL, II, 15.

[33] B.L., Stowe, CCCLIV, fol. 36 as quoted in Catherine S. Sims, "Policies in Parliament" An Early 17th Century Tractate on the House of Commons Procedure', Huntington Library Quarterly (1951), 54.

[34] S.T. Bindoff, 'The Making of the Statute of Artificers', Elizabethan Government and Society, S.T. Bindoff et al., ed. (London: 1961), 69.

[35] Neale, 'Supremacy and Uniformity', 312.

bill for supremacy. A third possibility is that the two entries represent two readings of the same bill — a bill for uniformity introduced by the government to complement the bill for supremacy. There is no certain way to choose the correct interpretation of these bills, but the odds favour the third one. The weaknesses in the first two are in their origin. They require someone to take direct action against the Queen within two weeks of the beginning of the session and only a few days after the introduction of the bill for supremacy. In addition, the second interpretation requires the clerk of the Commons to record a continuing debate on the content of the supremacy as readings of two separate bills. There is no precedent which would support this assumption. Then too, if the government had no intention of restoring the Protestant faith, how could Sir Anthony Cooke, who was in a position to know the government's mind, tell Martyr on 12 February that 'we are now busy in parliament about expelling the tyranny of the pope, and restoring royal authority, and re-establishing true religion?' The assumptions required to support these two theories are unprovable but improbable.

There are stronger reasons for suspecting that the two entries refer to a government bill or bills for reformation of the church. To begin with, Bacon had, at the opening of Parliament, called for the establishment of a uniform order of religion, indicating that the government intended to take the initiative in this. Moreover, if precedent and the 'Device' are considered, we would expect the bill for uniformity to be introduced separately from the supremacy. If we accept that the government had prepared its own uniformity legislation, the bill for 'order of Servyce and mynysters in the churche' was introduced at the logical moment. The supremacy had been brought in on 9 February, and the sittings on the 10th, 11th, 13th, and 14th were taken up with debate on it, the subsidy, and the Queen's answer to the Commons' petition asking her to marry. On the 15th, after the supremacy had been committed and the other important issues dealt with, the bill for order of service was introduced.

On the following day the clerk recorded that 'The boke for common prayer and mynystracon of sacraments' had been read. Beside it he wrote a number that may be either a one or a two, indicating either a first reading of a new bill, or a second reading of a bill already introduced. If the numeral is a one, then this bill would have established a prayer book and the one read the preceding day would have legalized the Edwardian ordinal or something similar. If, on the other hand, it is a two then it and the bill for 'order of Servyce' were the same piece of legislation.

After carefully examining the original Journal, I have concluded that the clerk probably wrote a 2 beside the 16 February entry, not the 1 shown in the printed edition. Seymour's ones and twos all tend to resemble zs, and I surmise that the 'z' in front of the 'boke for common prayer' was intended to be a two. If that is the case, then both entries refer to the bill variously described as the bill for 'order of Servyce and mynysters in the churche' and as the 'boke of common prayer and mynystracon of the sacraments'. Whether there were one or two bills, there is little doubt that its or their passage would have established a prayer book and an ordinal for the use of the Church of England — in all likelihood, the 1552 book with its purified ordinal attached. There is a possibility, however, that there was no ordinal included in the bill, in view of the fact that the Act of Uniformity's full title echoes of the clerk's description of the two readings without including one: The Act of the Uniformity of Common Prayer and Divine Service in the Church and the Administration of the Sacraments.

Whatever the contents of the first bill for supremacy and the bill for order in the church, they were fused together in Cooke's and Knollys' committee. The Commons, it was reported on 20 February, were examining the bill 'to give ecclesiastical authority to the Queen, and to annull almost all the public and private Acts (*cose*) enacted and ordained by the late Queen' clause by clause.[36] From this examination emerged a new bill for supremacy whose contents we can guess from the echoes of the debates, the reaction of Convocation, and the diplomatic correspondence.

The first evidence appeared on 4 March when the chancellor of the Duchy, Sir Ambrose Cave, angrily complained to the House that Sir Thomas White, a burgess for Southampton, had 'called hym to wytnesse not to lyke the booke of service'. White retorted that Cave had misunderstood him. He had really said that Mr. Chancellor 'wisshed the boke to be well consydered'. The House, however, decided in Cave's favour, and White was forced to beg his pardon.[37] Their squabble proves that the new bill for supremacy contained a service book. It also shows that Cave thought it important to assert his support for the book in the bill publicly.

The new supremacy bill, a complete reform package, came before the House of Commons on 21 February; on the 23rd it was

[36] *CSP Ven.,* VII, 35.

[37] H.L.R.O., Commons MS. Journals, I, fol. 197v.

passed, after a stormy debate.[38] Some members argued against its passage so strongly that, according to Feria, 'it was necessary, in order to succeed with his iniquitous scheme, for Secretary Cecil to throw the matter into confusion, and so passed it'.[39] The opposition encountered by the bill may be ascribed to several causes, and although the Catholic members were probably to the fore, there is evidence that there were Protestants in the House who did not agree with the proposed settlement. Richard Hilles, a wealthy merchant adventurer and a London alderman, told Henry Bullinger on 28 February that he no longer agreed with the theology Bullinger espoused, and that he desired no further contact with him. Hilles ended the letter by saying that he would do his utmost to promote true religion, 'of which the chief part is contained in the confession of faith exhibited to the invincible emperor Charles V at the assembly at Augsburg in 1530'.[40] Neale demonstrated that Hilles had, in the early 1550s, equated the 1549 prayer book with the Augsburg Confession and therefore argued that when he named the Confession he meant the 1549 book.[41] This is possible, but Hilles was very specific in labelling the creed to which he now adhered. It is an odd way to refer to Edward's first prayer book, if that was his intention: the one is a confession of faith, the other a manual for worship. It is more likely that Hilles was honestly a Lutheran. Strype tells us that Lutherans as well as papists opposed Elizabeth in the beginning, and Hilles may have been one of them. His letter is evidence for the presence of a Lutheran in the House of Commons, not for the theory that the prayer book of 1549 was considered as a possible foundation for the uniformity.

Hilles said something else which takes on the proportions of a riddle when considered in context. Writing the day after the supremacy was approved by the Commons, he added a postscript:

> The public assembly too, or common council of this realm, or parliament, as our people call it, has now been sitting

[38] Ibid., fol. 191v; 192; 193v.

[39] J.B.M.C. Kervyn de Lettenhove, ed., *Rélations Politiques des Pays-Bas et de l'Angleterre, sous le Regne de Philippe II* (Bruxelles: 1882-1900), I, 444-445: 'aunque huvo algunos que hablaron en favor de la razon, de maneral que fue necesario, para salir con su malad, que el secretario Sicel se metisese la cosa in garbullo, y asi paso.' This passage was mistranslated in the *CSP Span., Eliz.*, I, 33, which de-emphasized Cecil's role.

[40] ZL, II, 15.

[41] Neale, 'Supremacy and Uniformity', 318, citing *Original Letters*, I, 266.

nearly six weeks. Nothing however has yet been publicly determined with respect to the [*sic*] abolishing popish superstition, and the re-establishment of the Christian religion. There is however a general expectation, that all rites and ceremonies will shortly be reformed by our faithful citizens, and all other godly men, in the afore-mentioned parliament, either after the pattern which was lately in use in the time of King Edward the sixth, or which is set forth by the protestant princes of Germany, in the above-named Confession of Augsburg.[42]

This statement led Neale to hypothesize that, although the letter is dated 28 February, the postscript was added between March 1 and 8, after the bill had received its first reading in the Lords. It proved, he thought, that the Commons had revived the second Edwardian prayer book, and indicated that Hilles anticipated opposition to the Commons proposal from the Queen, who preferred the first Edwardian book. She would instruct the Lords to remove the more liberal book from the bill and substitute its predecessor.[43]

Upon close examination, however, Hilles 'letter will not support Neale's interpretation. Hilles was reporting rumour, 'a general expectation', about what Parliament would do, and he speaks as if he himself was not one of 'our faithful citizens and other godly men' in Parliament, even though he was a member. Did he really know any thing more than what gossip told him? Theoretically he must have known exactly what form of religion had been passed by the Commons, so we must assume that the rumour was just that. Hilles must have been indulging in some diplomatic obfuscation, in keeping with Elizabeth's attempts to keep the friendship of Lutheran states. By the end of February there were only two visible religious alternatives. Either the supremacy bill would be passed and its prayer book accepted, or it would be defeated. It is asking too much of Hilles to expect him to have forecast alterations in the bill on behalf of the court — especially since the changes that were made were certainly not ones Elizabeth could have liked.

Once the supremacy had passed through its mutations in the Lower House it was brought into the Lords for the consideration of the peers of the realm, to whom it was first read on February 28.[44]

---

[42] *ZL*, II, 17.

[43] Neale, 'Supremacy and Uniformity', 318.

[44] H.L.R.O., Lords MS. Journals, IV, 23.

Although the Journals of the two Houses do not mention one, there may have been a joint conference between them. A report from London sent to the Venetian ambassador in Brussels on March 7 was summarized by its recipient as follows:

> Advices . . . purport that the Lower House and the Upper House had debated together for three consecutive days about religion, without ever coming to any agreement; so five days passed without speaking further about this business, and in the meanwhile they discussed other matters; but it was reported that the Queen would attend Parliament in order to persuade them to comply with her wishes.[45]

Whether or not the Commons were requested to send members to confer with the peers, it is certain that the first reading of the bill caused an uproar in the Lords. Writing of that day Il Schifanoya told the Mantuan ambassador in Brussels that the reading had occasioned 'very great altercation and disputes on the part of the bishops and of other good and pious peers' before the House consigned it to silence for a few days.[46] John Francis Canobio told Paul IV the same thing and attributed the silence to an attempt by the bishops to table it.[47] It was two weeks before it was read a second time, and in the meantime the Catholics and the court were feverishly promoting their causes.

The Convocation of the Province of Canterbury reacted swiftly and strongly to the passage of the supremacy by the Commons. Fearing for the safety of their religion, the assembled clergy drew up a protestation of faith. 'Quoniam', they said, 'fama publica referente, ad nostram nuper notitiam pervenit, multa religionis Christianae dogmata . . . praesertim articulos infra scriptos in dubium vocari'. The articles which followed affirmed the real presence, transubstantiation, the sacrificial nature of the mass, and papal supremacy. The final one insisted that only the church could define matters of dogma and doctrine.[48] Written in reply to the bill altering religion, these articles explain the nature of the communion service in the proposed prayer book. Whether or not it went beyond the 1552 Book of Common Prayer, it certainly was not the 1549 book. In fact, the first three articles are the

[45] CSP Ven., VII, 48.

[46] Ibid., VII, 46.

[47] CSP Rome, 8.

[48] David Wilkins, Concilia Maganae Britanniae et Hiberniae (London: 1737), IV, 179-180. The original (or a contemporary copy) of the convocation journal for 1559 is at C.C.C.C. 121, 192-195.

same ones that were debated in 1554 at Oxford when the eucharistic doctrine of the 1552 book was attacked. To quote Henry Gee, the protest of Convocation was 'aimed as distinctly as could be against the Communion Service of 1552, and the Bill of Supremacy'.[49] The Bishop of London delivered the articles to Lord Keeper Bacon on 3 March, expecting that he would have them read to the Upper House. Bacon, according to the *Concilia,* accepted them gratefully but said nothing.[50] Nor did he do anything with them but suppressed the protest of the clergy, forcing Bonner to make it public by other means.[51] On 10 March the disgruntled clerics adjourned, after once more discussing whether or not they ought to grant Elizabeth a subsidy.[52]

To counter the protests of the Catholic clergy the government sponsored court preachers who did their utmost to convince the people that the Pope had no authority in England.[53] Cox, Parker, Grindal, Whitehead and Sandys repeatedly hammered home this lesson in their Lenten sermons before the Queen and large audiences.[54]

Before following the second bill for supremacy through the House of Lords it would be well to summarize what we know of its provisions. First, of course, it would have declared Elizabeth to be the supreme head of the Church of England and restored to her the powers that appertained to that position. Second, it contained the equivalent of an Act of Uniformity: it would have established a prayer book and enforced its use with penal statutes. Il Schifanoya wrote the only description we have of this section of the bill. It was, he said,

> a book passed by the Commons forbidding the Mass to be said or the Communion to be administered (*ne se communicassero*) except at the table in the manner of Edward VI; nor were the Divine offices to be performed in Church; priests likewise being allowed to marry, and the Christian religion and the sacraments being absolutely

[49] Gee, *Prayer-Book,* 82-3.

[50] Wilkins, *Concilia,* IV, 180.

[51] *Ibid.,* Sanders said, in 1561, that Bacon 'cum sciret eam rem suae nocere posse, conclusiones retinuit nec unquam promulgari passus est'. ASV, arm. LXIV, 28, fol. 258v.

[52] Wilkins, *Concilia,* IV, 180.

[53] *CSP Ven.,* VII, 46.

[54] *Ibid.,* and Machyn, *Diary, 189-90.*

> abolished; adding thereto many extraordinary penalites against delinquents.[55]

In all probability, then, the prayer book in the bill was the 1552 book or something similar. All of the testimony we have seen indicates that the second supremacy bill would have created a settlement similar to the one finally reached, with at least two important distinctions. If the second bill had passed, the penalties imposed on recusants would have been much harsher, and the clergy would have been permitted to marry. In these two differences are traces of modifications made in the government's bill by Protestants. Since it is unlikely that Elizabeth would have permitted her own ministers to introduce them as part of the bill,[56] they were probably amendments added by the committee that united the bills for supremacy and ministration of the sacraments. However, to see them as the work of Puritans is to stretch a point. It was a rare Protestant who opposed clerical marriage, and harsh anti-Catholic laws would have been a natural reaction to the Marian terror.

A more clearly radical Protestant motion was the bill for making ecclesiastical laws by 32 persons, a revival of an Edwardian Act intended to produce a revision as well as better enforcement of the Church's law. Introduced in the second week of March, the bill was the latest in a long line of attempts to strengthen the Church's disciplinary powers. A committee of 32 had actually completed the 'reformatio legum' and submitted it to Parliament in 1553, but the measure was defeated by the Lords at the behest of Northumberland. The new code, which was a source of contention among the Edwardians, called for synods on the diocesan and provincial levels, for increased power and efficiency in the Church courts, and for restoring the potency of excommunication.[57] The appearance of the bill in 1559 may not mean that it aimed to revive the 1553 'Reformatio', but it is likely that the new committee would have begun where its predecessor left off. Although the reform of the ecclesiastical law had been supported by the clergy in Edward's reign and was to become a standard plank in the Puritan platform, it was never passed by an Elizabethan Parliament. Whoever sponsored the bill, it died in the

---

[55] *CSP Ven.*, VII, 52.

[56] When, in 1563, Parliament passed harsh penalities against Catholics Elizabeth effectually quashed them by ordering the bishops not to enforce them. She never did officially sanction clerical marriage, although she did little to stop it.

[57] James C. Spalding, 'The Reformatio Legum Ecclesiasticarum of 1552 and the Furthering of Discipline in England', *Church History* (1970), 162-8; 166; 170-171. Jasper Ridley, *Thomas Cranmer* (Oxford: 1966), 331-4.

Lords in 1559, perhaps because, as Spalding says of its 1553 defeat, 'men who could live with the reformation of doctrine and worship were not prepared to accept the reformation of discipline. It would give a power to the Church which could be used against them.'[58]

The temporary silence surrounding the supremacy bill came to an end in the Lords on 13 March. After it had been read for the second time it was committed to a group of fifteen men.[59] The members of this committee were predominately conservative in religion, and it is possible that they were appointed in hopes that the government could win some of them over, splitting the opposition. In particular the appointment of the Bishop of Carlisle suggests this. If he, who alone among the bishops had consented to officiate at the coronation, could be persuaded to support the alteration, the opposition of the rest could be discounted and there would be continuity in the episcopal line. If this is what the government intended, they were soon disillusioned. When these fifteen, eight of whom later voted against supremacy, finished with the bill it had been reduced to a skeleton, changed almost beyond recognition.[60]

The peers who opposed the abolition of the mass had united behind the Archbishop of York to fight the combination of supremacy and uniformity. Their strategy was simple. Whenever a matter of religion was raised they challenged Parliament's right to discuss something reserved to the Church. All the bishops, said Sanders in 1561, argued in the same way:

> qui nullum articulum passi sund praeterire quem non ita persequirentur, ut nunquam ipsorum orationibus responderi potuerit. Erat res inaudita cum nihil habuerint laici quod in ulla causa possent dicere, cumque in episcopis admirari se et ingentium et doctrinam faterentur, tamen semper ab eisdem eos dissentire. Non aliam ob rem quam quod aliud reginae optatum esse intelligerent.[61]

[58] Spalding, 'Reformatio', 166. Among the M.P.s in 1559 were three who were on the committee: Sir Anthony Cooke, Sir William Petre, Sir Thomas Smith. Richard Goodrich, Richard Cox, Matthew Parker, John Scory, and William Barlow were also on the committee of 32.

[59] The committee members were the marquis of Winchester, the Duke of Norfolk, the Earls of Westmorland, Shrewsbury, Rutland, Sussex, and Pembroke, Viscount Montague, the bishops of Exeter and Carlisle, and Lords Clinton, Morley, Riche, Willoughby, and North. H.L.R.O., Lords MS. Journals, IV, 34.

[60] Winchester, Shrewsbury, Montague, Exeter, Carlisle, Morely, Riche and North voted against the Uniformity. See E. Jeffries Davis, 'An Unpublished Manuscript of the Lords Journal for April and May, 1559', EHR (1913), 538.

[61] Report to Moroni, ASV, arm. LXIV, 28, fol. 258v.

100

The Earl of Pembroke, the Earl of Shrewsbury, Viscount Montague, and Lord Hastings staunchly supported the bishops.[62]

Defending the Protestant cause, the earl of Bedford involved Anthony Browne, Viscount Montague, in a heated dispute. To illustrate the malignity and debauchery of Rome, Bedford asked if it was true that, when Browne and the Bishop of Ely had been in Rome delivering Mary's submission to the Pope, the cardinals had offered to procure whores for them. Reddening, Browne vehemently swore before God and the angels that it was a lie and affirmed the purity of the Curia.[63] At another time Browne tried to shame the Lords into defeating the bill. It reflected poorly upon their honour, he said, that three years after they had reaffirmed their obedience to Rome they were about to abandon that obedience at the whim of a woman. If they apostasized, he warned at the end of this ironic argument, they would be branded with everlasting disgrace for their levity in matters of religion.[64]

In the end the committee was persuaded to destroy those portions of the bill which would have altered the church service, leaving only the royal supremacy. The lay peers did not object to banishing the Pope from England, but they were not anxious to imperil their salvation by denying the fundamentals of the faith. The Catholic committee men received the thanks of Bishop Scot of Chester when he rose to speak at the third reading:

> ther be two things that do much move me, and, as it were, pull me backe from speaking any thinge in this matter. The first is, that I perceave the quene's highness . . . a partie therin . . . The second is, the reverence I have to those noble men, unto whom this bill was comyttide to be weyed and considerid, whose doings, I assure your good lordshippes, is a great comfort, not onely unto me, but also, as I do thinke, unto all that be of the profession that I am of, with manye other besides. First, for that their devocions towards Allmyghtie God, dothe appeare, seinge, they will not suffer the service of the churche, and the dew admynistraction of the holie sacraments thereof, to be disanulled or all reddye altered, but to be contened [retained] as they have ben heretofore. And secondlye, for that their charitie and pittie towards the poor clargie of this realme dothe appeare in

[62] CSP Ven., VII, 52.

[63] ASV, arm. LXIV, 28, fol. 258v-259.

[64] Nicholas Sanders, *The Rise and Growth of the Anglican Schism. . . with a Continuation of the History by the Rev. Edward Rishton*, D. Lewis, trans. and ed. (London: 1877), 255.

mytygatinge the extreme penalites mentioned in this bill for the gayne-sayers of the same.[65]

Il Schifanoya confirmed Scot's statement. He told his friend Ottaviano Vivaldino that the good Catholics had forced the modification of the book passed by the Commons which would have required the mass to be said in the manner of Edward VI's day. 'By a majority of votes,' he wrote, 'they have decided that the aforesaid things shall be expunged from the book, and that the masses, sacraments and the rest of the Divine offices shall be performed as hitherto'.[66] Feria described what was left of the bill after it came out of the committee:

By way of compromise . . . they brought forward the same as they had proposed at the beginning of Parliament, only more moderate. This was that she could take the title of supremacy if she chose, the Pope's authority being abolished in any case. This was to be sworn to by all who hold office or benefice from the Queen, and in case of refusal they were to be deprived. In the same manner all ecclesiastics, the graduates of the universities and the scholars would lose all the rights, places and profits they held.[67]

The committee members had refused to grant Elizabeth clear recognition of her claim to be supreme head of the Church of England. Rather than take the responsibility for giving a woman primacy they shifted it to her, declaring, in effect, that they would abide by her decision but would not sanction it. Their unwillingness to decide this issue, combined with qualms shared by Catholics and Protestants alike about the propriety of a female head of the Church, generated the rumours that said that Elizabeth would not accept the title.[68]

A proclamation printed on 22 March tells us about the religious changes permitted by the transformed bill. Although it was never issued, the proclamation reviving the statute for receiving communion in both kinds records the fact that the second bill for supremacy, as altered by the Lords, allowed communion in both kinds, but that was all. The proclamation admitted as much when it announced that it was legal to communicate *sub utraque specie,* but stated that no other 'manner of divine service for the communion of the said holy sacrament (than that which is now used in the Church) can presently be

[65] Strype, *Annals,* I, ii, 408.
[66] *CSP Ven.,* VII, 52.
[67] *CSP Span., Eliz.,* I, 38.
[68] *CSP Ven.,* VII, 58.

established by any law, until further time therefore may be had'.[69] The government's drive for a uniform Protestant order of worship had failed.

When the mutilated supremacy bill came to its third reading on 18 March there was more debate. The Protestants used history, law and English tradition to assert that England's independence and well-being required them to reject the Pope. English kings and Parliaments had always resisted the encroachment of papal power, they claimed, and by ancient right the kings of England were the rulers of the English Church. Moreover, Elizabeth, by the common law of the realm, had as much authority as any of her predecessors, and the primacy was rightfully hers. Failure to recognize this fact would leave her subjects in servitude, endangering the whole realm.[70]

In reply the Catholics argued that there could be only one true Church, and that Church was the one headed by the Pope, the steady rock of faith that had stood unchanging against the rip tides generated by squabbling Protestants. Fifteen hundred years of Church history were used as shot to demolish a mere forty years of Protestantism, and salvoes of scripture were fired against the idea that a prince could possess both the sword of justice and the keys to God's kingdom. The apostolic succession was launched against the inventions of the heretics: 'Whom can Cranmer name before hym in the sea of Canterbury? Whereupon it followithe that they are bastards, as men that cannot shew their fathers.'[71] The pivot for these arguments was the Nicene Creed, accepted by all Christians, through which the believer declared his faith in one holy catholic Church. The bishops in the Lords insisted that this meant the Roman Catholic Church and none other: if England was to be a part of the one true Church she would have to accept the Pope.[72]

When at last the vote was taken the Catholics failed to defeat the bill because most of the lords temporal would not vote against it. The bill 'for restoring of the supremacy of the Imperyall Crowne of this realme and avoyding divers Actes of Parliament made to the contrarie, with certain provisos added thereunto by

[69]Hughes and Larkin, *Proclamations,* II, 110.

[70]Strype, *Annals,* I, ii, 423-431.

[71]*Ibid.,* I, ii, 455.

[72]Two speeches made by Catholics in this debate over the supremacy exist. One was given by Bishop Scot and is printed in Strype, *Annals,* I, ii, 408-23. The other, anonymous, one is printed in the *Annals* at I, ii, 451-6.

the Lords and sondrie other amendments' passed in spite of the dissent registered by all of the spiritualty, Viscount Montague and the Earl of Shrewsbury.[73]

The approved bill was entrusted to the Queen's attorney and her solicitor for delivery to the Commons where news of the Lords' modifications had caused an uproar. With the reforms removed and the terms of the supremacy modified, the Lower House was in a quandary. Either they could reject the provisos and amendments and keep the Pope and his mass, or they could pass the bill and settle for the Roman service without the Roman pontiff.[74] The choice, if not good, was easy: they would approve the amendments. In the meantime someone tried a new tactic. If the Edwardian service could not displace the mass as the only national rite, toleration of both Catholicism and Edwardian Protestantism would be the next best thing. Thus it was moved that 'no persones shalbe punyshed for using the Religion used in kyng E[dward's] last year'.[75] This bill, which would have abolished the Marian heresy laws (something the Lords must have refused to leave in the supremacy bill), was rammed through the Commons. Read twice in one day, it was passed the day after, 18 March. This great haste was needed because it was expected that Parliament would be prorogued before the end of the month, ruining any further hopes of rapid reform.

The Protestant party was in agony. Scarcely two months before. Parliament had begun with the expectation that pure religion would be restored to England. They had been marching arm-in-arm with their godly Queen towards the new Jerusalem, when suddenly the holy gates were slammed shut. Now only Elizabeth could save the day for the reformed religion – but the omens were not auspicious.

II

As the drama surrounding the supremacy unfolded in the House of Lords, the Commons were busy with another facet of the Reformation. Taking advantage of the new religious climate,

---

[73] H.L.R.O., Lords MS. Journals, IV, 38.

[74] *CSP Ven.,* VII, 52. 'The members of the Lower House, seeing that the Lords passed this article of the Queen's supremacy of the church, but not as the Commons drew it up, — the Lords cancelling the aforesaid clauses and modifying some others — grew angry, and would consent to nothing but are in very great controversy, as they must of necessity ratify what the Lords have done in the Upper House.'

[75] H.L.R.O., Commons MS. Journals, I, fol. 202v.

private members clogged the agenda with bills designed to regain the lands they had lost when Mary restored the Catholic bishops to the sees from which they had been deprived by Edward. Some of these proposals were specific, dealing with certain estates, and others were general, attempting to solve the problem in one fell swoop. The debates and legal presentations they engendered monopolized the Commons' time for nearly three weeks in March, stalling the progress of other legislation and ruining any timetable the government might have had.

The appearance of this private legislation comes as no surprise, considering the mood of Parliament. The question of secularized Church lands had been bothering the nation throughout Mary's reign and had been a major obstacle to the reintroduction of Catholicism. In the present Parliament the path to royal supremacy over the Church was smoothed by ecclesiastical land, for men knew that the supremacy would assure their continued possession of the alienated Church property.

Most of the private bills dealing with episcopal lands had their roots in the deprivations of Edmund Bonner, Bishop of London; Nicholas Heath, Bishop of Worcester; and Stephen Gardiner, Bishop of Winchester. In 1551 Edward's Council, using the supremacy power, had removed these men and replaced them with Protestants, giving London to Nicholas Ridely, Worcester to John Hooper, and Winchester to John Ponet. Being, as they supposed, the legal possessors of their sees, these bishops gave the King various manors which the King granted, in turn, to others. In 1553 Queen Mary, who regarded Edward's use of the supremacy to deprive bishops as illegal, created commissions to investigate the deprivations. Not suprisingly, the commissioners reinstated the Catholics. All would have been well, but the commissioners complicated matters by decreeing that each Catholic 'should be restored to the bishopric . . . and to the estate in which he was when summoned' for his Edwardian trial.[76] The order to restore the bishops to their estates as they had been in 1550 or 1551 meant that the grants, leases, and other instruments executed by the Protestant bishops were invalid. As a consequence, those persons who held lands once granted to Edward VI by the bishops lost them when the properties were restored to the sees. Understandably, those who had lost that property sought its return in 1559.

In terms of time and numbers of people involved, the struggle for the lands of Winchester was the most important. After the bill for

[76] *Cal. Pat. Rolls, Phil. & Mary,* I, 121.

supremacy was committed on 15 February, the Commons heard the first reading of the bill to restore the patents of the Earl of Pembroke, Sir John Mason, Sir Henry Neville, Sir William Fitzwilliam, Sir Philip Hoby, Sir Henry Seymour, and Sir Richard Sackville to the late Bishop of Winchester's lands.[77] Heard a second time on 18 February, it was committed, with the result that a new bill was drafted and introduced ten days later. This new proposal was immediately given to Richard Kingsmill, either for articling or as a committal.[78] The next day Bishop John White, who possessed Winchester at the time, came in his own person to the House of Commons to ask for a copy of the bill concerning his lands. The House granted his request and gave him permission to return the next Saturday with his counsel to make his defence.[79] The patentees reacted to this by requesting that their lawyers be allowed to attend and hear White's arguments. The house gave them its permission.[80] When White appeared that Saturday he 'opened his title to the manors, saying they had been parcell of the bisshoprycke by xiii hundred years and required this house of Justice'. The Queen's attorney, after listening to the Bishop's arguments, requested that he be allowed to speak about the case on behalf of Her Majesty. The House was agreeable, and he and the Bishop were told to present themselves at 8:30 a.m. on the following Monday.[81]

That Monday morning, however, the members started a legal hare which had to be chased before the attorney could present his case. The trouble was caused by a debate 'touching cancellation of the records in the chauncery for the late bishop of Wynchesters lands'.[82] As rehearsed in the Act, this debate turned around the legality of the warrant, obtained by Bishop White from Queen Mary, which ordered the cancellation of all enrolments and deeds made by Bishop Ponet in favour of King Edward. Not only were these to be nullified, they were to be handed over to White, to be disposed of as he wished. This warrant established a precedent that disturbed the Commons deeply. Most of the possessions of the Crown and private subjects were assured to their owners by means of similar conveyances enrolled in the Chancery. If the

[77]H.L.R.O., Commons Ms. Journals, I, fol. 189v.

[78]*Ibid.*, fol. 194v.

[79]*Ibid.*, fol. 195v.

[80]*Ibid.,* fol. 196v.

[81]*Ibid.*, fol. 197v.

[82]*Ibid.*, fol. 198.

Queen could, by simply issuing a warrant, cancel an enrolment 'the possessions and inherytaunce of all men . . . may come in suche dowte and question in tyme to come that it should not be certenly knowen who should be the lawful possessor and owners thereof'.[83] Frightened by the implications of the charges made against White, the Commons asigned Sir Thomas Perry to investigate this matter. His report on 14 March moved the members to order that a bill be drafted for the punishment of the Bishop of Winchester and others for cancelling records.[84]

After the debate over the cancelled deeds the Queen's attorney was finally allowed to speak. He insisted that 'the appeale made by Gardyner was not of effect, for that in the commission at his deprivacion was conteyned omni appellacione remota, and so that grante made to kyng Edward the VIth by the bishop Poynet [is] in effect'. Later Mr. Nowell and Mr. Bell, counsel for the patentees, argued for their clients 'as Mr Attorney had shewed for the Queene'.[85] Although the commission depriving Gardiner was proof against all future appeals the preamble of the patentees' bill did not mention this as a reason for overturning Ponet's deprivation. Instead, it insisted that Gardiner had reinstated himself as Bishop of Winchester by chicanery, usurping the see and unlawfully taking the manors and other property.[86] When Gardiner died his successor continued to exclude the 'rightful' owners from possession of their lands. Sensing the insecurity of his hold over these manors (his 'fainte title', as the Act calls it) Bishop White had attempted, in conjunction with the Bishop of Worcester, to get parliamentary recognition of his possession of the bishopric.[87] When this ploy failed he gave Mary 'sinister informacions' and persuaded her to issue the warrant cancelling the deeds.

Elizabeth became involved with the bill, as written the second time, because it returned lost revenue to the Crown. Edward VI had reserved to himself certain services and rents to be paid upon the disputed manors, and under the terms of the bill these would be returned to the Queen. For her part, Elizabeth promised to renew the letters patent on the same terms as they had been granted by Edward.[88]

[83] H.L.R.O., Original Acts, 1 Eliz. I, no. 34.
[84] H.L.R.O., Commons MS. Journals, I, fol. 201.
[85] *Ibid.,* fol. 198.
[86] H.L.R.O., Original Acts, 1 Eliz. I, no. 34.
[87] *Journal of the House of Lords,* I, 530.
[88] H.L.R.O., Original Acts, 1 Eliz. I, no. 34.

Even after the bill passed the Commons on 18 March its repercussions continued to echo through the House. Dr. John Story, a noted lawyer and a member of Parliament, as well as a leading Catholic, had acted as Bishop White's counsel before the Lords. The Commons spent an entire sitting trying to decide how to punish him for this breach of parliamentary etiquette. In the end he apologized and was forgiven.[89]

In spite of the time spent on it, there was little resistance to this bill in the Commons. The Upper House, with its bishops in attendance, put up more of a fight. There is no record of the debate in the Lords, but the Journal shows that it passed by a slim margin. Archbishop Heath, all the bishops, the Abbot of Westminster, the Marquis of Winchester, and Lords Stafford, Dudley and North voted against it.[90]

Less than two weeks before the bill against Winchester finished its passage the Lords approved a Commons bill which assured 'lands late parcell of the bishoprycke of London' to Lords Darcy, Riche and Wentworth.[91] By having this legislation introduced the three peers sought to end a legal dispute arising from grants of land made to them by Edward and Ridley. Manors valued at several hundred pounds had been presented to them out of the Bishopric of London, and when Mary's commissioners restored Bonner to the see they ordered them to be returned to the Bishop.[92] Although the commissioners had decreed that Bonner should be given all his estates, the matter did not end there. The three peers refused to give them up without a struggle, and as late as July 1558 Bonner was still trying to get them. Seeking Mary's help he begged Cardinal Pole that, because 'the Lorde Darcye and other by unlawful accones did usurp with . . . Great Darcie Sudmynster and other thinges belonging to my church, I may, with her Graces favor, entre upon them lawfully again, saying I never did any acte whereby in lawe I have forgoune theym'.[93] The bill was meant to end this struggle by giving them a clear title to the land and forbidding Bonner, his grantees or the cathedral chapter to make any further claims to it.

[89]H.L.R.O., Commons MS. Journals, I, fol. 205.

[90]H.L.R.O., Lords MS. Journals, IV, 42.

[91]*Ibid.*, 31.

[92]*Cal. Pat. Rolls, Phil. & Mary,* I, 121.

[93]George C. Gorham, ed., *Gleanings of a Few Scattered Ears, During the Reformation in England. . . .1533 to A.D. 1588* (London: 1857), 375. Quoting Inner Temple, Petyt MS. 838, 47, no. 2, fol. 3.

This bill helps explain why some peers, like Riche, could support the supremacy while voting against the imposition of Protestant uniformity. Revival of the royal supremacy over the Church made it possible for Riche to get his land back on the grounds that Ridley had been a legal bishop — a claim which required the supremacy for support. As a consequence, Riche could vote in favour of Elizabeth's authority over the Church because it affected his material well-being; he could vote against the uniformity because he believed that the mass was important for the well-being of his soul.

Bonner did not make much of a defence against the claims of the three peers, but someone, perhaps one of his lessees, tried to protect him by introducing a bill which confirmed his right to hold the bishopric.[94] It died after its first reading.

Another motion, however, confirming all the grants and leases made by Bishop Ridley, stung Bonner into putting up a vigorous defence. He was angry when he came into the Commons, calling Ridley the usurper of his bishopric ('as he sayeth', commented the clerk with careful impartiality), and demanding a copy of the bill. The House granted him one and gave him permission to make a verbal reply to it the next Wednesday.[95] Bonner was angry because the bill specifically declared that his deprivation had been just, and that Ridley had been the legal Bishop of London. Strype, summarized it as follows:

> This bill set forth, 'How the said Edmond Boner, bishop of London, was upon good and just causes and considerations, by just sentences, and under the law of the realm, deprived, deposed, and put forth from his bishopric, and all other his spiritual promotions, for his contumacy; and that afterwards the said bishopric was justly collated and given to Nicholas Ridley, D.D. by letters patents by King Edward Vi. with all the lands and tenements thereunto belonging.'[96]

Of course, if Ridley had been the legal possessor of the bishopric's property his leases and grants were legitimate and Bonner's were not. Therefore, all leases, demises, grants, offices, bailiwicks and stewardships given by Ridley were effectual in law, 'as the same should have been, if the said Edmond Boner had been dead at the time of his deprivation'.[97]

[94]H.L.R.O., Commons MS. Journals, I, fol. 196.

[95]Ibid., fol. 200v.

[96]Strype, Annals, I, i, 94. A draft of this bill or a close relative can be found at B.L., Lansd. 97, fols. 185-89.

[97]Ibid.

Bonner made his defence, but the assembly was not convinced by his appeal to Mary and the letters patent she had issued on his behalf.[98] A month later the bill received its final reading and was passed.[99] The persons who would have benefited from this bill cannot be identified without further research; nor do we know who would have been injured by a wholesale nullification of Bonner's grants. Perhaps some of the laity in the Upper House stood to lose by it, for the Bishop had enough supporters in the Lords to defeat the bill there on 1 May.[100]

Like Bonner and White, Richard Pates, Bishop of Worcester found himself forced to defend his title to some of his lands because his predecessor in the see, Nicholas Heath, had been deprived by Edward and restored by Mary. After Heath's deprivation John Hooper had become bishop, presenting Edward with lands which he later passed along to the Duke of Northumberland, who in turn gave some of the manors to Sir Francis Jobson, Walter Blount, and John Throckmorton. Throckmorton complained to his brother, Sir Nicholas, about the unlucky results of these transactions:

> . . . not long before King Edward's death, my Lord of Northumberland, in an exchange with the king, took divers manors of that bishopric, assured to the King by Bishop Hooper, and sold and assured them to divers of his friends and followers, as the lordship of Hartlebury to Jobson, divers other manors to Mr. Walter Blunt, and the manor of Wellond to me for 40 years' purchase, which came to above 200 marks; this I paid, and had my assurance accordingly. Shortly after, upon the restitution of Dr. Heath to that bishopric, he entered without law or order into all again, so I lost my land and money also, and had no recompence . . .[101]

Sitting in Parliament in 1559, Jobson and Blount attempted to recover the lands, jointly introducing a bill which guaranteed their titles to the manors.[102] Bishop Pates defended himself with a plea

[98]H.L.R.O., Commons MS. Journals, I, fol. 201v. 'The bishop of London in his proper persone shewing the untrouthe of the bill as he takes yt dyd conclude that the comyssioners for his deprivacion dyd not according to ther commyssion and yet by his appeale as also by his lettres patents from Quene marye he standeth still bisshop and the graunts made by dr rydley voyde.'

[99]H.L.R.O., Commons MS. Journals, I, fol. 209.

[100]Davis, 'Unpublished MS.', 540.

[101]Sir John Throckmorton to Sir Nicholas Throckmorton, Dec. 29, 1565. *CSP Dom., Eliz., Addenda,* 575. For the details of the transaction concerning Hartlebury see *VCH Worcester,* III, 383; *Cal. Pat. Rolls Edw. VI,* V, 117. Blount had received Wychinford manor. See *Cal. Pat. Rolls, Edw. VI,* V, 273.

[102]H.L.R.O., Commons MS. Journals, I, fol. 197.

similar to Bonner's: 'Hooper was no lawful byshop by reason of thappeale of bisshop Heathe, and so the graunts not good, and [he] prayed the house to consider yt.'[103] His appeal was effective, for, although it was read a third time on 12 March, the bill did not pass the Commons.[104] Undaunted, Jobson and Blount introduced a new bill to the same effect on 15 April, but it disappeared after one reading.[105]

Acting alone, Sir Francis Jobson tried to get an act of Parliament returning to him two manors held by Cuthbert Tunstal, Bishop of Durham. When he was master of the jewels under Edward, Jobson was given the lordship and manors of Heveden and Hovedenshire in Yorkshire. Both of them had belonged to the bishops of Durham until Tunstal had been deprived and his bishopric abolished.[106] Worth more than £284 a year, the manors were valuable, and Jobson no doubt resented it intensely when Mary revived the bishopric and returned them to Tunstal.[107] Seeking to recover the revenue, Jobson on 24 February introduced a bill which would transfer the title back to him. For some reason it died after only one reading.[108]

Another member of Parliament, Thomas Fisher, saw the Protestant dawn as an excellent time to escape an increase in his rent. Pure opportunism seems to have guided him when, on 4 March, he introduced a 'bill to discharge a Fyne levyed by T. Fyssher to the Bishop of Conventry and Lychfeld for a rent'.[109] Twelve years before Bishop Sampson had alienated to Fisher the manor of Chadshunt, Warwickshire, for an annual rent of £50. Then, in 1548, Sampson sold him the estate outright, releasing him from the rent. This transaction was challenged by Bishop Bayne in 1558, with the result that Fisher agreed to pay the bishops of Coventry and Lichfield a yearly rent of £82.10s., chargeable on Chadshunt and three other manors.[110] Apparently Fisher hoped to avoid the expense by

[103] Ibid., fol. 200.

[104] Ibid., fol. 204.

[105] Ibid., fol. 208v. The VCH Worcester, III, 383 claims that Jobson, through the influence of the 'Earl of Leicester', obtained an Act confirming his title to Hartlebury in March, 1558, despite the protest of the Bishop. This is incorrect, for the bill did not pass. The county history seems to have been led astray by Throckmorton's statement that 'Sir Fras. Jobson, in the same case, obtained by my Lord of Leicester's help, and enjoys at this day £40 yearly at Hartlebury'. CSP Dom., Eliz., Addenda, 575.

[106] Cal. Pat. Rolls, Edw. VI, V, 133-4.

[107] Cal. Pat. Rolls, Mary, I, 377-8.

[108] H.L.R.O., Commons MS. Journals, I, fol. 192v.

[109] Ibid., fol. 197; 203v.

[110] VCH Warwickshire, VI, 31.

claiming that Bayne had used compulsion to levy the fine.[111] The ensuing debate brought Bayne into the Lower House on at least two occasions; once to request a copy of the bill, and once to explain why Fisher ought to continue his payments. After the Commons heard the Bishop's explanation they permitted the bill to die.[112]

In addition to the bills brought against individual bishops by specific people, the Commons saw several attempts to annul the Marian deprivations *in toto*. The first try was embodied in a bill confirming the grants and leases made by deprived bishops.[113] This motion died in committee. Thwarted, its supporters tried again, introducing two more bills. The first, 'to restore depryved bisshops', died after its first reading.[114] The other, a redraft of the original bill,[115] was described as 'The bill to make lawfull the deprivacion of the bisshops of London, Wynchester, Wigorn [Worcester], and Chichester in the time of k[ing] E[dward] the VIth'.[116] After its second reading the Commons heard no more of this bill to invalidate the work of Mary's commissions. However, two further attempts were made to get the deprived Edwardians recognized as legitimate incumbents. Having failed to restore the bishops by a single act of Parliament, men who wanted the bishop's grants reinstated introduced 'The bill that the Quene by commyssion may restore spirituall persons deprived'.[117] An attempt to get Elizabeth to do exactly as Mary had done when she restored the Catholic bishops, the bill was approved by the Commons and made it as far as a third reading in the Lords before the clerk there marked it 'rejecta'.[118] Two days before the Lords defeated this bill permitting restoration by commission, a bill 'to make deprivacions of Bisshops and spirituall persones in the tyme of K[ing] E[dward] the VIth pleadable' was read to the knights and burgesses.[119] After this single reading it disappeared.

Pollard called the Parliament's behaviour toward the attempts to restore the Edwardians 'conservative', but legalistic is a better description. The passage or defeat of these bills seems to have hinged

[111]H.L.R.O., Commons MS. Journals, I, fol. 200v. 'Mr Fysshers counsell alleged that the fyne was made by compulsion.'

[112]*Ibid.*, fol. 199; 200v; 203v.

[113]*Ibid.*, fol. 189.

[114]*Ibid.*, fol. 201.

[115]*Ibid.*, fol. 201v.

[116]*Ibid.*, fol. 204.

[117]*Ibid.*, fol. 212v.

[118]*Ibid.*, fol. 213; 213v. Davis, 'Unpublished MS.', 541.

[119]H.L.R.O., Commons MS. Journals, I, fol. 214.

on the legal strength of the claimant's arguments. Where the claim included the fact that the Marian bishop had obtained his rights by confiscation from a deprived predecessor, the claimant won. When the Marian bishop dealt in property that had come to him without such prehistory, the claimant lost. This is illustrated by the winning cases, all of which involved the actions of Mary's commissions. This principle probably saved Bishop Bayne from Fisher's attempt to escape his rent, and prevented Jobson from regaining the manors he had obtained in Durham diocese after its dissolution, which was not maintained in 1559. In Bishop Pate's case, arguments involving a forfeiture after Northumberland's treason may have protected him.

Moreover, most of the members of the Lower House were neither stupid nor fanatical. They must have recognized the complications that would arise if Parliament simply reinstated the Edwardians. In the first place, up to five years of Catholic episcopal rule would be overturned, causing endless disputes, making a travesty of the law, and establishing a dreadful precedent. If, at the beginning of each new reign, Parliament could invalidate grants made in the previous reign, there could be no security of tenure. In the second place, it would cost many of them money, just as Mary's action had cost the plaintiffs money. They were not opposed to allowing a royal commission to resolve individual cases, but wholesale deprivation, restoration and reinstatement threatened their interests. In short, they may have been Protestants, but they were not blindly zealous.

Whether crass attempts to exploit the change in religion for personal gain or pious motions, these bills and a few other similar ones had a profound impact on the Parliament of 1559. They made it impossible for the government to complete its legislative programme before Easter.

The impact of the land bills in the Commons before Easter is easily demonstrated. Between the day the first bill of the session was heard (January 25) and the day the last bill was read before the Easter recess there were forty-four meetings of the House. During the same period eighteen private bills dealing with land problems created by the Marian restoration were introduced, all of them after 10 February. Thus eighteen bills were introduced in thirty-five sittings, slightly more than one every other day. The eighteen received a total of twenty-seven readings before Easter, and nine days were spent hearing the requests and arguments of the bishops and their opponents. In all, the bills received thirty-six separate instances of consideration in thirty-five days. Of course some instances occurred on the same day, but the debates on these land bills dominated the period between 21 February and 15 March, creating a bottleneck. When Parliament recessed for Easter on 24 March, forty-eight bills were still pending in the Commons.

The surgery performed on the bill for supremacy in the Lords and the crush of unexpected legislation in the Commons put Elizabeth in a difficult position. She had intended to dissolve Parliament before Easter, but she had obtained few of the things she had sought from the session. Far from establishing a uniform order for religion, the Houses had passed a bill which tolerated Catholicism, did not provide for or protect Protestant worship, and did not clearly define the supremacy. Further, though she had obtained a subsidy, and the first fruits and tenths had been returned to the Crown, there had been no opportunity to introduce legislation dissolving the monasteries. Nor had the important bill for reforming the customs completed its passage. Moreover, her surest supporters, the Protestants, were upset and frightened by what had happened. Whether or not she dismissed the assembly, she had to do something to reassure them.

5

THE NEW STRATEGY FOR REFORM

The end of the third week in March found the young Queen and her principal secretary wrestling with the thorny problem presented to them by Parliament which had denied them a uniform Protestant order of worship and a definitive supremacy. Their first reaction was to accept the *fait accompli* forced upon them by the Lords, dissolve Parliament and use what little they had been granted to prepare for the next round. In keeping with this resolution, plans were made to issue a proclamation implementing the small reform in the service left in the bill for the supremacy. At the same time, preparations were begun for a disputation to discredit the Catholic bishops.

There is strong evidence that Elizabeth intended to follow this plan. The proclamation permitting communion in both kinds, which begins by referring to 'this present last session of parliament',[1] tells us that, as late as 22 March, she was going to send Parliament home before Easter. Since there had been no dissolution before or on the day the proclamation was printed, it can be assumed that this latter was destined to be issued after the dissolution and before Easter, which fell on 26 March. This is supported by Count Feria who reported that Elizabeth had intended, as late as the evening of 23 March, to go to Westminster on the 24th to give her assent to the bills and close the session.[2] It follows that the proclamation, if it had been issued, would have gone out on the 24th or 25th. Up to the night of the 23rd Elizabeth was prepared to accept the supremacy bill as passed by Parliament,[3] abandoning the struggle with the Lords and reverting to a strategy that had been developed since it had become certain that she could not secure Protestant uniformity until the Catholic bishops had been replaced.

John Jewel told Peter Martyr about the most important part of this ploy when he described to him the disputation scheduled to be held at Westminster before the Council, 'that our bishops may have no ground of complaint that they are put down only by power and authority of law'.[4] Evidently Elizabeth and Cecil were, at this point, determined

---

[1] Hughes and Larkin, *Proclamations,* II, 109.

[2] *CSP Span., Eliz.,* I, 44.

[3] The amended version was given the approval of the Commons on 22 March.

[4] *ZL,* I, 10.

to use the powers granted to the Queen by the reduced supremacy bill to remove the Catholic bishops from their sees. First, however, they would demonstrate to the nation the errors in the bishops' faith by exposing them in a debate with Protestant theologians. Once their self-delusion had been made plain, they could be deprived, and no one, theoretically, could say that they had not received a hearing. The disputation, however, was deliberately rigged to ensure a Protestant victory. Once the bishops had been expelled, the Queen would have a better opportunity to obtain a uniform order of religion.

This plan to remove the bishops may have been augmented by a bill introduced and read twice in the Commons on 21 March. The bill 'that the Quenes highnes shall collate or apoynt bysshops in bisshoprycks being vacant' or, alternatively, the bill for 'collating of bisshops by the Quenes highnes and with what rites and ceremonyes', was rushed through a third reading on the next day. That same afternoon it was carried to the Lords, where it was passed on the 23rd, having apparently received only a first and third reading.[5] This hastily passed bill, to which the Queen did not assent, did one of two things. Either it revived the portions concerning collation of bishops in the statutes restraining payment of annates (23 Henry VIII. c. 20 and 25 Henry VIII, c. 20), or it revived the Act for Election of Bishops, 1 Edward VI, c. 2. The need for a move to allow the Queen to appoint bishops tells us more about the amended supremacy bill, if nothing else. Apparently, it did not contain any provision which specified how bishops were to be chosen, not a large defect, but if Elizabeth wished to remove the Catholic bishops and replace them quickly she probably first wanted the replacement procedure ratified by Parliament.

If the March bill for appointing bishops was introduced at the behest of the Queen, as its handling indicates, why was it not approved? The answer is that the Act of Supremacy, as drafted in April, gave the Queen the necessary authority to fill vacant sees, replacing the bill passed before Easter.

The bill taking away pains and penalties made for religion in Queen Mary's time, which was passed by the Commons on 18 March, may also have been a part of the alternative plan for religion developed to solve the crisis created by the Lords. Whether it was is an open question. Undoubtedly, Elizabeth supported the repeal of these heresy laws — Goodrich had recommended this at the very beginning of the reign — but the handling of the bill in the Lords raises a problem in interpretation. Rushed through the Commons, the repeal

[5]H.L.R.O., Commons MS. Journals, I, fol. 204v; Lords MS. Journals, IV, 42. J.C. Sainty, ed., 'Further materials, from an Unpublished Manuscript of the Lords Journals, for Session 1559 and 1597-98', *H.L.R.O., Memorandum 33* (1965), 1.

died after the Lords had heard its contents. Did it disappear because the government did not want it passed, was it dropped because the Catholics in the House did not deign to hear it again, or did it become lost in the mad rush to get bills passed before Parliament dissolved? The Commons sent fourteen bills to the Upper House on the same day, and there were only three working days left before the dissolution was expected to occur. The government is unlikely to have been culpable, since the repeal of the heresy laws was desired by the Queen. Suspicion must rest heavily upon the Catholics, for exactly half the Lords present on the 20th, when the bill was read, are known to have been Catholics; in the remainder of the sittings before Easter the known religious conservatives kept a majority of between two and six members. It is not likely that this bill simply got lost in the shuffle, and so one is inclined to conclude that this attempt to legalize the Edwardian service met defeat at the hands of the same men who had cast the prayer book out of the bill for supremacy. They were willing to allow the Queen her prerogative to run the Church, but they would not license heresy.

In the week before Easter the Houses of Parliament were working with feverish haste to finish as much business as possible before they were sent home. Between 18 and 22 March the Commons heard twenty-nine bills, passing eleven.[6] The peers of the realm dealt with fifty items of legislation, passing seventeen bills between the 18th and 23rd.[7] Even with the help of an afternoon sitting the Lords and Commons could not dig themselves out from beneath the heap of legislation that had piled up as the Commons argued about ecclesiastical lands and the Lords refashioned the supremacy and uniformity bills. When the Easter holiday arrived several important bills, such as one regulating the landing and customing of sweet wines and another continuing the act against unlawful assemblies, were still unpassed. It had been rumoured that the dissolution would come by the 18th,[8] but by then the gossips were not so certain. 'Parliament', wrote Il Schifanoya,

> which ought to have ended last Saturday, was prolonged till next Wednesday in Passion Week, and according to report they will return a week after Easter; which report I believe, because of the three principal articles the first alone passed, viz., to give the supremacy of the Anglican Church to the Queen (nor have they yet spoken of the marriage), notwithstanding the opposition of

[6]H.L.R.O., Commons MS. Journals, I, fol. 203-205.

[7]H.L.R.O., Lords MS. Journals, IV, 38-42. Sainty, 'Further Materials', 1-2.

[8]*CSP Ven.*, VII, 46; 52.

the bishops, and of the chief barons and lords of this kingdom. . . .[9]

Whoever the Italian's informants were, they had guessed the course of events before the Queen had resolved to continue the session and obtain the other two articles.

The Queen decided to continue the Parliament on 24 March, only hours before she had intended to dismiss it. Feria, in a letter to his king, told how his scheduled meeting with Elizabeth at 9 o'clock that morning was cancelled at the last minute because she was very busy, intending to go to Parliament at 1 o'clock to give her assent to the bills. Instead, she postponed going until after Easter, and the members were instructed to reconvene on 3 April.[10] 'For weighty affyres to be doon this parlament according to the example of the upper house', wrote the clerk of the Commons, the Parliament was adjourned over the holiday.[11] Elizabeth had changed her mind.

What persuaded her to scrap her plan? Probably a combination of two factors. One was the knowledge that if she ended Parliament now many private and public bills would be left undecided, to the dissatisfaction of many and the disadvantage of her coffers. The other was the realization that the supremacy bill as passed did not define her position properly, so that religious order would be difficult to maintain with the legal tools Parliament had granted her.

While the backlog of bills waiting to be dealt with would not have prevented Elizabeth from dissolving Parliament, she must have been aware of the discontent she would cause if the members were not offered a chance to see more of the legislation passed. Moreover, matters of importance to the Crown were still pending: notably the badly needed reform of the customs prepared by Winchester's committee. The numerous bills aimed at the bishops' lands had kept the Commons from dealing with this other legislation, perhaps because Cecil had failed properly to manage the session to the Queen's benefit. Nearly all the statutes of 1559 were passed after Easter; if Elizabeth had ended the session in March, as she had intended, the supremacy, a subsidy, and the restoration of first fruits would have been the sole results of the Parliament. It is not surprising that she continued the session. The failure of the religious legislation also called for continuation. About 21 March Elizabeth received a letter from Philip Melanchthon which expressed her dilemma over the missing uniformity. 'Hoc moneo, ut initio de omnibus doctrinae

[9]*Ibid.,* VII, 52.

[10]*CSP Span, Eliz.,* I, 44.

[11]H.L.R.O., Commons MS. Journals, I, fol. 205v.

membris, et de ritibus, re deliberata, proponatur certa forma, ne postea dissensiones oriantur,'[12] he wrote, and Elizabeth must have agreed. By refusing to sanction a firm order for religion the Lords were endangering the peace of the commonwealth.

The lack of a uniformity statute might not have been so dangerous if Elizabeth had been given clear and full supremacy over the Church, but, if we can accept Feria's report, the amended bill did not grant this. The Queen was in an untenable position. Her claim to control the Church rested on the recognition, by Parliament, that the rulers of England were masters of the English Church by virtue of their office, as proven by historical precedent. Now the estates were telling her that they did not know if she had the right to call herself head of the Church, but if she wanted the title she could take it. Such an arrogation of power, unbacked by a clear parliamentary mandate, would leave Elizabeth open to attack from both the religious left and right. Not only was papal supremacy to be abolished without a clear replacement, the reform was to be left to the Queen without the mandate of Parliament. The Lords had told Elizabeth that she could do as she wished about religion, but they would not take the blame. Then too, Elizabeth's staunchest supporters, the Protestants, were angry and frightened at what had happened. If she accepted the supremacy and kept the mass she would alienate them and do violence to her own beliefs, without gaining the trust of the Catholics. Moreover, she could hardly make the supremacy work as long as the episcopal bench was full of Roman Catholics. Quite clearly, there was a danger that she could not remain master of the situation if she accepted a crippled supremacy over a Church that had no distinct legitimate order. After a week of indecision she decided to try again for an acceptable religious settlement, instead of dissolving Parliament and imposing reform as a self-proclaimed caesaro-papistical Queen.

When Neale discovered that Elizabeth had intended to end the session and relenting, had introduced new bills for supremacy and uniformity, he suggested that her change of heart had been caused by the news of the conclusion of a peace with the French at Cateau Cambrésis. Now, he thought, Elizabeth felt that she no longer needed to humour the Spanish into protecting her, and she could permit a full reform of the Church.[13] This theory he rested on two pieces of evidence.

First there is a statement by Feria who, writing about the passage of the second bill for supremacy in the Lords, said that he was sure

[12]P.R.O., SP 70/III/fol. 9.
[13]Neale, 'Supremacy and Uniformity'. 325-326.

'that the news of peace made Parliament come to the decision'. The English, he believed, had been afraid that Philip would make a separate peace and abandon them to the French if they broke with the Roman Church.[14] Feria's analysis is here very dubious, since the bill for supremacy, first introduced in February, had completed its slow passage through Parliament on the day before the first report of the peace settlement reached London on 19 March.[15] It is difficult to see why the bill should have been introduced more than a month earlier if the government was afraid to allow its passage before there was news of a treaty with the French. The alleged effect of the news of peace before Easter is made even more doubtful by the fact that there was no peace until after Easter. The report received in England on the 19th was not news of the signing of a treaty. That despatch from the English commissioners told the Queen that a set of articles had been agreed upon and asked her to look at the enclosed copy of them.[16] The next news from France, received on the 21st or 22nd, was less optimistic. Sir John Mason informed the Queen that there was little likelihood that peace could be concluded before Easter, for the French and Spanish could not agree on the details of the treaty.[17] Not only did the French and Spanish disagree, Elizabeth was not satisfied, either. On 22 March she sent instructions to her commissioners at Cateau Cambrésis telling them that the amount of the indemnity to be paid by the French was insufficient, and that the article concerning 'defensive uppon inovation' ought to be more clearly drawn.[18] As Easter approached the chances of peace seemed to recede, and on the 29th or 30th a report was received that the French and Spanish were on the verge of breaking off the talks.[19] It was not known in London that a peace had been signed on April 2 until near the end of the first week of the month. It is thus quite impossible that Elizabeth could have based her decision to adjourn Parliament and reform religion on the peace of Cateau Cambrésis.

The second bit of evidence for the argument that the peace prompted the decision to proceed with an Act of Uniformity comes from Edmund Grindal, soon to be bishop of London. On 23 May he wrote to Conrad Hubert that the Parliament had delayed the reform and made no change in religion until peace had been concluded

[14]*CSP Span., Eliz.,* I, 43.
[15]*Ibid.,* I, 42. H.L.R.O., Lords MS. Journals, IV, 38.
[16]P.R.O., SP 70/III/fol. 48.
[17]*Ibid.,* fol. 57.
[18]*Ibid.,* fol. 64.
[19]*Ibid.,* fol. 72; 76.

between Philip, the French king and England.[20] When used to prove the Queen's intentions, his comment has a flaw. There is no way of knowing whether he meant that Parliament had purposely delayed the change, or if the events simply had occurred in chronological sequence. Nor did he impute any motive.

The clinching argument against seeing the peace as the stimulant for reform is found in a letter from Henry II of France. Dated 20 January, 1559, long before the prorogation, it assured Elizabeth that Henry and the Scots were ready to make a separate peace with England. In other words, if Elizabeth had so desired she could have abandoned the Spanish to the French while securing a peace for herself.[21]

The news of the peace did not prompt Elizabeth to change her mind. The failure of the religious legislation did. Il Schifanoya explained:

> Parliament was not adjourned on Holy Wednesday as supposed; but has continued to sit, not being able to come to an agreement, for though the Lords have passed the article of the superiortiy (*sic*) of the Church, they have done so under such conditions that the Lower House will by no means concur therein; whereby they are in greater discord than ever. And on Thursday, the celebrations being done, they will set to work again and begin rediscussing the matter.[22]

Having decided to continue the Parliament, Elizabeth had to do something with the activities she had set afoot when she had intended to dissolve the meeting. The bills connected with the plan — if they were connected — were quietly forgotten, and the disputation was incorporated into the new scheme. The proclamation for communion in both kinds was not issued even though it had been printed. J.H. Pollen was the first to suggest that this proclamation, which plays an important role in many histories of the Settlement, was never proclaimed. In a partisan article on the passing of the Elizabethan supremacy, Pollen argued that, bearing the date of 22, March it was to have been used on Good Friday (24 March), after Elizabeth had confirmed the supremacy bill. Because she suddenly decided not to sign the bill it never became law and the proclamation was

---

[20] *ZL*, II, 19.

[21] *CSP For.*, I, 94-5.

[22] *CSP Rome*, 8. This passage is paraphrased in *CSP Ven.*, VII, 57. Because of the difference in the two I checked ASV, Lettere di Principi, XI, fol. 288. The Roman *Calendar's* translation is the best.

suppressed.[23] Pollen, loyal Catholic that he was, credited Feria with stopping its issuance, which is wrong, but it is very likely that the edict was scrapped. No contemporary documents mention that it was publicly announced that people could communicate in both kinds at Easter: a thing so highly significant to Catholics and Protestants alike was not likely to be overlooked by the diplomats and theologians whose letters tell us the story of the Parliament. Nor is there any record of the proclamation in the archives of the English cities. Contrary to custom, it was neither enrolled in the Journal nor mentioned in the Repertories of the Corporation of London. The city government of York did not receive it, and neither did Lincoln, if we can believe the silence of their records. There is no mention of its being issued in the act book of the privy council, either. We know only one thing about the proclamation: it was printed. At least three copies exist, and Il Schifanoya knew that it had been sent to the presses of Jugge and Cawood.

Il Schifanoya's report of this matter also seems to indicate that it was printed but never used. His language is, however, ambiguous and the translations of his report in the Venetian and Roman State Papers do little to help the mystery, so it is safest to quote the original and let the reader compare it with the translations, which are appended. On 28 March, Il Schifanoya told Vivaldino:

> Fra questo mello havevano, et stampato una proclamatione, che ciascuno si dovesse communicare sub utraque specie, con alcune altre sue reformni: et ordinato anche che se publicare ma poi non si fatto altro, che Sua Maesta asci il giorno di pasqua in capella, dove fa cantato la messa in Inglese secondo il modo del re Eduardo sua fiello, et si communicare in ginochioni sub-utraque specie. . . .[24]

The Italian seems to be saying that the proclamation was printed and was ordered to be proclaimed, but then was withdrawn, the only sign

[23] Pollen, 'Passing of Elizabeth's Supremacy', 57-8.

[24] ASV, Lettere di Principi, XI, fol. 288. *CSP Rome*, 8, has a rather good translation: 'In the meantime they have ordered and printed a proclamation to the effect that everyone is to communicate *sub utraque specie* with certain other reforms. They have also ordered that it be published, but nothing more is done save that her Majesty came on Easter day into the chapel where Mass was sung in English according to the mode of her brother King Edward, and communicated on her knees *sub utraque specie*.' Compare this with *CSP Ven.*, VII, 57: 'During this interval they had ordered and printed a proclamation for everyone to take the Communion in both kinds. Some other reforms of theirs had also been ordered for publication, but subsequently nothing else was done, except that on Easter day her Majesty appeared in Chapel, where mass was sung in English, according to the use of her brother, King Edward, and the Communion was received in both kinds, kneeling'. It is possible that some of the variations between these two are caused by differences between the letters in the Venetian archives and the *avissi* in the Vatican archives.

of it being the Queen's reception of both the body and the blood at Easter. If this interpretation of his words is correct, he has explained why there is no other contemporary mention of the proclamation. It was not issued, and the Protestants of London were not free to communicate in both kinds at Easter. The last line of Il Schifanoya's letter confirms this: 'Mass and other Divine offices are performed in the Churches.'[25]

Things had changed in the royal chapel, however, and the divine offices of the Roman Catholic Church were no longer performed there. As shown above, the Easter celebration was conducted in English in the form of Edward's service, and the kneeling communicants received in both kinds. Il Schifanoya went on to say that the priest made Elizabeth avow her faith in the body and blood before she received, and that the priest wore vestments while he sang the mass, but that he served the communicants clad in 'the mere surplice (*la semplice cotta*)'.[26] All of these changes are reminiscent of the prayer book of 1552, and prefigure the visitation injunctions of 1559.

Another description of Elizabeth's Easter worship was missed by the editor of the Roman *Calendar of State Papers* when he searched the Vatican archives. The letter, from Canobio to Paul IV, is dated 28 May, 1559 and has some obvious errors, but it may contain one very important fact. Reported to Canobio by Philip's confessor, Father Reggio, the information was sent from Brussels to Rome. Canobio wrote:

> mi ha detto ancora che la regina Inglese il giorno di pasqua prossima si communico alla mensa coperta d'un panno negro, et dov'era un calice con vino, consecrando ella medesima l'hostia, et che in gli giorno fecero il medesimo molt'altri sclerati.[27]

If we can trust Reggio not to have invented the table used in Elizabeth's eucharist, this passage is important. The visitation injunctions proclaimed by the Queen in June 1559 specified that a holy table 'covered as thereto belongeth' was to be used for the communion, in the place of an altar.[28] The use of the table was a remarkable feature of the injunctions, for, to quote Dixon, it 'traversed the rubrics of the established Book of Common Prayer'.[29] If Elizabeth had introduced a table into her chapel by Easter it proves that, conservative as she was reputed to have been, she preferred the reformers' table to the sacrificial altar.

[25] *CSP Rome*, 9.

[26] Hughes and Larkin, *Proclamations*, II, 128; 126.

[27] ASV, Lettere di Principi, XI, fol. 316v.

[28] Hughes and Larkin, *Proclamations*, II, 131.

[29] Dixon, *History*, V, 137.

By Easter Elizabeth's chapel was as reformed as it ever would be, and she was ready to make another attempt at extending her chapel service to the rest of the English church. Her immediate problem was how to weaken her Catholic opponents in the Lords while preparing new, more palatable bills for supremacy and uniformity.

The already scheduled disputation became Elizabeth's weapon against the opposition. On Good Friday she ordered eight Catholics and eight Protestants to meet on March 31 to debate three propositions:

> (1) It is against the worde of God, and the custome of the auncient churche, to use a tongue unknown to the people, in common prayer, and the administration of Sacraments.
>
> (2) Everie Church hath authoritie to appoynt, take awaye, and chaunge ceremonies and Ecclesiastical rytes, so the same bee to edification.
>
> (3) It cannot bee proved by the worde of God, that ther is in the Masse offred up a sacrifice propitiatorie for the quicke and the dead.[30]

Carefully chosen by the Protestants, these three propositions were a trap for the Catholics. By appealing to the word of God and the custom of the ancient Church for their proofs, they robbed the Catholics of their best arguments — the customs developed by Christians during the previous centuries. The propositions were designed to answer the doubts that some of the lords felt about their right to meddle with religion, and to refute the arguments the bishops were using to bolster their defences. The Protestant party in the Upper House lacked debating power, as Jewel testified, and the disputation gave their theologians a chance to supply this lack. When Jewel and his brethren had proved the bishops wrong, the Queen could introduce a new bill for reformation of the Church.[31] After Archbishop Heath had selected the men who would uphold the Catholic cause they took steps to defend themselves and their faith. At the prompting of Feria[32] the eight delivered a protest to Her Majesty. Affirming that they were sons of the true Church and mystical members of Christ's body, they declared that they would do nothing contrary to the decretals and

---

[30] Raphael Holinshed reprinted the original government report of the disputation in his *Laste Volume of the Chronicles of England, Scotlande, and Irelande* (London: 1577). The quotation is from page 1801 of that work. The original report is in the P.R.O., SP 12/III/fol. 163 ff.

[31] Pollen, 'Passing of Elizabeth's Supremacy', 59-60. It was here first noted that the disputation had great importance for Elizabeth's parliamentary programme.

[32] *CSP Span., Eliz.*, I, 45.

traditions of the Church. This declaration was followed by a set of demands. As the representatives of the true faith, the Catholic disputants required that the arguments and counter arguments of both parties be submitted in writing so that misrepresentation and falsification could be avoided. They also asked that the writings be in Latin and that no oral arguments be permitted because speeches were useless, except for subversion. Finally, they tried to counter the Protestant bias in the formulation of the propositions by asking that the interpretations of the Church and the Fathers be recognized as correct.[33] The Queen at first agreed that the arguments should be in writing and in Latin, but she soon changed her mind.[34] According to the official report, she ordered that it be verbal and in English because the nobility and Commons had requested her to make the change, 'for the better satisfaction and inhabling of theyr owne judgements, to treate and conclude of such lawes as myght depende hereupon'.[35] Feria protested, but the Queen was unmoved.[36]

Out of this change in the rules grew confusion. The partisan accounts do not always agree on what happened when the disputants met, but the Catholics seem to have believed that oral arguments would follow formal opening speeches made by representatives of each side. The judges and the Protestants, however, followed the rule that only formal arguments, read *de scripto* and subscribed by the disputants, would be permissible. These written presentations would then be submitted to the Council, which would judge their merit. When the representatives of the two sides met in Westminster Abbey it quickly became apparent that either the Catholics had misunderstood the rules, or they were being deliberately obstructive.

There is evidence which hints that the Catholics knew the rules before the meeting, although they claimed otherwise. The report published by the privy council says that both sides had agreed to put their arguments in writing and deliver them to their opponents for their consideration. Evidently the Protestants did hand their arguments to the Catholics ahead of time, because the oration of Dr Cole, who opened for the Catholics, shows an intimate knowledge of the arguments the Protestants would advance after he had finished.[37] Also, Cole had prepared a long speech in writing, even though the

---

[33] P.R.O., SP 12/III/fol. 161.

[34] *CSP Span., Eliz.,* I, 45.

[35] Holinshed, *Chronicles,* 1779.

[36] *CSP Span., Eliz.,* I, 45.

[37] What appears to be the original of Cole's speech is in C.C.C.C., 121, 183-191. The Protestant reply to his speech begins at 179 in the same volume.

Catholics claimed they could not present a written statement because they had lacked time to prepare. The published report indicates that the Catholics knew that they should have a 'book' but, they said, it was not ready.[38] William Dey lent credence to the Privy Council's version of the story, when he wrote to someone, possibly Matthew Parker, that the Catholics 'provided not as their adversaries had don and as their promise was'.[39] John Jewel, whose testimony is heavily biased, insisted that the Catholics had had ten days in which to prepare, and time to assemble their 'auxiliary troops' from Oxford and Cambridge.[40] All this evidence suggests that the Catholics were obstructing the proceedings. Il Schifanoya, however, explained the trouble on the first day of the disputation as stemming from a deliberate trick played on the Catholics.[41]

Whoever was at fault in the beginning — and neither side can be suspected of innocence — the Catholics were soon obliged to take a stubborn defensive position. An audience of peers and commoners heard Dr Cole open the disputation on 31 March. Under the watchful eyes of the moderator, Lord Keeper Bacon, Cole attacked the proposition that a foreign language should not be used in worship. He began by asserting, correctly, that the Protestants could only muster one place of scripture and a few Greek doctors to support their contention that Latin was not permissible.[42] Turning himself 'towards all quarters, and into every possible attitude, stamping with his feet, throwing his arms, bending his sides, snapping his fingers, alternately elevating and depressing his eye-brows' Cole argued, with the strength of 1300 years of English religious tradition, that Latin could be used in worship.[43] When he had finished, Dr Robert Horne rose and, after praying for guidance with his back to the altar, read the Protestant's 'book', which insisted that their position was based on the doctrine of the Christian Catholic Church and built on the scriptures, the prophets and the apostles.[44] When Horne ended his speech the Catholics expected to make a rebuttal, but Bacon would not permit them to do so. At this, Bishop White of Winchester complained that so far only Dr Cole had spoken for them, and yet all of them had much to say about this proposition. Demanding that they

[38]Holinshed, *Chronicles,* 1779.

[39]C.C.C.C. 118, 383.

[40]*ZL,* I, 14.

[41]*CSP Ven.,* VII, 64-5.

[42]C.C.C.C., 121, 383.

[43]*ZL,* I, 14.

[44]*CSP Span., Eliz.,* I, 46. Holinshed, *Chronicles,* 1800.

be given another day to debate the first article, he asked that if they could not be heard at that moment they be allowed to reduce what they had to say to writing. With much bad grace Bacon agreed that on the following Monday, 3 April, they could read their reply to the Protestants.

The sour ending of the first day's debate made way for the bitter beginning of the second day of argument. That morning Lord Keeper Bacon caused a real misunderstanding. The impressions of both a Catholic and a Protestant, Feria and Dey, were that the Catholics would be given more time to answer the Protestants' arguments on the first point.[45] Bacon, however, began the session by insisting that they speak on the second proposition, about the right of a church to alter its ceremonies. The government's official apology for the proceedings insisted that when the first meeting ended it had been agreed that at the second session the second proposition would be raised, the Catholics submitting their written reply to the first proposition to the Protestants.[46] The Catholics did not understand it that way at all, and they arrived on Monday ready to continue the fight over the use of a foreign tongue in worship, not to dispute the rights of local Churches. Bacon quickly set them straight, telling them that the first proposition had been dealt with on the first day and they must now proceed to the second. To this the Catholics replied that they were ready to present their opinion on the first and begged permission to read it. Four times Dr Harpsfield rose to begin only to be stopped and urged to pass on to the second question. Adamant, the Catholics insisted that since the Protestants had been allowed to present their arguments in full, it was not just to prevent them from doing the same. Prevented they were, and Bacon ordered them, in the Queen's name, to present their case on the second point.[47] 'And thereupon', says the carefully edited official report, 'what sinister or disordered meaning is not yet fully known (though in some part to be understanded) the Bishop of Winchester and his colleages, and especially Lincolne, refused to exhibit or read. . . .'[48] Insisting that they would not debate the second

---

[45] *CSP Span., Eliz.*, I, 46-47. Feria's report is verified by William Dey's letter, C.C.C.C. 118, 383. That the Protestants also believed that there would be oral arguments after the 'books' had been read is proven by the conclusion of their written argument on the second proposition. Referring to the arguments against their position, they wrote: 'Theis and other obiections shall be by goddes grace answered more at large when the contrarie booke shall be exhibited.' C.C.C.C. 121, 228. In other words, they were waiting for the Catholics to present their side of the question before rebutting them.

[46] Holinshed, *Chronicles*, 1800.

[47] *CSP Span., Eliz.*, I, 47.

[48] Holinshed, *Chronicles*, 1800.

question until they had answered the first, the Catholics quarrelled violently with the lord keeper. Abbot Feckenham, who was not one of the disputants, intervened and, in a desperate attempt to keep the peace, offered to argue the second point. It was not allowed.[49] Archbishop Heath chided his colleagues for being so stubborn, but he was ignored. Finally Bacon declared that if they would not speak on the second proposition he would dissolve the debate. Bishop White of Winchester replied:

> Contented, let us be gone; for we will not in this point give over. I pray you, my lords, require not at our hands that we should be any cause of hinderance or let to our religion, or give any such evil example to our posterity, which we should do, if we gave over to them; which in no wise we may, or will do.[50]

Hearing this, Bacon dismissed the assembly.

Writing after it was over, Feria thought the Catholics had won the disputation; Jewel was sure the spoils belonged to the Protestants.[51] Jewel was a better guesser. Elizabeth had only intended the disputation to provide propaganda to support her new attempt to establish uniformity, but the recalcitrance of the Catholics gave her a golden opportunity to weaken their party. Within hours after the adjournment of the debate White of Winchester and Watson of Lincoln were arrested and sent to the Tower, charged with disobedience to common authority.[52] That same afternoon Sir Ambrose Cave and Sir Richard Sackville were ordered to go to Winchester's and Lincoln's London houses, 'to peruse their studyes and wrtyinges'.[53] On April 4 the other six Catholic disputants were called before the Privy Council and bound to make a daily appearance before that body, ordered not to leave London and Westminster, and fined for contempt of the Queen's order.[54]

There is no record of what Cave and Sackville found in the bishops' houses, but they were probably looking for proof that there was a plot afoot to excommunicate Elizabeth. Allen, Parsons, Sanders and Camden all say that some of the bishops wanted to pronounce the ultimate censure. Parsons wrote that White and some of the others wished to go to Paul's Cross and excommunicate the

[49] *CSP Span., Eliz.,* I, 47.

[50] Foxe, *Acts,* VIII, 691.

[51] *CSP Span., Eliz.,* I, 48, ZL, I, 15.

[52] *APC,* VII, 78. Holinshed, *Chronicles,* 1800. *CSP Ven.,* VII, 65.

[53] *APC,* VII, 78.

[54] *Ibid.,* VII, 78-79.

heretical Queen, but that they were dissuaded by Archbishop Heath.[55] Allen told a very similar story in 1584,[56] and Sanders, working under Allen, connected these reports with the arrest of the bishops after the Westminster disputaton.[57] The first edition of Camden's *Annals* followed Sanders exactly, naming several bishops who desired to pronounce the curse. In later editions of the *Annals* the entry was changed to read:

> Adeoque indignati sunt Lincolniensis and Wintoniensis, ut Reginam, et huic ab Ecclesia Rom. defectionis authores, excommunicationis censure feriendos censuerint qui hanc ab causam incarcerati.[58]

If, however, the arrests were made to forestall an excommunication, the government did not publicize the fact, for obvious reasons. Instead, they did their best to advertise the disloyalty and disobedience of the Catholic disputants who, because they obeyed a foreign authority, had wilfully disobeyed their Queen. First, the Council prepared a carefully worded explanation of what had happened and ordered it to be printed and circulated. The draft of this report is very informative since it shows that the councillors edited it, changing words and phrases in order to make the bishops look as bad as possible. A good example of the distortions in the official account is the change made in a passage which seems to admit that the Catholics could have reasonably expected to resume debate on the first proposition on the second day. Speaking of the Catholics' desire to rebut Horne's address, the original draft says:

> if their tyme might to serve, before Mondaye, they might in both parties also bring in their answers to the same. Thus both partes assented thereto. And before Monday uppon suit made by the other partie, D. Cole was required if it myght be to send their booke touching the fyrst matter, but he answered it cold not be so sone redie, and therefore the like assemblie began agayn at the place and house appoynted.

The edited draft with more clarity and less accuracy, and beginning at the same place, says,

> and uppon Mondaye it should be agreed what daye theye shuld bring in their answer to the same, and the assembly quietly

[55] Persons, 'Memoirs', 59.

[56] William Allen, *A True Defence of English Catholiques that Suffer for Their Faith* (Ingolstadt: 1584), 52.

[57] Nicholas Sanders, *De Origine ac Progressu Schismatis Anglicani Liber* (Cologne: 1585), 382.

[58] William Camden, *Annales Rerum Anglicarum et Hibernicarum, Regnate Elizabetha* ....(London: 1615), 28. On this matter see also C.G. Bayne, *Anglo-Roman Relations, 1558-1565.* (Oxford: 1913), 53 n. 41.

dismissed. And therefore uppon Mondaye the lyke assemblie began agayn at the place and house appoynted.[59]

It is notable that according to the first draft they all agreed on the 31st to prepare their rebuttals before Monday (3 April, the second day of the disputation), while the version that was printed had it that upon Monday they would agree on a day upon which to present their answers. The Council had no intention of leaving the Catholics an excuse.

More propaganda was wrung from the disputation on 9 April, the day before the new bill for supremacy was introduced. Preaching at Paul's Cross, Dr Bill explained to the crowd why the bishops had been sent to the Tower.[60] The abortive debate was still doing duty for the Protestant cause two and a half decades later when Clerke, refuting Sander's accusations about the unjust punishment of the bishops, maintained that they had been proven ignorant and disloyal at the disputation.[61]

The Queen's power in the House of Lords was increased by the outcome of the meeting at Westminster Abbey. Where before the Catholics had managed to maintain a small majority, they now lost their lead. Two of the hottest papists had been removed, leaving men like Heath, who was a moderate, a respector of authority, and a fatalist to lead the opposition. 'There is nought to do,' Heath once told Feria about the state of religion, 'but to bear that God shall ordain'.[62] Some of the laymen were changing their tunes, too. Lord Howard of Effingham, the Earl of Arundel and the Earl of Derby were all castigated by the diplomats for their lack of courage.[63] Although the number of votes on each side was nearly equal, Elizabeth could be more confident that her bills would receive the assent of the peers, especially since some of the things which the lords found objectionable were being removed from the new legislation.

Having done what they could to weaken their opponents, Elizabeth and Cecil turned their attention to preparing the new bills for supremacy and uniformity and a bid for greater control over the lands of the Church.

---

[59] P.R.O., SP 12/III/fol. 173.

[60] Machyn, *Diary*, 194.

[61] Bartholomew Clerke, *Fidelis Servi, subdito infideli responsio, una cum errorum et calumniarum quarundam examine quae contientur in septimo libro de Visibili Monarchia a Nicholao Sandero conscripta* (London: 1573), Sig. L. (iiii$_v$).

[62] *CSP Rome*, 62.

[63] *CSP Span., Eliz.*, I, 66-67. *CSP Ven.*, VII, 52.

How the third bill for supremacy was drafted is a mystery, but it is safe to assume that Cecil and his fellows had a hand in it. One thing is certain about this bill: it was shaped by its two forerunners in this Parliament. Except that it did not authorize a prayer book, the bill that became the Act of Supremacy was very similar to the second bill for supremacy as passed by both houses before Easter, with a few important changes and concessions. Its most important feature was the abandonment of the title 'Supreme Head' and its replacement by the formula 'Supreme Governor,' a clear compromise with the critics of both camps. It also included the revival of the Act licensing communion in both kinds, the repeal of the Marian heresy laws, and the revival of the Henrician Act for consecrating bishops. Cecil and Elizabeth were attempting, apparently, to send a supremacy bill to Parliament which made clear the constitutional position of the monarch and which was more to the lords' liking. It embodied some shrewd, political manouevres. The revival of the Act for communion in both kinds had been the limit of religious change allowed by the Lords before, and it remained in the new bill, perhaps as an insurance policy in case the uniformity bill was defeated once again. The bill, already passed, for consecrating bishops was now incorporated into it, and the repeal of the heresy laws was attached as a rider. Thus, if this latest bill passed the Queen would have a sure legal position and the Protestants would have freedom of worship. The inclusion of the repeal of the heresy laws in the bill for supremacy, rather than in that for uniformity where it belonged, was a shrewd move. Indications were that the supremacy, which most of the lay peers were willing to accept, would pass without major opposition. The section ending prosecutions for heresy would slip through on the coat-tails of the supreme governorship.

The opposition of all parties to the idea of a female head of the Church must have been an important factor in the Queen's decision to seek the governorship instead. Of course, the Catholics recognized the Pope as the head of the Church and would have no other, but they did not oppose her headship on petrine grounds alone. Their arguments from scripture found sympathetic ears among the Protestants. Archbishop Heath propounded some of these reasons to the House:

> Now whether your honours have authority, by this high courte of parliamente, to say unto our soveraign ladie. *Pasce, pasce, pasce,* you must shewe your waraunte and commyssion. And further, that her highness, beyinge a woman by birthe and nature, is not qualyfied by God's worde to feed the flock of Chryst, it appeareth most playnlye by St. Paul on this wise, saying, *Taceant mulieres in ecclesiis: non enim permittetur eis loqui,*

sed subditas esse, sicut dicit lex: and it followethe in the same place, *Quod turpe est mulieri loqui in ecclesiis:* and in his first epistle to Timothy, the second chapter, saythe, *Docere autem mulieri non permitto, neque dominari in virum, sed in silentio esse.* . . . so by Paul's doctryne her highness may not entermeddle her self with the same: therefore she cannot be supreame head of Chryst's church here in this realme . . . one chief pointe of spiritual government is to confirme his brethren, and ratifie them bothe by holsome doctryne, and administracion of the blessed sacraments. But to preach or mynister the holy sacraments, a woman may not . . . But a woman, in the degrees of Chryst's churche, is not called to be an apostel, nor evangelst (*sic*), nor to be a shepherd, neyther a doctor or preacher. Therfor she cannot be supreme head of Christ's militant churche, nor yet of any part thereof.[64]

The Protestants entertained fears of the headship in their own right. As Hallam has noted, the Queen took pains to relieve the worries of those who had imbibed from Calvin a fear of Erastianism.[65] Calvin, watching the behaviour of Henry VIII, had stated his unequivocal opposition to the combination of royal and ecclesiastical power. 'Erant enim blasphemi', he said 'qui vocarent eum [Henry VIII] summum caput ecclesiae sub Christo'.[66] Rishton, in his continuation of Sanders, contended that it was Calvin's opposition to the headship which convinced the Protestants that it would be improper for Elizabeth to accept the title.[67] For whatever reason, the Protestants were the ones who persuaded her to make the change. 'Mr Lever', wrote Edmund Sandys, 'wisely put such a scruple in the Queen's head that she would not take the title of supreme head'.[68] John Jewel fleshed out the Queen's objections to the title: 'she seriously maintains', he wrote, 'that this honour is due to Christ alone, and cannot belong to any human being soever; besides which, these titles have been so foully contaminated by antichrist, that they can no longer be adopted by any one without impiety'.[69] He was pleased with her decision.[70]

[64] Strype, *Annals,* I, ii, 406-407. See also, B.L., Cotton Vespasian D. 18, fols. 101v-102.

[65] Henry Hallam, *Constitutional History of England* (London: 1827), I, 120.

[66] Calvin, *Comment. in Amos,* c. vii, 13.

[67] Sanders, *Origin of Schism,* 244.

[68] Parker, *Correspondence,* 66.

[69] *ZL,* I, 33.

[70] *ZL,* I, 24.

Cecil told the Commons that Elizabeth, out of humility, was unwilling to accept the headship.[71] Not all the members of the Lower House were pleased by this news, however. If Feria had his information straight, members objected that it was against the word of God and the scriptures for her to refuse the title and expressed their surprise at the new proposal.[72] Evidently some of them were shocked by Elizabeth's sudden about-turn. After all, English Protestant tradition and the constitutional developments caused by the Reformation in England were closely intertwined with the idea that the king was the supreme head of the Church and Elizabeth's refusal of the headship in a way contravened the constitutional principles upon which she based her claim to rule it. The monarch theoretically inherited the supremacy and could not voluntarily give it up or trade it for some new formula. All, however, can be justified in politics, and no one in England was going to use the arguments against her that they had used against Mary's abandonment of the title.

The frequency of the rumours that the Queen would not accept the headship indicates that Elizabeth, motivated by personal conviction or not, abandoned it because she was trying to circumvent a problem. Information reaching Paulo Tiepolo, the Venetian ambassador in Brussels, made the situation look like this:

> The result (*la reuscita*) of the proceedings of Parliament would make it appear that the Queen has determined not to adopt either in documents or otherwise the title of 'Head of the Church,' but to act like the Princes of Germany, who use the power and not the title. (*che usano la potesta, et non il titolo.*)[73]

His information was correct. Elizabeth would not take the title, but neither would she relinquish the power over the Church that she believed was hers by right. In terms of her prerogative, the change from headship to governorship was meaningless. True, Christ was the only Head of the Church, but as an institution the Church needed an administrator, a governor who would keep it safe and unified in this sinful world. It was a lesson that the German Protestants had learned, their theologians had rationalized, and their princes had acted upon. Toepolo's informant understood Elizabeth's position very well.

To his delight, Neale found a trace fossil in the third bill for supremacy which allowed him to put forward the theory that Elizabeth had intended to return to the prayer book of 1549,

---

[71] *CSP Span., Eliz.*, I, 52. *CSP Ven.*, VII, 73.

[72] *CSP Span., Eliz.*, I, 52.

[73] *CSP Ven.*, VII, 64.

instead of that of 1552. This fossil, section 5 of the Act of Supremacy, revived the Act against persons who spoke irreverently of the sacrament of the altar, and for receiving it in both kinds, (1 Edward VI, c. 1). It was, in Neale's reconstruction, included at the drafting of the first bill for supremacy when the government intended only to copy Edward's progress to reform, and was left in the third bill as an insurance policy, just in case the uniformity bill was defeated.[74] However, as every paleontologist knows, you cannot reconstruct the history of a fauna from one fossil, especially if that fossil can only be surmised to belong to a particular stratum. In order to know where the fossil belongs, the geological history of its site must be understood. In the same way, the historical forces that brought 1 Edward VI, c. 1. into the third bill need to be re-examined.

The most acceptable explanation of the revival of this Edwardian Act is that it was considered a part of the royal duty to prevent religious disturbances at a time when religious change was abroad in the land. This first Act of Edward VI's first Parliament, although it did express a eucharistic doctrine (a memorialist one) and license communion *sub utraque specie*, was designed to prevent disputes about the sacrament which might damage the concord of the Commonwealth. It was introduced in 1547 because the repeal of the Act of Six Articles and the Lancastrian heresy laws left the government no way to control religious agitation. G.R. Elton describes it as 'an attempt . . . to balance the dangers of excessive liberalism — which worried Paget and other more practical members of the administration'.[75] In conjunction with a Protestant prayer book the Edwardian Act had its value as a statute which could be used to safeguard the legal eucharist from Catholics and dissenting Protestants. Resuscitated by the Act of Supremacy, this statute gave Elizabethan justices of the peace the power to investigate and indict persons who had 'condemned in their harts and speche' or had 'depraved dispised or reviled' the sacrament of the altar verbally or in print. Offenders were to be tried by jury, and, if found guilty, could have been punished with fines and imprisonment.[76] The whole Act is concerned with silencing criticism of or disputes about the eucharist, with the exception of the last section. Almost as an afterthought the

[74]Neale, 'Supremacy and Uniformity', 309.

[75]G.R. Elton, *Reform and Reformation: England 1509-1558* (London: 1977), 342.

[76]1 Edw. VI, c. 1, § § 1-7.

framers of the bill added a paragraph which declared that people should receive in both kinds, after the custom of the primitive church.[77] Parliament gave Elizabeth back this power against religious dissent in 1559, and, although it was seldom if ever used in the early part of the reign, the High Commission later found it useful.[78] Thus when the prayer book was stricken from the bill for supremacy Elizabeth seized upon the revival of the Act for communion in both kinds as a means whereby she could legally permit the celebration of the eucharist in a Protestant manner. The proclamation of 22 March, which announced the revival of the statute and emphasized the section permitting reception in both kinds 'to quiet the consciences of such great numbers', confirms the Queen's intent.[79] A godsend, the Edwardian Act gave Elizabeth the wherewithal to circumvent the Catholics and to encourage the Protestants.

After Elizabeth changed her strategy and suppressed the proclamation, the section reviving 1 Edward VI, c. 1. (no fossil) was put into the new bill for supremacy both as a legitimate penal statute and as a way to ensure a Protestant eucharist. Proof of its value to the government as insurance comes, according to Neale, from the Irish Act of Supremacy which omitted the section concerning communion in both kinds. Instead, a separate bill was made of it which, along with the Act of Uniformity, was certified to the Irish Parliament in October 1559. However, this Irish bill for communion in both kinds did not become law, even though the uniformity bill did, which indicates that it was probably introduced as an alternative to the uniformity in case that should fail.[80] Neale's theory, unconvincing for the history of the English supremacy bill, cannot be saved by what happened at Dublin.

The history of the Act of Supremacy is obscure; the history of the Act of Uniformity is impossible to discover. The preparation of the

---

[77] 1 Edw. VI, c. 1, § 8.

[78] Hughes, *Reformation in England,* III, 430.

[79] Hughes and Larkin, *Proclamations,* II, 110.

[80] Neale, 'Supremacy and Uniformity', 309. Robert Dudley Edwards, *Church and State in Tudor Ireland* (London: 1935), 177. For what it is worth, it ought to be noted that a paper explaining the alterations made in bills, drawn from English statutes, which were sent to Ireland in 1559 exists in the P.R.O. It lists several changes made in the Act of Supremacy to ready it for the Irish Parliament, most of which resulted from the fact that some Acts revived by the English statute had never been passed in Ireland. The Act for Restraint of Annates is one instance. This list says that the section for communion in both kinds had been deleted because a new bill was being drawn. Beside that someone, in a different hand, has written 'Concordat' and drawn a large cross. The content of this new bill is puzzling, since it seems rather a drastic way to revive a statute — if that is what it would have done. What 'Concordat' means in this context is also a mystery, since the bill did not become law. See P.R.O., SP 63/II/fol. 1.

bill left no traces between the 'Device for Alteration of Religion' and the introduction of what became the Act of Uniformity. Probably got ready in the manner suggested by the 'Device' some time in January or February, the Act of Uniformity is a direct descendant of the Edwardian Acts of the same name. Eleven of the Elizabethan Act's fourteen sections are copied directly from the earlier ones. Where changes do occur, they were made, in most cases, to correct dates and change offensive or unclear language. The fact that the bill is little more than a revised version of the Edwardian Acts may account for the mystery which surrounds its preparation. It could not have taken long to write it. There are only two important differences between this Act's prayer book and its predecessors: the ornaments rubric and a change in the words of administration in the communion. Diplomatic analysis of the original parchment copy of the Act tells us little about the origin and evolution of the bill. After studying it, we can echo F.W. Maitland, who wrote: 'If I have to sing a *Nunc dimittis,* it will run "quid occuli mei viderunt originalem Actum de Uniformitate primi anni Reg. Eliz." Few can say as much. It was hardly so well worth seeing as I had hoped it would be . . .'[81] The parchment proves only that the bill was, in every important particular, already in its final form when it was engrossed after its second reading in the Commons.[82] There is nothing in the Journal of the House of Commons that hints of any changes made in the bill in its paper form, so we can assume that Elizabeth and her advisers were responsible for both the ornaments rubric and the change in the communion service.

The rubric, which provided that the ornaments of the Church and the dress of its priests should be the same as those in use in the second year of the reign of King Edward VI, caused violent disputes in both the sixteenth and nineteenth centuries, but Elizabeth had intended just the opposite. This section of the Act of Uniformity established a mean for ecclesiastical ornamentation which, the Queen presumably hoped, would prevent iconoclasm and keep the externals of the Church from undergoing violent and shocking changes. Ornaments — which were, after all, *adiaphora* — were included in the Queen's prerogative, and the Act reserved to her the right to change ornaments, rites, and ceremonies whenever such alterations would benefit religion and the Church.[83] The aim of the rubric was therefore threefold. First, it would establish uniformity in ornaments,

[81] Maitland to R. Lane Poole, 8 Oct. 1899. Fifoot, *Letters,* 249.

[82] Maitland's diplomatic analysis may be seen in his 'Elizabethan Gleanings', *Papers,* III, 204-7. I have checked his remarks against the original parchment roll, H.L.R.O., Original Acts, 1 Eliz. I, no. 2.

[83] 1 Eliz. I, c. 2. 13.

forestalling disputes about clerical dress or church decor. Secondly, it made it clear that ornaments, rites and ceremonies were reserved to the Queen, not the clergy. Lastly, by accident or design, the wording of this section left the door open for change, encouraging men who might otherwise have opposed it to tolerate the rubric. Edmund Sandys's interpretation of it shows both his hope and his comprehension of the Queen's role. 'Our gloss upon this text', he wrote, 'is that we shall not be forced to use them, but that others in the meantime shall not convey them away, but that they may remain for the Queen'.[84]

Elizabeth did not foresee the trouble the ornaments rubric would cause. To her, ornaments and ceremonies were matters which she, as guardian of the Church and nation, had to control. So strongly did she believe this that she later told Archbishop Parker she would not have agreed to 'divers orders' in the prayer book if the Act had not given her the right to control them. Naturally, interpreting as she did her role as head of the Church, she expected her subjects to be ordered as she saw fit.[85] Doubtless, she agreed with Thomas Starkey when he wrote that hymns, clerical celibacy, adoration of saints, tradition and ceremonies were all things unnecessary for salvation. Nonetheless, said Starkey, 'when they be set out with authoritie... the people are to them bounde'.[86] When the battle over 'popish rags' began, Elizabeth's conservatism only helped to strengthen her resolve that no one should be allowed to impinge upon her prerogative. Matters of theology aside, men who would not abide by the Act were disobedient subjects and a threat to the kingdom's peace.

The two sentences added to the communion service are the best proof that Elizabeth and Cecil altered the bill in order to improve its chance of passage. The change in the words of administration legalized by the Act of Uniformity joined the 1549 formula with that of 1552. The result was a compound which read, in the 1559 book, like this:

> The body of our Lord Jesus Christ which was given for thee, preserve thy body and soul into everlasting life: and take and eat this, in remembrance that Christ died for thee, and feed on him in thy heart by faith, with thanksgiving.[87]

[84] Parker, *Correspondence,* 65.

[85] Parker recalled Elizabeth's statement in a letter to William Cecil written in 1571. See Parker, *Correspondence,* 375.

[86] As quoted in Kurt-Wilhelm Beckmann, 'Staatstheorie und Kirchenpolitik im Werke das Englischen Humanisten Thomas Starkey', (Ph.D. dissertation, Hamburg University, 1972), 128-129.

[87] John E. Booty, ed., *The Book of Common Prayer 1559. The Elizabethan Prayerbook* (Charlottesville, Va.: 1976), 264.

This union of the two formulae has been interpreted in various ways. To some it was an attempt to comfort Catholics and Henricians by preserving the formula of 1549 with its implication of a real corporeal presence. To others it appears to be an affirmation of the Calvinist doctrine of a real, but not corporeal, presence. The existence of these two schools of thought proves the value of the formula as a political tool. It could mollify the conservatives without incensing the more radical Protestants. To the lords who wished to keep the mass this change in wording was important. The 1552 formula had been plainly memorialist – 'take . . . this . . . and feed on him in thy heart by faith, with thanksgiving'. In the 1559 prayerbook, however, this memorialism was softened by the 1549 sentence. On the other hand, the history of the passage of the Act of Uniformity through the Commons in April makes it plain that the Protestants did not object to the new formula, either. The change was true to scripture and it did align English theology more closely with Swiss thought on the eucharist. No Protestants protested against the new formula, and Jewel could tell Martyr that their doctrine had not departed from the *Consensus Tigurinus*.[88]

If the formulae were joined as a concession to the Catholics, it made good political sense. As we have seen, the laymen in the Lords did not object to the supremacy but several of them did refuse to give up the Catholic eucharist. It is probable that the revised form of institution was an attempt to win over a few crucial votes in the Upper House. However, this assumes that the change was made after Easter. There is the possibility that the combined formulae were in the bill for order of service introduced in February. If this was the case the political motive would be less likely — although not impossible — and it would be more likely that the new formula reflected Her Majesty's preference (which it also may have done).

The other legislation touching the Church prepared in early April concerned ecclesiastical land. In the tradition of her father and brother, Elizabeth was preparing to fill her shrunken purse with the lands of the bishops, the monasteries, and the chantries. Once the new bills were ready to be sent to Parliament, the government could begin the next bout in its fight to get a clearly defined supremacy, a properly established uniformity, and a pleasant increase in the Queen's revenues.

[88]*ZL*, I, 21.

6

PARLIAMENT AFTER EASTER

On 7 April, three days after Parliament had returned to its work, the body of a woman was borne to its grave in the church of St. Thomas of Acre in Cheap. Following the corpse were the solemn mourners, walking in pairs and accompanied by priests who, gowned like laymen, performed the burial service in English, completing the obsequies with a sermon.[1] Unlicensed by authority, change in religion was being instituted by the people of their own accord. Catholicism in England was beginning to shake and fall,[2] and the Protestant Queen who had started the shaking was trying to settle religion before too much of the structure collapsed.

Elizabeth was in an awkward position by the beginning of April. A devotee of political caution, she was working like a racing tortoise to establish the reformed service in the church. Her caution led her along the smooth path of moderate religion, not to the peaks of religious enthusiasm, and those who yearned for freedom to practise a thoroughly reformed faith were impatient with her insistence upon establishing the legality of the reform before permitting it. The Reverend Doctor Jewel was among those who fidgeted while the Queen plodded toward reformation. 'O Mary and the Marian times', he lamented,

> With how much greater tenderness and moderation is truth now contended for, than falsehood was defended sometime since! Our adversaries acted always with precipitancy, without precedent, without authority, without law; while we manage every thing with so much deliberation, and prudence, and wariness, and circumspection, as if God himself could scarce retain his authority without our ordinances and precautions. . . .[3]

Seething with frustration, Jewel, admitting that Elizabeth had reformed her own chapel, found the root of the delay. The Queen,

> excellent as she is, and earnest in the cause of true religion, notwithstanding she desires a thorough change as early as possible, cannot however be induced to effect such change

[1]Machyn, *Diary,* 193.
[2]The expression is Jewel's, *ZL,* I, 10. See also, *ZL,* I, 18.
[3]*ZL,* I, 17.

without the sanction of law; lest the matter should seem to have been accomplished, not so much by the judgment of discreet men, as in compliance with the impulse of a furious multitude. Meanwhile, many alterations in religion are effected in parliament, in spite of the opposition and gainsaying and disturbance of the bishops. These however I will not mention, as they are not yet publicly known, and are often brought on the anvil to be hammered over again.[4]

A multitude of Catholics and Protestants were furious with the pace of the reform. The Catholics wanted it stopped, the Protestants wanted it hastened, and both groups were growing restive. From Wales the Earl of Pembroke received word that the Welsh were threatening to kill any Protestant preachers sent into their country. Good Protestant though he was, the Earl of Sussex, lord deputy of Ireland, was forced to voice his fears that if Protestantism was introduced in Ireland the country would revolt.[5] In London the Protestant rabble was being incited by plays performed in the taverns, and, in order to keep the city quiet, the Queen issued a proclamation banning these performances.[6] In the meantime, Elizabeth and Cecil renewed their attempt to obtain a workable settlement of religion.

Officially, Parliament reconvened on 3 April, but because the second meeting of the Westminster Disputation was also held that day the Commons postponed their business until the next morning.[7] Beginning where they had left off before Easter, two bills were given their second readings on the 4th. It took a few days to pick up the pace of work, and attendance was not good. During the Easter recess the Council had written to the sheriffs, ordering them to inform members who had departed without licence that they had to be present on 3 April.[8] This measure had little effect, for on the 10th it was announced that the names of the members would be called on the following Wednesday.[9] There is no record of any penalties inflicted as a result of the roll call.

[4]ZL, I, 18.

[5]CSP Span., Eliz., I, 50.

[6]The original of this proclamation is lost, but it is mentioned in CSP Ven, VII, 65. It must have been issued near the end of the second week in April, for the London Repertory has the following entry: 'At this Court yt was orderyd that the Quenes Maiesties proclamacion lately set fourth and made within this cytie for the steyinge of interludes with in the sayd cytie should fourth with be entered in the iornall of Records and then be conveyed to Mr Recorder to be delivered over ageyn unto Mr Secretarye Sicell for asmoche as he hath sent to my lorde mayor for it.' Corp. London R.O., Repertories, XIV, 13 April 1559.

[7]H.L.R.O., Commons MS. Journals, I, fol. 206.

[8]APC, VII, 74.

[9]H.L.R.O., Commons MS. Journals, I, fol. 207.

The peers spent the first four days on the new government bill that granted the Queen the right to take the temporalities of vacant sees. The bishops argued against it, but the laymen were not sympathetic, and the bill was passed on 7 April with all the clerics dissenting.[10]

The morning of 10 April saw the first reading of the third and last supremacy bill in the Commons, the introduction of which surprised many of the members.[11] Cecil, according to Feria (whose information on this point contains some obvious inaccuracies), responded to their confusion at the appearance of yet another supremacy bill by explaining that although Elizabeth appreciated their good will in offering her the title of supreme head of the Church, she chose, out of humility, to decline the offer. Someone replied that it was against the word of God and the scripture for the Queen to refuse the title, and members marvelled 'at his coming to them every day with new proposals and objections'.[12]

Although it mystified them, to most of the Commons the bill's content was agreeable, if not preferable. There is no record of any opposition to the new supremacy bill in that House. Read a second time and engrossed on 12 April, it was passed on the 13th.[13] When, however, the bill entered the Lords on 14 April an old story repeated itself: the bishops fought it tooth and nail. 'The cause of the pope is now agitated, and with much vehemence on both sides', wrote Jewel, 'for the bishops are labouring that they may seem not to have been in error; and this delays and hinders the progress of religion. . . .'[14] The Lords heard the bill's contents on the 15th, and on the 17th it was read again and committed. Archbishop Heath, according to Feria, was the one responsible for getting it sent to committee.[15] Unlike the first time the supremacy was committed in the Lords, the men chosen to study the bill were not overwhelmingly sympathetic to the conservative point of view. This time the government had no illusions about its ability to win over the Catholics. Moreover, since this new bill dealt only with the supremacy, the laymen on the committee were more inclined to its aims than they had been to those of the previous bill for supremacy. A majority of the committee appointed were known

[10]H.L.R.O., Lords, MS. Journals, IV, 44-48.

[11]H.L.R.O., Commons MS. Journals I, fol. 207.

[12]*CSP Span, Eliz.,* I, 52.

[13]H.L.R.O., Commons MS. Journals, I, fol. 207v-208.

[14]*ZL,* I, 20.

[15]*CSP Span., Eliz.,* I, 55.

Protestants. Eight of them had been on the March committee, but of the fifteen on this new panel only six were conservatives.[16] The influential Protestant Earl of Bedford's membership suggests that its numbers were chosen with an eye to its tractability.

Although the bill's existence was not threatened by this committee, it pulled some of the teeth from the proposed act. An examination of the original roll in the House of Lords Record Office shows that the Upper House made at least four amendments and attached three provisoes to the bill, nearly all of them designed to protect people who disagreed with the Crown about religion.

The first amendment was made in section 4, which decrees that all statutes repealed by Mary and not specifically revived in the present Act shall continue repealed. One clause, of two lines, was erased from the middle of this section. What the missing lines said is unknown, but, with Maitland, we may conjecture that they excepted some Henrician and Edwardian Acts and were removed by the conservatives in the Lords.[17] An interpolation, which was either an amendment or a correction, was made in the oath of supremacy in section 9. There, the person taking the oath swore, originally, that the Queen was supreme governor 'in all Spirituall Thinges or Causes'. This was amended to read, 'in all Spirituall or Ecclesiasticall Thinges or Causes'. Maitland suggested that, if it was an amendment, 'or Ecclesiasticall' was inserted to explain 'Spirituall' in such a way that any claim to jurisdiction *in foro conscientiae* would be excluded. This argument, however, is weak, for the changes would not have excluded matters of the *forum conscientia* from 'Spirituall'. In all likelihood, the change was either a verbal improvement made to balance the sentence or a lawyer's recognition of the fact that there were matters of Church administration which 'Spirituall' might not cover.[18] Section 14, which established the penalties for maintaining a foreign spiritual jurisdiction within the realm, was altered in four places. One change simply added clarity. Another, an erasure of perhaps sixteen letters, left no clue that would explain why it was made. The others are identical and informative. In both, the words 'in maner and fourme aforesaid' were inter-lined in order to ensure that the Act was strictly construed to refer only to offences named in it. For example, one line was made to read: 'comit or doo the said Offences or any of them in the

[16]Davis, 'Unpublished MS.,' 536.

[17]Maitland, 'Gleanings,' *Papers*, III, 189. I have verified Maitland's observations by comparing them with the original parchment roll.

[18]*Ibid.*, III, 190. I am indebted to G.R. Elton for his criticisms of Maitland's interpretation of this amendment.

142

maner and fourme aforesaid'.[19] The Lords were hedging the power to prosecute about with safeguards.

Three schedules attached to the parchment roll were introduced and read twice in the Upper House on 25 April.[20] The first of these, section 20 in the printed Act, shows that the conservatives realized that unless some limitation was placed on the High Commission it might soon begin judging the old beliefs heresy. Therefore, a proviso was added which defined its powers. After it was written, it was amended by a clause limiting heresy to beliefs condemned by general councils. Thus amended (the amendment is underlined) the proviso reads:

> [The Commission] shall not in any wise have Aucthoritie or Power to order determine or adjudge anny Matter or Cause to bee Heresie but onelye suche as heretofore have been determined ordred or adjudged to bee Heresie *by thaucthoritee of the Canonicall Scriptures, or by the first fowre generall Councelles, or any of them or by any other generall Councell wherin the same was declared Heresie by thexpresse and playne woordes of the sayd Canonicall Scriptures,* or suche as hereafter shall bee ordred judged or determined to bee Heresye by the Highe Courte of Parlyament of this Realme withe thassent of the Clergie in their Convocation. . .[21]

This proviso originated in the Lords, for it bears the order for delivery to the Commons and the usual note saying that the Commons assented, which means that both the original form and the amendment were the work of the peers. Maitland, noting the interlined addition to the schedule, suggested that the clause came from the reforming side.[22] A speech by Archbishop Heath may support the argument that this clause was prompted by the conservatives, either as a safeguard or as a compromise. Heath propounded the belief that if England broke with Rome it must also break with the Councils of the Church, especially the first four, which, he believed, recognized the primacy of the Pope and condemned many heresies which 'thinhabitants of this realme, are much more inclined to rayse uppe'.[23] By adding this clause specifying that heresy could be defined by reference to the General Councils and the canonical scriptures, the conservatives were making it difficult to turn recognition of the Pope, belief in

[19] *Ibid.*
[20] Davis, 'Unpublished MS.,' 537.
[21] H.L.R.O., Original Act, I Eliz. I, no. 1.
[22] Maitland, 'Gleanings', *Papers,* III, 192.
[23] Strype, *Annals,* I, ii, 400.

transubstantiation, or other basic Roman Catholic beliefs into heresy. Interestingly, the last clause of the schedule leaves room for the definition of new heresies in case, perhaps, Anabaptists invented some new ones which were not covered by the decisions of the councils. Moreover, ever since Henry broke with Rome the definition of heresy at law had been uncertain. This clause helped stave off any precise definition of it.

The proviso known as section 21 of the Act replaced a clause which stood at the end of section 15 until it was cancelled. Both the proviso and the deleted portion of 15 stated that at least two witnesses were necessary before there could be a conviction under the Act. The Lords, recognizing that the original language was very clumsy, replaced it with a better version. They wanted to clarify a rule which was favourable to accused conservatives.[24] Section 22 also constitutes a proviso designed to replace a clause whose language was too murky. Originally the clause, at the end of section 18, had merely provided that anyone who unwittingly aided an offender against the Act should not be prosecuted.[25] Anxious to establish clear rules of evidence to protect persons accused of helping offenders, the Lords replaced this with the following:

> Provided also and be it enacted by thaucthoritee aforesaid, That yf anny person or persons shall hereafter happen to gyve anny Relief Ayde or Comforte or in any wise be ayding helping or comforting to the person or persons of any that shall hereafter happen to bee an Offendour in any Matter or Case of Preminire or Treason revived or made by this Acte, that then such Relyef Ayde or Comforte given, shall not bee judged or taken to bee anny Offence, onelesse ther bee twoo sufficient Witnesses at the least that can and will openly testifie and declare that the person or persons that so gave suche Relief Aide or Comforte hadd Notice and Knowledge of suche Offence committed and doon by the said Offendour at the tyme of suche Relief Ayde or Comforte so to him gyven or ministred. . . .[26]

These changes show that the conservatives in the Lords, while unable to stop the bill's final passage, did have enough strength to modify it in ways which gave them some protection from persecution for their opinions.

The bill for supremacy, with its provisos engrossed on a single membrane, was read for a third time on 26 April. It passed in spite of

[24]Maitland, 'Gleanings', *Papers,* III, 192.
[25]*Ibid.,* III, 193.
[26]*Ibid.,* and H.L.R.O., Original Acts, I Eliz. I, no. 1.

the dissent of all the ecclesiastical peers present. Only one lay peer, Viscount Montague, joined the bishops in resisting its passage. After the vote had been taken Richard Weston, serjeant-at-law, and the Queen's attorney carried the bill to the Commons.[27]

The Commons, too, were concerned about persecution for heresy, and they passed a proviso to protect themselves from condemnation for their part in ejecting the Pope and his religion from the realm. 'Be it enacted', said the proviso, 'that no maner of order Acte or Determinacion for annye Matter of Religion or Cause Ecclesiasticall had or made by thauthorite of this present Parliament, shalbe accepted demed interpretate or adjudged at any time hereafter to be any Error Heresie Scismes or Scismaticall Opinion'.[28] What prompted this odd provision, which would certainly have been useless if the Catholic party had returned to power, is unknown. Perhaps the Lower House was remembering how easily Edwardian Protestantism had turned into heresy. It might also be that they were considering the distinct possibility that their unmarried Queen might soon be replaced by a Catholic. Whatever their reasons were, the existence of this proviso is proof that the godly in the Commons had little faith in a secure political future for their religion.

The last two schedules attached to the Act also came from the Commons. Both of these were private provisions in a public Act, resolving two appeals then pending in the Court of Rome and implicitly exempting the appellants from charges of praemunire. Richard Chetwood, Robert Harcourt and their wives had lost suits in the consistory court at Paul's. Refusing to accept the court's ruling, they had appealed to Rome. Now that the Act of Supremacy was about to outlaw appeals to the Pope the two men sought to protect themselves. Accordingly, the two provisos added to the bill declared that if the decision did not come from Rome within sixty days after the end of Parliament, Chetwood and Harcourt could appeal their sentences in the manner in which they would have been appealed in the 28th year of King Henry VIII.[29]

Having agreed to the Lord's provisos and added their own, the Commons sent the supremacy bill back to the Upper House on 28 April. On the 29th the peers voted their approval of the Commons' provisos, and the third bill for supremacy was ready for the royal assent.[30]

[27]Davis, 'Unpublished MS.', 537.
[28]H.L.R.O., Original Acts, I Eliz. I, no. 1. Section 19 in the printed editions.
[29]H.L.R.O., Original Acts, I Eliz. I, no. 1.
[30]Davis, 'Unpublished MS.', 539.

The story of the passage of the Act of Uniformity parallels that of the Act of Supremacy. The Commons made no objections and rushed it through; the Lords fought over it and amended it. The bill 'for the unytye of service of the churche and mynystracion of Sacraments' was read to the knights and burgesses for the first time on 18 April. The next day, read again, it was engrossed. On the 19th it was passed.[31] Sent to the Upper House on 25 April, the bill received its first reading on the 26th, its second on the 27th, and its third on the 28th.[32] Once again the men who opposed altering the service rallied to defend their faith, attacking the bill resolutely and with good effect.

After its third reading, Bishop Scot of Chester made an excellent speech which illuminates the arguments on both sides. Opening with references to the lamentable nature of the bill, Scot questioned Parliament's right to meddle in matters of religion, partly because faith was a matter of unchangeable certainty, and partly because acts of Parliament were mutable and often abrogated. Moreover, the members of Parliament, though worthy men, were 'not so studied nor exercised in the scriptures, and the holie doctors and practyses of the churche, as to be competent judges in suche matters. Nor dothe it apperteine to thier vocation. . . .'[33] The Lords, said Scot, should also consider that this bill would reject the religion practised by their forefathers for a thousand years. 'But nowe I do call to remembraunce', he said,

> that I did here yesterday a nobleman in this howse say, makinge an answer unto this as it were by procurance, that our fathers lyved in blyndness, and that we have juste occasion to lament their ignorance; whereunto me thinkethe it may be answered, that if our forefathers were here, and heard us lament their doings, it is very lyke that they woulde say unto us as our Savyour Christe said unto the women which followed hym when he went to his death, and weepted after him, *Nolite flere super nos, sed super vos.*[34]

Comparing the missal and the Book of Common Prayer, Scot maintained that the prayer book removed the additions made by the Fathers to adorn and perfect the service, that it ignored the ordinances of the apostles for the performance of the sacraments, and that it did

---

[31]H.L.R.O., Commons MS. Journals, I, fols. 210-210v.

[32]Davis, 'Unpublished MS.,' 538.

[33]B.L., Cotton Vespasian D. 18, fols. 112-113v. There is another contemporary copy in Emmanuel College, Cambridge, MS. 76. It is appended to a manuscript copy of Harpsfield's life of Thomas More.

[34]B.L., Cotton Vespasian D. 18, fol. 115v.

not follow the forms established by Christ.[35] Since the new book denied transubstantiation, Christ, Scot insisted, was not present in its communion.[36]

> Ther did yesterdaye a nobleman in this howse say, that he did beleve that Christe is ther receaved in the communyon set owt in this booke; and beyng asked if he did worshippe hym ther, he said, no, nor never woulde, so longe as he lived. Which is a strange opynyon, that Christe shoulde be any where, and not worshypped. They say they will worshippe hym in heaven, but not in the sacrament: which is much lyke as if a man would saye that when themperor syttethe under his clothe of estate, princely apparelled, he is to be honoured; and yet if he come abroad in a freez coat, he is not to be honoured; and yet he is all one emperor in clothe of golde under his clothe of estate, and in a freez coat abroad in the street. As it is one Christe in heaven in the forme of man, and in the sacrament under the formes of bread and wyne.[37]

Concluding, Scot charged again that it was not Parliament's place to discuss matters of religion, illustrating this with numerous examples of councils acting without the aid of an assembly of nobles and commons.[38] He left the Lords with a solemn warning: 'If you passe this bill, you shall not onely . . . erre you selves, but ye also shalbe the awthors and cawsers that the whole realme shall erre after you. For the which you shall make an accompte before God.'[39]

Dr Feckenham, Abbot of Westminster, provided three rules by which the Lords could determine for themselves the difference between true religion and false. Antiquity was the first test. Which religion had been observed by all men, at all times, in all places? The second test was stability. Which religion was the most steadfast and consistent? The third question he urged the lords to ask themselves was 'which of these religions dothe brede the more humble and obedient subjects, first unto God, and next unto our sovereigne ladie the quene's highness, and all superior powers?'[40] The first trial was easily passed by the Roman Church, as was the second. Protestantism,

[35] *Ibid.*, fols. 116v-117.

[36] *Ibid.*, fols. 118-119.

[37] *Ibid.*, fol. 119v.

[38] *Ibid.*, fols. 121-122v.

[39] *Ibid.*, fol. 121.

[40] *Ibid.*, fol. 86v. A copy is also included in the Harpsfield manuscript mentioned in note 33. Another manuscript copy is in C.C.C.C., 121 fol. 127 ff. A note is on the title page of this manuscript: 'hic desunt pagine 12', after which follows this comment in Parker's red chalk: 'quia superfluae'. Strype printed the speech in his *Annals*, I, ii, 431-438.

on the other hand, was damned by its own history. 'The new religion, here now set forthe in this booke', he declaimed, 'is no stedfast religion, nor allwayes one, neither agreeable with it self. Who seethe it not when in the late practice therof in kinge Edward the 6th his dayes, howe changeable and variable was it in and to it self?'[41] The new religion's failure to breed subjects who were obedient to authority was proven by the Abbot in an interesting, if shortsighted, argument.

> I shall dissier your honours to consider the sudayne mutation of the subjects of this realme, sythence the deathe of good quene Marye, onely caused in them by the preachers of newe religion: when in quene Marye's daies your honours do know right well, howe the people of this realme did live in an order, and wolde not runne before lawes, nor openlye disobey the quene's highness's proceedinges and proclamations. There was no spoyling of churches, pullinge downe of aultars, and most blasphemous tredinge the sacraments under their feet, and hanging up the knave of clubs in the place thereof. There was no skurching nor cuttinge of the faces and lages of the crucifix and image of Christ. There was no open flesh eatings, nor shambles kepeinge in Lent and the daies prohibited. The subjects of this realme, and especially the nobilitye, and suche as were of the honourable councell, did in quene Marys daies knowe the waye unto churches and chappels, there to begyne their daies worke, with callings for helpe and grace, by humble prayers and servinge of God. And nowe, sithence the comynge and reigne our most soveraigne and dear lady quene Elizabeth, by the onely preachers and scaffold players of this newe religion, all thinges are chaunged and turned up side downe, and notwithstandinge the quenes majesties proclamations most godly made to the contrarye, and her vertuous example of lyvinge, sufficyent to move the hearts of all obedyent subjects to the divine service and honour of God. But obedyence is gone, humilitie and mekeness cleare abolyshed, vertuous chast and straight livinge abandoned, as thoughe they had never ben heard of in this realme; all degrees and kindes beynge desirous of fleshely and carnall libertie, whereby the springalls and children are degennerate from their naturall fathers, the servants contemptors of their masters commandments, the subjects disobedyent unto God and all superior powers.[42]

In conclusion, the Abbot called upon the Lords to take the opportunity to expel the new religion, whose evil fruits were so well known, from the realm.[43]

[41] B.L., Cotton Vespasian D. 18, fols. 87-87v. Strype, *Annals*, I, ii, 432-33.
[42] B.L., Cotton Vespasian D. 18, fols. 90v-91. Strype, *Annals*, I, ii, 436-37.
[43] B.L., Cotton Vespasian D. 18, fol. 91. Strype, *Annals*, I, ii, 437.

Aided by this kind of strong rhetoric, the conservatives altered parts of the bill to protect their interests. One change they may have made was the deletion of the harsh words used about the Pope in the second Edwardian prayer book. To quote Maitland, "'twas a Lords' amendment that spared the feelings of the detestably enormous bishop of Rome'.[44] Maitland believed the change had been made by means of an interpolation, indicated here by brackets:

> withe one Alteracion or Addition of certayne Lessons to bee used on every Sundaye in the yere, [and the fourme of the Letanie altered and corrected,] and twoo Sentences onelye added in the delyverye of the Sacrament to the Communicantes, and none other or otherwise. . . .[45]

Conjecturing that some peers, though willing to vote for the prayer book as a whole, could not stomach hearing the Pope referred to in such a manner, Maitland qualified his argument. He was forced to admit that there was a little evidence that the phrase had already been dropped from the litany used in the Queen's chapel.[46]

Two alterations in section 2 of the Act were made in order to protect patrons of livings from the effects of the law. These changes were inserted in the midst of a section copied verbatim from the first Edwardian Act of Uniformity. One was written over an erasure (italicized here) and the other was interlined (bracketed words).

> And yf any such persone once convicte of anye offence concerning the Premisses shall after the first conviccion eftesoones offende and bee therof in fourme aforesaid lawfully convicte, that then the same person shall for his second Offence suffer Imprisonment by the Space of one hole yere, and also shall therefore be deprive ipso facto of all his Spirituall Promocions; and that it shalbe lawfull to all Patrones or Donors of all and singler the same Spiritual Promocions *or any of them, to present or collate to the same, as thoughe the person and persons so offending were deade:* And that yf anye suche persone or persones after he shall bee twise convicted in Fourme aforesaid shall offende against any of the Premisses a thirdde tyme, and shalbee thereof in fourme aforesayd lawfully convicted, that then the person so offending and convicted the thirdde tyme [shall be depryved ipso facto of all his Spirituall Promotyons, and also] shall suffer imprysonment during his Lyef.[47]

[44]Fifoot, *Litters,* 249. Written to R.L. Poole, 8 October 1899.

[45]H.L.R.O., Original Acts, 1 Eliz. I, no. 2. The interpolation occurs in section 2 of the printed Act.

[46]Maitland, 'Gleanings', *Papers,* III, 205.

[47]H.L.R.O., Original Acts, 1 Eliz. I, no. 2. Other than the noted changes, all of section 2 is copied verbatim from 2 & 3 Edw. VI, c. 1, except that the punishments for unbeneficed persons are taken from 5 & 6 Edw. VI, c. 1.

Both of the alterations were made by the Lords in order to clarify and guarantee the rights of the patron of a benefice whose occupant had been convicted under the Act. Once the occupant had been found guilty, nothing would prevent the owner of the benefice from putting a new man in his place, and there was no chance that the culpable party would be able to hold his benefice while imprisoned. 'It is not, perhaps, uncharitable', wrote Maitland, 'to suppose that some wavering noblemen may have been reconciled to the bill by thoughts of patronage.'[48] In relation to this observation, it is worth noting that nowhere in the Elizabethan Settlement was there any test for patrons. No one with the power to present to a benefice could be deprived of that right on religious grounds. It is probably that this loophole, which Catholics and Puritans alike were to exploit, was no accident. It would have been dangerous to enforce the Settlement with too much strictness on the influential men of the realm.[49]

When Maitland did his diplomatic analysis of the Act of Uniformity he was puzzled by the apparent absence of any indication of assent by the Commons to the amendments made in the Lords.[50] Working with the printed Journals of Parliament, he did not have access to the then unpublished copy of the missing portion of the Lords' Journal that recorded the passage of the Act of Uniformity. Therefore, he did not know that, although the printed Commons' Journal does not indicate it, the amended uniformity bill was sent back to the Commons. It passed in the Lords on 28 April. On 29 April the Inner Temple manuscript of the Lords' Journal notes: 'introducte sunt a domo communi 3 bille viz. An Acte for unforitie of commen praier and service in the Churche and thadministraction of the Sacramentes conclus.'[51] This entry elicited a comment from Robert Bowyer, who made the Petyt copy of the Journal. He said it had been made by error or negligence of the clerk, 'for it came originally from the Commens and was not with any addition or amendment, nor for any other cause returned to them whereby they shoulde or might send yt agaien backe'.[52] Knowing as we now do that the Lords did amend the bill, we can see that both Bowyer and Maitland were mistaken. The entry is proof that the amended bill was returned to the Commons, who approved the changes and sent it back to the Upper House.

[48]Maitland, 'Gleanings', *Papers,* III, 206.

[49]*Ibid.*

[50]Maitland, 'Gleanings', *Papers,* III, 207-8.

[51]Davis, 'Unpublished MS.,' 539.

[52]*Ibid.*

150

The Catholics' arguments were potent and they almost succeeded in wrecking the religious uniformity. When the vote was taken eighteen peers voted against its passage, and twenty-one voted for it. It was marked 'conclus' by the clerk, but it had been a near thing for the Queen's party.[53] If the bishops of Lincoln and Winchester had not been in the Tower, if Abbot Feckenham had not been unaccountably absent during the vote, if Asaph or Durham had attended, or if a few laymen had not been kept away or persuaded, the uniformity statute would have been defeated. Catholic apologists ascribed their defeat in this crucial vote to force and corruption. Cecil and Bacon, wrote Person, 'partly by violence and partly by fear . . . gott the mager part of the voices by two or three to chaung religion'.[54] Rishton's continuation of Sanders says that the change in religion would have been impossible if Elizabeth had not won the peers over by promises, flattery and bribes. The Earl of Arundel, Rishton maintained, was persuaded by his hope that he might marry the Queen.[55] The Duke of Norfolk was charged with joining the reforming party in order to win a dispensation for his marriage which he could not obtain from the Pope.[56] 'And yet after all, the schismatics obtained their end against the Catholics only by three votes.'[57] Count Feria summed up the feelings of his co-religionists: 'It is all roguery and injustice.'[58]

The Act of Uniformity's narrow escape made constitutional history. For the first time a change in religion had been enacted without the consent of a single churchman and over the protest of Convocation. This impressed itself upon Feria who tried to protect England's loyal Catholics from inclusion in the excommunication he thought to be imminent. He wrote to King Philip:

> It is to be supposed that when the Pope knows what has happened he will proceed against the Queen and the people here, and it would be of great importance for him to be informed that in the time of Henry VIII. the whole Parliament consented without any contradiction whatever, except from the bishop of Rochester (*Rofense*) and Thomas More, wheras now not a single

[53]The margin of victory has been noted by two sources. Persons, 'Memoirs', 59, and *CSP Span., Eliz.,* I, 67. The dissentients are named above in chapter 3 and in Davis, 'Unpublished MS.,' 538.

[54]Persons, 'Memoirs,' 59.

[55]Sanders, *Origin of Schism,* 255-256. Arundel was accused of desiring to marry Elizabeth as early as October 1554. *CSP Span., Mary,* 64.

[56]Sanders, *Origin of Schism,* 255-56.

[57]*Ibid.,* 256.

[58]*CSP Span., Eliz.,* I, 67.

ecclesiastic has agreed to what the Queen has done and of the laymen in the lower chamber, and in the upper some opposed on the question of schism, and a great many opposed the heresies.[59]

It was something that the Catholics would not let Elizabeth forget.

The bill for uniformity had passed, but its opponents still had arows in their quiver. If they could persuade Elizabeth that there was something wrong with the prayer book, they might convince her to withhold her assent to the bill. Matthew Parker was informed of this attempt by Edmund Sandys. After the prayer book had passed, wrote Sandys,

> Boxall and others quarrelled with it, that according to the order of the scripture we had not *gratiarum actio*; 'for,' saith he, '*Dominus accepit panem, gratias agit,* but in the time of consecration we give no thanks.' This he put into the Treasurer's [Thomas Parry] head, and into Countie de Feror's head, and he laboured to alienate the Queen's Majesty from confirming of the act, but I trust they cannot prevail. Mr Secretary is earnest with the book, and we have ministered reasons to maintain that part.[60]

As Sandys had hoped, these quibbles failed to persuade Elizabeth to veto the bill.

There was another weapon in the Catholic arsenal, and that, too, was brought to bear on the Queen. Count Feria tried to scare her into abandoning the reform. King Philip personally ordered this strategem. Writing to Feria on 24 April, he ordered him 'to endeavour to confirm the Queen and her friends in the fear you say they feel of the peril and danger in which they stand'. After he had frightened her in a subtle manner, Feria was to open her eyes to 'the only true remedy, which is to forbid any innovations in religion which usually cause risings and turbulence in countries and in the hearts of subjects'.[61] Acting on these instructions, Feria visited Elizabeth on the 28th. In the interview which followed Elizabeth was her usual evasive self, and the two argued about religion for a while before Feria came to the point. He told her of Philip's good offices with the Pope in her behalf, and warned her that a king of Navarre had been deprived of his kingdom for a schism less grave than heresy. Although he assured her that if the king of France himself told her how to govern she could not find a surer course to ruin than the one now being followed, she remained

[59]*Ibid.*, I, 68.

[60]Parker, *Correspondence,* 65-6. Bishop Scot argued a similar case in Parliament. B.L., Cotton Vespasian D. 18, fols. 118v-119.

[61]*CSP Span., Eliz.,* I, 60

unmoved.[62] Elizabeth's refusal to be frightened led Feria to complain that she was fickle and that her advisors were so 'blind and bestial' that they did not understand the state of affairs.[63] During this meeting Feria seems to have delivered some sort of petition to her on behalf of some English Catholics, who had begged him to speak to her before Parliament closed.[64] Perhaps this refers to the attempt to convince the Queen that the form of communion in the prayer book failed to require the giving of thanks when the bread was consecrated.

One shaft fired by the Catholics struck the Protestant preachers in a vulnerable spot. During the debates in Parliament and at the Westminster Disputation the defenders of the old faith repeatedly raised the charge that the Protestants could not agree about the essentials of their faith. In one instance, the Bishop of Coventry and Lichfield demanded to know to which of the many churches of Germany the English Protestants claimed to belong.[65] Speaking against the bill for uniformity, Abbot Feckenham went to great lengths to prove that the reformers were far from unanimous about a doctrine of the eucharist. Feckenham said that Luther had disagreed with Carlstadt and Zwingli about the eucharist; Peter Martyr had invented a fourth interpretation; and Cranmer had affirmed the real presence one day and denied it the next. Nicholas Ridley vacillated, too, and the confusion over this matter was so great that in the second Edwardian prayer book 'this is my body' became 'this my body'.[66] The moral, said Feckenham, was that this new religion, filled as it was with discord over essential beliefs, could never be constant or settled. 'And therefore of your honours not to be receyved; but great wisdome it were for your honours to refuse the same, untyll you shall perceyve better agreement amongest the awthors and setters furthe of the same.'[67]

The reaction of the Protestant preachers to these accusations proves how much they were hurt by them. 'We are forced, through the vain bruits of the lying papist . . . to shew forth the sum of that doctrine which we profess, and to declare that we dissent not amongst ourselves,' wrote Sandys to Parker.[68] The result was a declaration of

[62] *Ibid.*, I, 62.

[63] *Ibid.*, I, 63.

[64] *Ibid.*

[65] Foxe, *Act*, VIII, 691.

[66] B.L., Cotton Vespasian D. 18, fols. 88-90. Strype, *Annals,* I, ii, 433-436.

[67] *Ibid.,* fol. 90. Strype, *Annals,* I, ii, 435-436.

[68] Parker, *Correspondence,* 66.

doctrine, written in April and delivered to Elizabeth soon after Parliament closed. In the preface to their declaration the preachers explained how they had been goaded into writing it:

> Yet at no tyme hathe the subtile serpent been more stronge in his wicked members and deceitful workers to deface the doctrine of the gospell, and to slaunder the setters furthe of the same, then he hathe shewed him self at this present. And namely against us which have of late preached before the Quene's Majestie and against our bretherne teachers of the same truthe most untruly reporting of us that our doctrine is detestable heresie, that we are fallen from the doctrine of Christes Catholick churche, that we be subtile sectaries, that we dissent amonge our selves, and that everie man nourisshethe and mayntaynethe his peculiar opinion, and that we be teachers of carnall libertie, condempning fasting, praier, almes, and lyke godly exercises, that we be disordered personnes, disturbers of the common wealthes, persuaders of rebellion, teachers of disobedience against magistrates, and what not . . . .[69]

The declaration is a valuable document for it names the arrows that had wounded the reformers and shows them trying to justify themselves to their Queen. Three-quarters of it is concerned with questions of doctrine. Beginning with the statement that they believed in the Nicence, Athanasian and Apostles' creeds, the preachers wrote of their belief in the original, sinful nature of man, of free will and grace, and of election and predestination. Discussing the latter point they showed that they were aware of the danger to Church discipline if it was widely known that men were predestined to salvation or damnation: 'It were best that suche articles be passed over in sylence (in dede we do thinke discrete ministers will speake sparrely and circumspectly of them . . .).' They included them in their declaration only because others denied their truth. 'A man is justified by faithe onely' says the next article, but fasting, prayer, good works and mortification of the flesh are worthy. Several articles thereafter deal with the Church and its authority and condemn Catholic beliefs about purgatory and Latin masses.

Only baptism and the Lord's Supper were accepted as true sacraments by the preachers, and they carefully elaborated their eucharistic doctrine. This article, designed to show exactly where they stood on the complex question, is worthy quoting at length.

> The supper of the lorde is not onely a signe of the love that Christians ought to have amonge them selves one to another, but rather it is a sacrament of our redempcion in Christes deathe, in so moche that to suche as rightly, worthily, and with faithe

[69]C.C.C.C., 121, 141-42.

receyve the samme, the breade which we breake is the communion of Christe, lyke wise the cuppe of blessing is the
communion of the bloude of Christ. So that in the administracion
of this holie supper we do not denye all manner of presence of
Christes bodie and bloude, neither do we thinke or saie that this
holie sacrament is onely a naked and a bare sign or figure in the
which nothing elles is to be receyved of the faythfull but common
bread and wyne, as our adversaries have at all tymes most
untrewly charged, and yet do we not alow the coporall, carnall,
and reall presence which they teach and mayntayne affirming
Christe's bodie to be sensibilie handled of the priest, and also
corporally and substantially to be receyved with the mouthe
aswell of the wicked as of the godly. For that were contrary to the
scripture, bothe to remove him out of heaven where concerning
his natural bodie he shall contynewe to thend of the world, and
also by making his bodie bodiely present in so many sundrie and
severall places at once to destroye the properties of his humane
nature. Neither do we allow the fonde error of transubstantia-
cion . . . . But we affirme and confesse that as the wicked in the
unworthy recyving of the holie sacrament eateth and drinketh his
won dampnacion: so to the belever and worthy receyver is verily
geven and exhibited wholie Christ god and man with the fruites
of his passion. And that in the distribucion of this holie
sacrament as we with our outwarde senses receyve the sacramental breade and wyne: so inwardly by faithe and through the
working of goddes spirite we are made partakers *vere et
efficaciter* of the bodie and blood of our saviour Christe, and are
spiritually fedde therewith unto everlasting lyfe.[70]

Rejecting Zwinglianism, strict Lutheranism and Roman Catholicism,
the preachers expressed a doctrine of the Eucharist that fell between
the reformed and 'crypto-Calvinist' doctrines of the Supper.[71]

Ironically, although their confession was designed to prove their
unity, the five articles that delineated the role of magistrates were
obviously written to assure the Queen that they had no sympathy with
the political ideas of John Knox. Special emphasis was laid upon the
sinfulness of rebellion and the assassination of magistrates, and it
was explicity stated that the Word of God does not condemn 'the
government or regiment' of a woman.[72]

The confession ended with a paragraph which, whether or not it
was honestly written, shows that the reformers were acutely aware of
the importance of appearing to uphold the Edwardian Reformation:

[70]*Ibid.,* 154-55.

[71]Haugaard, *Elizabeth and the English Reformation,* 266.

[72]C.C.C.C., 121, 158-159.

And although in this our declaracion and confession we do not precisely observe the wordes, sentences, and orders of certen godly articles by authoritie setfurthe in the tyme of kinge Edwarde of most famous memorie (for the malice of our adversaries hathe occasioned us otherwise, to whose wrongful disfamacions we must of necessitie make answere otherwise) yet in altering, augmenting, or diminishing, adding, or omitting, we do neither improve nor yet recede from any of the said articles, but fullie consent unto the whole as to a most true and sounde doctrine grounded upon goddes worde, and do referre our selves unto such articles there as in this our confession for shortness sake we have omitted.[73]

The preachers were reassuring Elizabeth and their public that the doctrine represented by the revived 1552 prayer book was correct and would be upheld by them. Their enemies could not accuse them of inconsistency.

We have followed the bills for supremacy and uniformity through the Houses of Parliament. It remains to examine bills concerning the clergy and religion which were moved in 1559, but which did not become law. Excluding the bills aimed at placing ecclesiastical land in laymen's hands, there were three. One, which would have created a committee of thirty-two persons to reform the ecclesiastical law, has already been discussed. The other two, which were both introduced before Easter, were the bill to revive the Edwardian Act for holy days and fasting days, and the bill to restore persons deprived for heresy or marriage.

The bill which would have revived the Act for the Keeping of Holy Days (5 & 6 Edw. VI, c. 3.) was introduced in the Commons on 21 March.[74] By or for whom is unknown, but it was undoubtedly someone who believed that, since holy days and fasts are for edification and worship, and are not holy in themselves, any Church has a right to determine, alter or abolish them as it wishes. The bill was much too conservative to have come from the radical end of the reforming party. Even though it reduced the number of holy days and fasts in the Church calendar, it required the observance of twenty-seven holy days, in addition to Sundays.[75] The evening or day before each of the enumerated feasts was to be a fast day, and abstinence from meat was required during Lent, on Fridays and Saturdays, and on any other days appointed to be kept.[76] This law would have been

[73]*Ibid.*, 160.

[74]H.L.R.O., Commons MS. Journals, I, fol. 204.

[75]5 & 6 Edw. VI, c. 3. 1.

[76]5 & 6 Edw. VI, c. 3. 2, 4.

enforced by the bishops who were required to use the censures of the church against offenders, enjoining infractors to perform the penance ordered by the spiritual courts.[77] The measure may not, however, have been sponsored by a religious faction. There is a very good possibility that the interests of mariners and fishmongers were more in the minds of its sponsors than were the dogmas of the Christian Church. Whatever its aim, the bill to enforce the keeping of holy days did not worry anyone very much. There is not a single mention of it in the sources that have come down to us. Its passage through the Commons was uneventful. Read a second time on 4 April, it was engrossed the same day and passed on the 12th.[78] Carried into the Upper Chamber on 14 April, it was read immediately.[79] The next day it was read a second time, after which it drops from the record.[80] Its death cannot be explained with any certainty. It may have been stopped by some group in the Lords, Catholic or otherwise. It is more likely, though, that it died of neglect. A minor bill, it along with many others may have been terminated by the Queen when, having finally obtained her ends, she dissolved Parliament.

Two attempts were made to restore deprived Edwardian clergy to their livings, ousting the Catholic appointees who had supplanted them. As early as 8 March a bill was read in the Commons which, had it passed, would have returned benefices to spiritual persons who had lost them because of heresy or marriage.[81] It was almost a month before the bill was given another hearing, after which it was committed to Francis Goldsmith. The problems that forced it into committee must have been serious, for it never reappeared. We can only conjecture about the content of this curious bill. The clerk's description of it hints that it would have restored all the Edwardian clergy deprived during Mary's reign which in theory would have affected a large number of men. In Essex eighty-eight incumbents had been deprived for marriage, out of a total of 319.[82] In the conservative diocese of York there had been fifty-three deprivations between March 1554 and March 1555.[83] However, most of those

[77]5 & 6 Edw. VI, c. 3. 3.

[78]H.L.R.O., Commons MS. Journals, I, fol. 206.

[79]Davis, 'Unpublished MS.,' 536.

[80]*Ibid.*

[81]H.L.R.O., Commons MS. Journals, I, fol. 199.

[82]Oxley, *Reformation in Essex,* 180.

[83]A.G. Dickens, *The Marian Reaction in the Diocese of York: The Clergy.* (London: 1957), 1-2.

deprived had been moved to other livings rather than ejected from the Church, so that the main effect of the bill would have been to supply jobs for the returning exiles.

The sponsorship of this bill is shrouded in obscurity. The only person connected with it is Francis Goldsmith who chaired the committee that considered the bill. All we know about him is that he also chaired the committee which considered the legislation that would have encouraged artificers to dwell near the sea in Kent. It would come as no surprise if, when the History of Parliament Trust publishes its volumes on the sixteenth century, Goldsmith turns out to have been an ardent Protestant. The bill to overturn the deprivations is the only genuinely radical bill seen in 1559, and its premature death may be an index to the support the exiles could muster.

Also derived from the attempt to restore completely those deprived for heresy or marriage, the bill 'that the Quene by commyssion may restore spirituall persons deprived'[84] was another move to get her to reinstate the Edwardians. The clerk also referred to this bill, informatively, as one 'to restore suche persones to their benefices as were unlawfuly deprived', and the exiles staked their hopes on it.[85] Edmund Sandys wrote of it: 'The bill is in hand to restore men to their livings; how it will speed I know not.'[86] It was defeated in the Lords after its third reading, and the returned clerics must have been bitterly disappointed. However, by the time it died the Acts of Supremacy and Uniformity had at last been passed, and they could look to the future with optimism. 'Not one of us has yet had even his own property restored to him,' lamented John Jewel.

> Yet, although this long waiting is very tiresome to us, we doubt not but that in a short time all will be well. For we have a wise and religious queen and . . . religion is again placed on the same footing on which it stood in king Edward's time.[87]

All would not, necessarily, be well, but in the weeks after the passage of the Acts the letters written by the returned exiles were full of hope. Popery was at last cast out, and they were home to stay.

So the ministers and the government could at last look forward to the future with some certainty. This was felt even by men as highly placed as Sir Nicholas Bacon. Early in the reign he had discussed with Matthew Parker the possibility of Parker's appointment as Archbishop

---

[84]H.L.R.O., Commons MS. Journals, I, fol. 212.

[85]*Ibid.*, fol. 213.

[86] Parker, *Correspondence,* 66.

[87]*ZL,* I, 33.

of Canterbury. Their correspondence had ended in March, with Parker awaiting a reply from Bacon to his appeal to be excused from that office. In mid-May Bacon finally responded with a letter which shows how uncertain he had been about the outcome of the government's attempt to push reform through Parliament: 'That before this time I have not sent you answer to your last letters, the cause hath been for that I could by no means understand to what end the matter mentioned in those letters would certainly grow unto.'[88] He knew at last, and it was a moment of relief.

There were, however, a few clouds on the religious horizon which prevented the reformers from basking too indolently in the light of Elizabeth's sunny smile. For one thing, clerical marriage had not been legalized. Although it had been included in the first attempt at uniformity, it was not in the Act, perhaps because Elizabeth had a pathological dislike of matrimony. No doubt this was reinforced by the widespread dislike of clerical marriage. The continuing illegality of their marriages worried the wedded ministers. '*Nihil est statutum de conjugio sacerdotum, sed tanquam relictum in medio,*' wrote Sandys, 'the Queen's Majesty will wink at it but not stablish it by law, which is nothing else but to bastard our children.'[89] Others were concerned that the newly restored Edwardian forms would not be energetically imposed; that religion would be treated as a tool of policy, not a beloved faith. The ornaments rubric and Elizabeth's moderation boded ill for pure religion. John Jewel expressed these fears.

> As to religion, it has been effected, I hope, under good auspices, that it shall be restored to the same state as it was . . . under Edward. But, as far as I can perceive at present, there is not the same alacrity among our friends, as there lately was among the papists. So miserably is it ordered, that falsehood is armed, while truth is not only unarmed, but also frequently offensive [hated].[90] The scenic apparatus of divine worship is now under agitation . . . [and is] now seriously and solemnly entertained by certain persons (for *we* are not consulted), as if the Christian religion could not exist without something tawdry. Our minds indeed are not sufficiently disengaged to make these fooleries of much importance. Others are seeking after a *golden,* or as it rather seems to me, a *leaden* mediocrity; and are crying out, that the half is better than the whole.[91]

[88] Parker, *Correspondence,* 68.

[89] *Ibid.*, 66.

[90] Although *ZL,* I, 23 says 'offensive' the original Latin makes 'hated' seem more accurate.

[91] *ZL,* I, 23.

Jewel and his fellows were soon going to collide with this mediocrity.

In his reply to the Speaker at the closing of the Parliament, Lord Keeper Bacon made it clear that the government was on the side of mediocrity and unquestioning obedience to the laws regulating religion. They were to endeavour, Bacon told the members of Parliament, to maintain the uniformity established by them in the session now ending.

> And here great observation and watch should be had of the withdrawers and hinerers thereof; and especially of those, that subtilly, by indirect means, seek to procure the contrary. Amongst those I mean to comprehend, as well those that be too swift, as those that be too slow; those I say, that go before the laws, or beyond the laws, as those that will not follow; for good government cannot be where obedience faileth, and both these alike break the rule of obedience; and these to be those, who in likelyhood should be beginners, and maintainers, and upholders of all factions and sects, the very mothers and nurses to all seditions and tumults, which necessarily bring forth destruction and depopulation; . . . upon these being found, sharp and severe correction (according to the order of laws) should be imposed; and that in the beginning, without respect of persons, as upon the greatest adversaries that can be to unity and concord, without which no common-wealth can long endure and stand. . . .[92]

Bacon's speech brought the government's policy full circle. The plans for the alteration of religion announced by the 'Device' had stated the same attitude toward those who wanted either to impede the established religion or advance beyond it. Even the language of the 'Device' reminds one of Bacon's speech; 'Strayte laws' and 'severe execution' were called for in the beginning to ensure the peace.[93] The *via media* had been created because keeping the nation tranquil was always foremost in the royal mind.

[92] D'Ewes, *Journals,* I, 34.

[93] B.L., Cotton Julius F. VI, fol. 168v.

7

APPROPRIATION OF ECCLESIASTICAL REVENUE, 1559

No study of the legislation considered by Parliament in 1559 is complete without some analysis of the Crown's attempt to make a profit from the Church. By the time Elizabeth came to the throne it had become an established Tudor tradition that the Church's lands and revenues could be expropriated by the monarch. True, Mary had piously attempted to reverse this policy by turning some of the ecclesiastical revenue back to its proper recipients, but it was a momentary aberration that had been strongly opposed by the nation. When Elizabeth acceded she looked to the precedents set by her father and brother. During the first two months of her reign the Privy Council investigated the problem, and as the Parliament progressed the councillors introduced bills redirecting the first fruits and tenths back into the royal treasury, confiscating the lands of the new monasteries and chantries, and giving Elizabeth the pick of the temporalities belonging to vacant sees. Acting on the theory that Mary had no right to diminish Elizabeth's inheritance, the Council set up a committee in mid-December 1558 'to understand what lands etc. hath been graunted by the lat Quene during hir reign'.[1] At the same time, steps were taken to determine the value of the temporalities possessed by the sees then vacant.[2] The records of the late Court of Augmentation were searched, the bishops were interrogated about payments they had received, and they were forced to prove their rights to their revenues.[3] One product of this research was a detailed list of Queen Mary's grants. According to it, she gave lands worth £3,982 a year to religious houses of her creation. Upon Cardinal Pole's institution as Archbishop of Canterbury she granted him parsonages impropriate, first fruits and tenths, and tithes worth £25,000. Counting the gifts made to secular persons, Mary gave away over £49,000 of yearly income.[4] Of this sum Elizabeth sought to recover some £29,000 — Mary's gift to the Church.

By far the largest source of income abandoned by Mary was the first fruits and tenths, and the first bill dealt with by the Lords in 1559

[1] P.R.O., SP 12/I/fol. 125. Here Lord Riche, Lord North, Sir Richard Sackville, Sir Ralph Sadler, and the Auditor are named. *APC,* VII, 28 has Winchester, Bacon, Riche, North, and Mildmay on the committee.

[2] *APC,* VII, 28.

[3] *Ibid.,* VII, 48. P.R.O., SP 46/125/item 1.

[4] P.R.O., SP 12/I/fols. 138-143. According to fol. 143v the list we have was copied in 1608.

was designed to return them to the Crown. It passed that House very quickly, over the unanimous protest of the peers spiritual.[5] Brought into the Commons and read for the first time on 6 February, the bill was immediately committed to William Fleetwood, the future recorder of London.[6] After Fleetwood's committee had worked on it for eleven days the bill, with new provisos, was read a second time. Apparently the House was still not satisfied, for it was again committed, this time to the care of Sir Richard Sackville of the Privy Council.[7] Three days later another proviso was added, and on 21 February 21 the entire package was passed by the Commons.[8] The Lords, after only two readings, agreed to the 5 provisos and sundry amendments added by the Commons.[9] The bill's mutations, however, did not end there. Three weeks later a schedule containing six new provisos to be annexed to the bill for the first fruits and tenths was passed in the Upper House.[10] Although it was unusual, these additions to a previously approved bill received the assent of the Commons on 22 March.[11]

A glance at the parchment copy of the Act for the Restitution of First Fruits (1 Eliz. I, c. 4) shows that a great deal of cancelling, blending and amending went on before it assumed its final shape. For example, the printed Act contains only eight provisos, even though the Journals tell us that eleven were produced — five by the Commons and six by the Lords. A diplomatic analysis of the original explains what happened to the missing provisions. The parchment roll in the House of Lords Record Office is the final copy of the bill, stitched together out of the pieces cut from the membranes of the original engrossed bill and the various schedules which bore the provisos. In all likelihood, the first two membranes, which contain the first, second and third sections, belonged to the bill introduced by the government in the beginning. Section 4 starts at the bottom of the second membrane and follows unimpeded on to the third membrane, so that sections 4 and 5 may also have belonged to the primary bill.

Up to this point everything about the parchment Act is proper, but at the end of the third membrane, which is a very short one, the peculiarities begin. At one time, membrane 3 was much longer and

[5]H.L.R.O., Lords, MS. Journals, IV, 5; 6; 8.
[6]H.L.R.O., Commons MS. Journals, I, fol. 187v.
[7]Ibid., fol. 190v.
[8]Ibid., fols. 191-191v.
[9]H.L.R.O., Lords MS. Journals, IV, 17; 28.
[10]Ibid., 35.
[11]H.L.R.O., Commons MS. Journals, I, fol. 204v.

contained at least one more section. Instead of letting this section stand, the Lords cancelled it and replaced it with a proviso, section 11 of the printed Act. This we know because, in order to leave room for a hem, the dropped section was left on the bottom of the membrane and a new schedule was stitched over it.[12] The eight provisos that are sewn to membrane 3 are all written on a single membrane in the same hand and ink, even though some came from the Lower House and some from the Upper. Moreover, although the sections that appear on the first three membranes have suffered extensively from the erasing knife and interlining pen, the membrane of provisos has escaped with only two interlineations, one of which is the correction of a scribal error. The conclusion to be drawn from this evidence is that the provisos added by the Lords to the already completed bill incorporated or replaced some of the provisos put in by the Commons. As a consequence, only eight provisos remain, all on one membrane. The clinching proof of this is that the eight were sent to the Commons for their approval, as the instructions at the bottom of the fourth membrane indicate: 'Soit baille aux Communes.'[13] The additions and changes made by the Lords were designed to focus and define the effects of the Act.[14]

Related to the restitution of the first fruits was a bill that would have exempted farmers and lessees of benefices from paying the tenth. Introduced on the last day of February, this bill disappeared after it had been engrossed.[15] Its death was probably caused by the realization that farmers leasing from spiritual persons were already exempted from paying the tax by the revival of 26 Henry VIII. c. 17 in the bill which returned the tax to the Crown.[16]

The bill restoring the ecclesiastical taxes to the Crown completed its passage two days before Parliament recessed for Easter. After Easter the government pressed ahead with legislation which would abolish the monasteries and give the Queen her choice of temporalities in church hands. The first step in this direction was taken on 10 March, when a piece of legislation was proposed which was called by the clerk 'The bill touching colleges and chauntryes surrendered to kyng henry the VIIIth.'[17] This description suggests that it would

[12]H.L.R.O., Original Acts, 1 Eliz. I, no. 4. The remnant of the section occupies two and a half lines beneath line 266.

[13]*Ibid.* This fourth membrane, lines 267 to the end of the parchment, contains sections 6-13 of the printed Act.

[14]Jones, 'Faith by Statute,' 223.

[15]H.L.R.O., Commons MS. Journals, I, fol. 194v; 196.

[16]1 Eliz. I, c. 4, § 1.

[17]H.L.R.O., Commons MS. Journals, I, fol. 199v.

have revived 37 Henry VIII, c. 4, for the dissolution of chantries, guaranteeing the rights of the Crown and its grantees to hold chantry lands. Five days later a bill 'touching the overplus of chauntrye lands' was read. It may have been the second reading of the previous bill, or it may have been a new bill intended to confiscate any chantries founded during Mary's reign.[18] Both these bills disappeared, and after Easter a new one was introduced: 'that all suche colleges and chauntryes graunted to kyng E[dward] the VI shalbe also in the Quenes maiestie.'[19] This bill, in turn, was replaced by yet another, which became the Act annexing monasteries, chantries, and other religious houses to the Crown. As its preamble indicates, it was predicated upon the Crown's supremacy over the Church and on the truth of reformed religion:

> certayn Abbeys Pryories Hospitalles Nunreyes Howses of Fryers Chantryes and other Religious and Ecclesiasticall Howses, by procurement of certayne persons meaning to reduce this your Realme reither to darknes and supersticion then to the true knowledge and honoring of Almightye God, in tyme of the late Quene Marye. . . . were restored or of newe entredd unto founded and incorporated; and divers Howses manors landes tenementes hereditamentes liberties franchises goodes chattels commodities and profits, all whiche or the most parte therof before and untill that tyme were apperteining to the imperiall Crowne of this Realme, have been given and assured to the same corporacions aswell by the late Quene Marye, (to the decaye of the possesions of the same Imperiall Crowne,). . . . whiche. . . ar nowe wholly and onely possessed and enjoyed by a fewe persons born within this Realme. . . [who] under the collor of certayne supersticious Relygions and professions, have not onely vowed professed and acknowledged them selfes to be subjecte and obedyent to forreyn power and aucthoritee, to the manifest derogacion of the . . . aucthoritee regall of the sayd Imperiall Crowne of this realme. . . .[20]

Making the assumptions its does, this bill could not logically be introduced until Parliament had recognized the Queen's claim to supremacy and the evil of Catholicism. The men who drafted it realized this when they wrote it, as the Commons recognized when they ordered it engrossed, for the scribe left a blank for the name of the yet-to-be-passed Act of Supremacy in section 4. Someone else, in a different hand and ink, later added the Act's full title.[21]

[18]*Ibid.*, fol. 201.

[19]*Ibid.*, fol. 206v.

[20]1 Eliz. I, c. 24, § 1.

[21]H.L.R.O., Original Acts, 1 Eliz. I, no. 41, lines 67-68. (c. 24 in *Statutes of the Realm*).

Whatever the theoretical basis for the annexation of the monasteries and chantries, greed lent its support to the Queen. Il Schifanoya reported that the bill was very popular: so popular that Elizabeth might not reap much profit from it.

> In the Lower House they have carried the Bill to expel all friars and monks, nuns and hospitallers, destroying everything (*et gia nella Casa Bassa havevano portata la cedula di cacciar tutti i frati e monaci, monache et hospitalieri, destruendo tutto*), and assigning the revenues to the Queen, who will gain but little in the end; for they all make demands of her, some for a piece of land, some for a garden, some for a house, and some for the fee simple of estates for their residence (*et chi il territorio, avero fondo delli luochi per accomodarsi*); nor can she refuse, not having anything else to give them, from the poverty of the Crown. . . There is no doubt of the Bill passing, as it favours personal interests, and also because they will not hear mention made of friars and nuns, whom they call rabble (*canaglia*). . . .[22]

When it was first submitted to the Commons, the bill for annexation consisted of eleven sections. These presented the goods and possessions of the religious houses and chantries to the Queen, provided for pensions for those religious who would take the oath of supremacy, guaranteed the continued legality of grants of stewardship and leases for the period of twenty-one years, and saved the rights of schools, colleges in the universities, and hospitals — all of which the Queen was empowered to reform. A section of the original bill also decreed that the Queen would be responsible for the debts of the religious houses and that all debts owed to them were payable to her.[23] This was changed by the Lords, who replaced it with section 13 of the printed statute, providing simply that 'all the Goodes Cattalles and Dettes dewe or belonging' to any of the houses should be applied against their debts. The remainder, if any, would be divided among the inmates of the house.[24]

It was introduced on 24 April. On 28 April the Commons tacked two provisos onto the bill and changed the date when its retroactive clauses took effect. One of the provisos enabled the newly ex-religious persons to sue and be sued, in the same way that Henry VIII had provided for them.[25] The other was made in order to protect the religious and financial interests of the legal community: it guaranteed that the stipend and wages of the master and priests of the Temple

[22] *CSP Ven.*, VII, 73.

[23] H.L.R.O., Original Acts, 1 Eliz. I, no. 41, lines 145-156.

[24] 1 Eliz. I, c. 24, § 13.

[25] 1 Eliz. I, c. 24, § 11.

Church would continue to be paid out of the revenues generated by the lands of the Knights of St John.[26] The Commons passed the bill on 29 April and sent it to the Lords, where four provisos were added. According to the Journal the bill itself was given its final reading, the provisos were read three times, and the whole package was passed. As we might expect, not a single ecclesiastical peer voted for it, and neither did Viscount Montague.[27] The Lords' provisos, written on three schedules, were concerned with protecting the innocent from injury. One, discussed above, tried to guarantee that the debts of the religious houses would be paid.[28] Two protected lessees of the Abbot and the chapter of Westminster from revocation of their leases.[29] The fourth proviso made certain that the Church of Great St Bartholomew's next Smithfield in London, which was the conventual Church of the Black Friars, would be returned to the inhabitants of the neighbourhood for use as their parish church, instead of being seized by the Crown.[30] Once again the Upper House had acted to soften the effect of a government bill.

The last public bill touching ecclesiastical lands and taxation was undoubtedly sponsored by the government, with the intent of improving royal finances and, perhaps, of giving force to a certain Protestant opinion about the role of bishops. Introduced in the House of Lords immediately after the Easter recess, 'An Acte giving Authoritie to the Quenes Majestie uppon thavoidance of any Archebishoppricke or Bishoppricke to take into her Handes certain of the Temporall Possessions therof, recompensing the same with Parsonages Impropriate and Tenthes,'[31] met resistance in both Houses. A short Act, it enabled Elizabeth to take lands, castles, manors and other temporal property belonging to an empty see, equal to the yearly value of the parsonages impropriate and tenths held by the Crown in that diocese. In exchange, the Queen would grant the affected bishopric tenths, tithes and parsonages within the see 'as shalbe of asmuche or more yerely valewe' as the temporalities taken.[32] Only the bishops' and archbishops' dwellings and lands required for the maintenance of hospitality were exempted from the exchange.[33]

[26]1 Eliz. I, c. 24, § 12.
[27]Davies, 'Unpublished MS.,' 541.
[28]1 Eliz I, c. 24, § 13.
[29]1 Eliz. I, c. 24, § § 14, 15.
[30]1 Eliz. I, c. 24, § 16.
[31]1 Eliz. I, c. 19.
[32]1 Eliz. I, c. 19. § 1.
[33]1 Eliz. I, c. 19, § 2.

Felicity Heal has shown that there is reason to believe that the government was trying, through this Act, to clip the bishops' wings and put their possessions to better use. For instance, Armagil Waad, in his 'Distresses of the Commonwealth', advocated that the bishops should be deprived of their temporal property. In its place, he argued, they ought to be given spiritualities worth £1,000 in the case of an archbishop and 1,000 Marks for a bishop. Although Waad urged that the lands thus acquired should be given to needy nobles, this proposal bears enough resemblance to the legislation enacted to suggest that the Council liked his idea, if not his purpose.[34] Cecil shared Waad's dislike for powerful bishops, seeing their wealth as a danger to the pre-eminence of the Crown and a potential source of royal revenue. In 1552 he had expressed himself about this to Cranmer, and in 1559 he strongly denounced wealthy prelates. Writing to the Lords of the Congregation in Scotland about the lessons the English had learned in their Reformation, Cecil said:

> if the prelacy had been left in their pomp and wealth, the victory had been theirs. I like no spoil, but I allow to have good things put to good use, as to the enriching the Crown, to the help of the youth of the nobility, to the maintenance of the ministry of the Church, of learning in schools, and to relieve the poor members of Christ, being in body and limbs impotent.

He closed his letter by recommending the example of Denmark, where Lutheran superintendents, paid by the state, had replaced the bishops.[35] Cecil's letter was propaganda — the lands Elizabeth took were not used for such laudable ends — but it may have reflected his personal opinion. Whatever its authors thought about the morality of clerical riches, the bill permitting the exchanges had a very practical purpose: it would augment the Crown's revenue. This was specifically stated in the bill's preamble.

> Perseyving howe necessarye yt ys for the Imperyall Crowne of this Realme to bee repayred withe Restitucion of Revenues meete for the same, and having assented and fully accorded to restore to the same Imperyall Crowne the Firste Fruites of [sic] Tenthes and Parsonages Impropryate, for thencrease of the Revenue Therof, bee also desirous to devise some goode Meanes wherby the said Revenue of Tenthes and Impropryate Benefices might bee in the governance and dispocision of the Cleargie of this Realme, being most apte for the same, in suche

---

[34]P.R.O., SP 12/i/fol. 66, and Felicity Heal, 'The Bishops and the Act of Exchange of 1559', *Historical Journal* 19 (1974), 233-4.

[35]Heal, 'Act of Exchange', 234.

> sorte as yet therby the sayd Imperyall Crowne shoulde not bee
> in any wyse dyminished in the sayd restored Revenue.[36]

It seemed fair, but in practice the bishops would lose money on the exchange.[37]

Like its near relative, the Act restoring first fruits to the Crown, the bill for exchanging the bishops' temporalities was first introduced in the Lords. Presumably, this was because the government did not expect any objections from the laity there, and perhaps because the Lords, unlike the Commons, were not swamped with legislation. As introduced, the bill probably consisted of the first three sections of the Act: allowing the exchange, protecting the bishops' residences, and saving the titles of strangers.[38] Section 4 of the Act may have originated with a bill, introduced in the Lords, which would have prohibited the making of spiritual leases for longer than the life of the incumbent.[39] Originally intended to revive or replace 28 Henry VIII, c. 11, 5, which limited the maximum duration of spiritual leases, it was subsumed by section 4. That section decreed that gifts, fines and conveyances of the bishop's temporalities made to anyone but the Crown after 25 January 1559 would be void. An exception, however, was made for leases no longer than twenty-one years or three lives from the time of the grant. By exempting the Queen from the limitation on the length of leases and grants, it guaranteed that only the Crown would hold ecclesiastical land in perpetuity.

On 7 April the Lords approved the exchange, in spite of the dissenting voices of all the men on the episcopal bench. Not one layman opposed it.[40] In the Commons the resistance was vigorous enough to cause a division of the House. When the bill's supporters had filed back into the chamber it was found that it had passed by a vote of 134 to ninety.[41]

There are several theories to account for the strong opposition voiced by the Commons. Neale, assuming that the Lower House was united behind radical Protestants, was convinced that the ninety negative votes represented the 'irreducible Puritan core' who 'would

[36] 1 Eliz. I, c. 19, § 1.

[37] Heal, 'Act of Exchange', 242-3.

[38] Introduced on 4 April. H.L.R.O., Lords MS. Journals, IV, 45.

[39] H.L.R.O., Commons MS. Journals, I, fol. 204v; Lords MS. Journals, IV, 46.

[40] *Ibid.*, IV, 48.

[41] H.L.R.O., Commons MS. Journals, I, fol. 209v.

not betray the Church in the interest of the state'.[42] William Haugaard, who assumed that Neale was right about the Puritans' control of the Commons, disagreed. He suggested that at least part of the resistance to the bill came from men who thought that their own interests would be endangered if the Crown had tight control over episcopal patronage. Men who lacked influence at court would be excluded from the enjoyment of Church lands.[43] Felicity Heale, however, doubted that men who were solely concerned with the danger that episcopal patronage would be controlled by the Crown would have voted against the government, 'unless given active leadership and encouragement by the Protestant group in the House'.[44] Lacking proof of the existence of a united Protestant party, we are led to believe that the votes cast against the bill were prompted by a variety of motives. Certainly some of the Catholic members followed the bishops' example and opposed it. Men who feared that the episcopate and the Church would be crippled by the exchange of lands presumably baulked at it, too. Antagonized by fears of shrinking patronage, some of the land-hungry members may have voted against it, regardless of their religious feelings. In the end, however, the objectors could not override the majority of the Commons who probably believed that royal control over the revenue of the Church was a legitimate part of the supremacy.

These bills recouped for the Crown the revenue lost by Mary's piety and added a little extra. They also provided food for historical speculations about a Queen and her subjects who spent half a Parliament seeking to restore the true religion and the other half casting lots for the spoils of the church.

[42]Neale, *Elizabeth I and her Parliaments,* I, 74-5.

[43]Haugaard, *English Reformation,* 154.

[44]Heal, 'Act of Exchange', 233 n. 30.

8

THE PARLIAMENT OF 1563

The Parliament of 1559 re-established the Anglican Church but it left several loose ends which were not tied until Parliament met again in 1563. Because of the strength of the conservatives in 1559 few teeth had been put into the laws defending the settlement: this was done in the next Parliament. Elizabeth's first Parliament was preoccupied with the transfer of Church revenue to the Crown; by 1563 it was obvious that something had to be done about the poverty of the clergy. These and other ecclesiastical problems — created by the new settlement or inherited from the more distant past — were dealt with in Elizabeth's second Parliament. Its actions cast further light on the events of 1559. Juxtaposed, the pressure groups in the two Parliaments stand out in relief. Look as we may, however, there is no sign of a strong Puritan party at work on behalf of reformed religion, even though we might expect to find one in 1563. By then the puritan clergy were restive enough to disturb the lower House of Convocation, introducing Puritanical proposals for reform of the Church. However, their lay followers in the Parliament were quiet, overshadowed by the bishops and the government, the two groups which determined the success of religious legislation.

Various clerics and laymen began to be troubled by precisian scruples shortly after Parliament dissolved in 1559. Kneeling during communion, the rubric detailing clerical vestments, keeping the communion table 'altar-wise' in the east end of the churches, and other reminders of Roman Catholic ways were required by the visitation injunctions of 1559, to the scandal of many. Shortly after the visitation Elizabeth's insistence on keeping a crucifix and lighted candles in her chapel further offended many of her clergy, reminding them too vividly of Catholic idolatry. These royal policies, however, did not serve to unite the reformers against her. Instead, whatever unity of opinion and intent they might have had was ruined by the election of several of them to bishoprics. Now they had to choose between their consciences and the influential positions offered them by the Queen. Many decided, like Edmund Grindal, 'not to desert our churches for the sake of a few ceremonies, and those not unlawful in themselves, especially since the pure doctrine of the gospel remained in all its integrity and freedom'.[1] Having accepted the responsibilities

[1]ZL, I, 169.

of a bishopric, men like Cox, Sandys, Jewel, Grindal, Parker, Parkhurst and Bentham grew conservative in the defence of the established Church. Some important reformers — men like Sampson, Foxe and Coverdale — refused or were not offered positions in the new Protestant establishment. Too few in number to be a major political force, these clerics were distinguished enough to make their unemployment a scandal to conscientious Protestants. Undistracted by political necessity, they formed a group which kept alive the pure ideal of a fully reformed Church, in loyal opposition to Elizabeth and her bishops.[2] Where they could, men of this sort introduced usages contrary to the orders of the Queen. Clerics married, congregations sang Genevan hymns, and the black Geneva gown was seen in the pulpits. The bishops, who were usually sympathetic, tended to ignore these doings when they could, and, thanks to Elizabeth's leniency, there was a period of uneasy peace between 1559 and 1563 which was aided by the widespread assumption that there would be further reforms made from above. It was understood that the 1559 settlement was an interim during which the nation was to be readied for the completion of the reformation. Not until Convocation met in 1563 did it become apparent that Elizabeth had no intention of going beyond the 1559 settlement.[3]

The clerics who came to Convocation in 1563 had diverse and often conflicting expectations about how the Church could be improved. The more militant members of the Lower House were concerned with liturgical and disciplinary reform; the bishops in the Upper House were hoping for a clearer definition of the Church's doctrine. The declaration of doctrine — the Thirty-nine Articles — was passed, but the Puritans failed to achieve their ends. Although approved by a healthy majority in the Lower House, the proposal for a 'book of discipline' and a catechism were quashed by the bishops who refused to act on them. Blaming the episcopate and Elizabeth for their defeat, the Puritans became disillusioned with the bishops and distrustful of the Queen's pious intentions.[4] Out of the frustration caused by the failure of the precisians' programmes in Convocation was born the Puritan party within the Church. The lines had been drawn and the resentment of those who sought a purer, better disciplined Church was focused on the bishops. This, however, did

[2]Knappen, *Tudor Puritanism,* 181.

[3]*Ibid.,* 184.

[4]The Convocation of 1563 has been well studied by William Haugaard in his *Elizabeth and the English Reformation* (Cambridge: 1970).

not come to pass until it was too late for the Puritans to carry their struggle into Parliament in 1563.

As a consequence, in 1563 the Lords and Commons heard numerous bills which would have affected religion and the Church, but none of the legislation they considered can be properly termed 'Puritan'. The proposals presented to them — whether they embodied reforms urged by Convocation, reflected the desires of the government, or attempted to solve pressing ecclesiastical and social problems — were moderate and did not reflect the thought of the Puritan clergy.

The Act 'for the assuraunce of the Quenes Majesties Royall Power over all Estates and Subjectes within Her Highnes Dominions' (5° Eliz. I, c. 1) was the most important piece of religious legislation seen in 1563. Put simply, this Act made it praemunire and, ultimately, treason either to claim that the Pope had any authority within the realm or to refuse the oath of supremacy. Introduced by the government, it continued the process of restoring England's laws to their pre-Marian state. Without admitting its parentage, its authors copied its crucial clause from the Act extinguishing the authority of the Bishop of Rome (28° Henry VIII, c. 10).[5] The penalties it ordered reflect the debt the statute owes to Edward VI's first Treason Act, which made it high treason to deny the supremacy or to uphold the Pope's authority in England (1⁰ Ed. VI, c. 12, §§ 5, 6). Mary had repealed these laws, and an attempt had been made in the second supremacy bill of 1559 to reinstate them. The Lords committee that considered the bill in that Parliament, however, mitigated 'the extreme penalties . . . for the gayne-sayers' of the supremacy, and they were not revived.[6] With the Catholic bishops deprived and replaced by Protestants, the government tried again in 1563 to strengthen the forces guarding the royal ascendancy over the Church.

The Catholics, although they no longer controlled the episcopal bench, were still a threat to the nation. Having taken the Protestant side in the French civil war, the English had become acutely aware of the danger represented by a strong Catholic presence in the kingdom. Consequently, Cecil and the other Protestant councillors wanted a law they could use to protect the Settlement and keep the peace; the Protestant public wanted revenge on the hated Catholics, and the clergy demanded that the 'caged wolves' — the imprisoned Catholic bishops — be killed. By the time Parliament met it was common

---

[5] Comparison of 28 Hen. VIII, c. 10, § 1 with 5 Eliz. I, c. 1, § 1 shows that the enactment was taken almost verbatim from the earlier law.

[6] Strype, *Annals,* I, ii, 408 and above.

172

knowledge that the government would seek a statute which would inflict harsh penalties on the papists.[7]

It is debatable how tough a law the government wanted, because the bill which was engrossed and enacted was not the one originally introduced. The paper bill was committed after its second reading in the Commons, and the committee rewrote it to such an extent that the clerk described the finished project as 'the new byll'. This new bill became law, and Neale has contended that it was much harsher than the government had planned, arguing that the Puritans in the Commons put in the rigorous penalties in spite of the government's objection. To support this he quoted Cecil:

> A law is passed for sharpening laws against Papists wherein some difficulty hath been, because they be made very penal; but such be the humours of the Commons House, as they think nothing sharp enough against Papists.[8]

Neale may have been right: there is no doubt that the radical Protestants wanted a severe law. However, there is evidence which indicates that the bill first introduced by the government was the harsher of the two, and that the new bill was softened in order to win support from the Catholic laymen in the Lords.

Our witness in this instance is de Quadra, the Spanish ambassador, who did his duty by sending King Philip detailed reports on the progress of the anti-Catholic legislation. On 15 February, the day that the initial bill was committed, de Quadra noted:

> It is announced today that Parliament has passed an Act relating to religion containing three principal provisions. The first is that all those who hold any office, stipend, or public charge, or receive any learned or ecclesiastical degree or any sort of benefice dependent on the Crown are to be obliged to swear the supremacy of the Queen in spiritual affairs. The second that any person who is held to be suspect in this particular may be compelled by the Bishop to subscribe to this oath, although he may have no obligation to do so on any of the above grounds. The third, that no person shall presume to defend, either by argument, conversation, or writing, the doctrine of the Apostolic See on pain of loss of goods and imprisonment for life for a first offense, and death for the second.[9]

[7]*CSP Span., Eliz.,* I, 291; 269; 279: 'since the commencement of the present war in France and the demonstrations made against the heretics in Paris the preachers here in every sermon incite the people to behead the papists, and Cecil himself and his gang never say anything else. If they dared I believe they would behead every Catholic in the country . . . .'

[8]Neale, *Elizabeth I and her Parliaments,* I, 117.

[9]*CSP Span., Eliz.,* I, 302.

The bill had not been passed as he claimed, but he had very accurately described the core of the Act for the assurance of the Queen's power.[10] After the rewritten bill was passed on 20 February he explained to his King how it had been changed, and why.

> On the 15th instant I advised your Majesty of the course of events here, and since then they have been discussing the publication of the law which I said they wished to pass against the Catholics. It was agreed to in the Lower House, as I already wrote, on the aforementioned date but not without some opposition and, to meet this, and for fear the Upper House would throw it out they have modified the bill as follows. The Lords and Councillors are not to be constrained to swear, since it is presumed that they, being pillars of the State, will hold no opinions contrary to the Crown. The other people who refuse to swear are to lose their personal property only for a first offence and are to be imprisoned at the Queen's will. They are to be punishable by death for a second offence, but their real property is to go to their children, as they say it would be inhuman to deprive them of all their estate, and if they were well brought up they may hold different opinions to their fathers.

Once again de Quadra had misunderstood the mechanics of Parliament, but his information about the bill was very accurate.[11] This report encourages us to surmise that the changes in the bill were made in response to protests against its rigour. In this light Cecil's comments about the difficulties met by the bill may indicate a struggle between the conservatives and those members who wanted the harsh penalties proposed by the government.

The debate on this was heated. In the Commons Robert Atkinson, a member of the Inner Temple, attacked it on the grounds that supporting the Pope was an offence in religion, not treason, and that excommunication, not death, was the ultimate spiritual penalty. With bitter irony he pointed out that the Protestant preachers had used this argument against the Marian executions. Then, he said, the Protestants had insisted that religion could not be forced on people, it could only be taught. Now these same Protestants were preparing to coerce men into declaring their belief in the new religion.[12] Atkinson's

[10] 5 Eliz. I, c. 1, § 1 makes it praemunire to uphold the jurisdiction of the See of Rome, the penalty for the first offence being forfeiture and imprisonment at the Queen's pleasure. Section 4 requires all persons taking degrees, holy orders, etc. to take the oath of supremacy. Those refusing the oath commit praemunire (section 7). The penalty for upholding the pope or refusing to swear a second time is the traitor's death (section 9). Section 6 permits the lord chancellor to appoint commissions to tender the oath to anyone he might authorize. Section 5 gives bishops the power to tender it to all ecclesiastics.

[11] *CSP Span., Eliz.*, I, 302. 5 Eliz. I, c. 1. 10; 14 contains the provisions he describes.

[12] Strype, *Annals*, I, i, 446-455.

174

argument was answered by the counterproposition that refusal of the oath of supremacy was a temporal matter, not a spiritual one. It was the duty of every subject to recognize the Queen's sovereignty, and refusal of the oath was a denial of her royal authority, which was clear treason. This line of argument reflects the rationale expressed in the bill's title. Incidentally, this speaker noted that only the penalties to be inflicted on nonjurors were arousing opposition and said that, in his opinion, praemunire was too lenient for first offenders.[13]

Cecil, 'when some of the members showed that the severity of this enactment did not please them', rose and asserted the government's case. As he presented it, the bill was necessary for national security. de Quadra summarized his remarks:

> Cecil . . . said that those who questioned the supreme power of the Queen acted ungratefully, and if she found herself embarrassed and troubled it was solely in consequence of her defence of the said authority, and her refusal to admit the authority of the Pope or the *Concilio*, for which reason your Majesty [Philip II], after having pressed her very urgently to send representatives, was now threatening war with her. He said the pressure was brought to bear by your Majesty because the Pope had hired you (this I am told was the word he used) for the purpose with three million in gold which he had paid your Majesty to make war on those who could not send representatives to the *Concilio*, but that the Queen was determined to die before consenting, and he therefore exhorted them not only to defend the royal authority with this necessary law but also to serve the Queen with their property and their lives as was their duty.[14]

This speech shows Cecil at his political best, skilfully playing upon the strings of nationalism, anti-Catholicism, hatred of the Spanish, and loyalty to the Queen.[15]

The final vote on the bill, taken by a division of the House, showed 186 for it and 83 against it. We may suppose that the eighty-three were Catholics and others who thought that the bill's penalties were too harsh.

The Spanish ambassador wrote that some parts of the bill were modified 'for fear the Upper House would throw it out'. In reality,

[13]*Ibid.*, I, i, 455-59.

[14]*CSP Span., Eliz.*, I, 302-303.

[15]Neale, *(Elizabeth and her Parliaments,* I, 119) has rejected de Quadra's report of Cecil's speech because de Quadra 'would almost have us believe that Sir William Cecil sided with the extremists'. I do not believe that this rejection is warranted. The speech is an extended explanation of the bill's preamble, and it accurately explains why the government wanted the bill so badly. Then too, if de Quadra's account of the original government bill is correct, Cecil was supporting the harsh penalties which were originally written into it.

there was little chance that the Lords would have rejected it altogether: the Protestant party was too strong. There were, however, many important laymen in the House of Lords who remained Catholics, and it would have been impolitic to force them into resistance. Consequently they were in a position to demand and get concessions. One of the leading Catholics was the Marquess of Winchester, lord treasurer and member of the Council. Winchester had voted with the bishops in 1559, and in 1563 he again came to the defence of his faith. Shortly before Parliament met he and other Catholic lords told de Quadra that although they did not have enough strength to defeat the harsh penal laws which were about to be proposed, they would try to prevent 'more harm being done than is already effected'.[16] On 27 January 1563 the Earl of Northumberland spoke his mind on the bill, which had not yet been introduced. He said that he thought the proposed Act was unnecessary, and that the heretics ought to be content to enjoy the property taken from the Catholic clergy without seeking to cut off their heads as well. He went on to say that 'when they had beheaded the clergy they would claim to do the same to the lay nobles, and he was moved by his conscience to say that . . . so rigorous an Act should not be passed. . . .'[17] Afraid for his own neck and those of his class, Northumberland undoubtedly had the sympathy of many peers. Hence the clause exempting peers from taking the oath: it was a plain attempt to get the support of these men. In passing it should be noted that Northumberland knew, more than two weeks before the bill was introduced in the Commons, that it called for the death penalty, which shows that the cruel terms of the bill were not added by the Protestant zealots in the Lower House.

When the bill assuring the Queen's power was debated in the House of Lords, Viscount Montague attacked it. Like Northumberland he insisted that it was unnecessary because the Catholics were not a threat to the realm. Then he delivered a veiled threat which, although it was politically astute, probably confirmed the suspicion and fear with which the Protestants regarded the Catholics. 'What man is there so without courage and stomach, or void of all honour,' he enquired, 'that can consent . . . to receive an opinion and new religion by force? . . . it is to be feared, rather than to die they will seek how to defend themselves.' Montague ended with an appeal to class solidarity, upbraiding those who wished to despoil the houses of noble and ancient men.[18]

[16] *CSP Span., Eliz.,* I, 275-276.

[17] *Ibid.,* I, 293-294.

[18] Strype, *Annals,* I, i, 442-446.

To no one's surprise the Lords eventually passed the bill, but first they added four provisos protecting the accused.[19]

The events surrounding the passage of the Act for the assurance of the Queen's power tell us that the government wanted the death penalty and wrote it into the bill they introduced in the beginning. In asking for the power to force men to take the oath and abjure the Pope they were not moved by a simple desire to kill Catholics. They were seeking a weapon which could be used to defend the royal sovereignty and the religious settlement attached to it against the sort of Catholics they saw active in the French Civil War. Undoubtedly many in the Parliament hated Catholicism for religious reasons, but many also feared it and its leader in Rome. The Pope was, to them, the head of a bloody-minded ideology which threatened Protestant princes all over Europe. Therefore, the bill against the Pope's authority cannot be seen as a simple indication of religious feeling. Patriotism, paranoia and political reality are all reflected in it. The resistance of the Catholics to this measure is also notable. As in 1559, they had fought to preserve some safe standing ground for themselves. In 1563 they were not as successful as they had been in the first Parliament of the reign, but their obstruction was resented by the other members who saw to it that the Commons would never again be bothered by papists. The Act assuring the Queen's power ordered that in future Parliaments all members would be required to take the oath of supremacy before they would be allowed to sit in the House.[20]

Ironically, when Parliament had established the English Book of Common Prayer as the manual of worship, it had by so doing, imposed worship in a tongue as foreign as Latin on the people of Wales. Manifestly against the principles of the reformed Church, this inequity was corrected by the 28th Act of Elizabeth's second Parliament. Ungraciously announcing that because the Welsh did not understand English they remained as ignorant as they were when they lived in popery, this statute ordered the Bible and prayer book translated into Welsh. Until March 1566, the Welsh could use a service in which the epistle, gospel, and Lord's Prayer would be in their language. In the meantime, five bishops were ordered to haste the translation to its conclusion: any of them who failed to co-operate were liable to a £40 fine. The Act closes with a flash of

---

[19]H.L.R.O., Lords MS. Journals, IV, 98. H.L.R.O., Original Bills, 5 Eliz. I, c. 1 shows that sections 15 (giving alms to offendors), 16 (peers to be tried by peers), 17 (only certain persons compellable to take the oath a second time), and 18 (killing of persons attainted for praemunire unlawful) were amendments added by the Lords. Section 18 was further amended by the Commons to permit execution of those convicted.

[20]5 Eliz. I, c. 1. 13.

cultural nationalism, ordering that the English Bible and service book be kept in every church for those who knew or wished to learn English.[21]

The Parliament of 1559 had been dominated by the fight over episcopal lands, and the echo of that battle could still be heard four years later. Striking this familiar note, someone introduced a bill in the Lords 'for the assurance of certaine lands assumed by the Quenes Maiestie from certaine Bisshopps during the vacacion of there Bisshoppricks'.[22] Designed to confirm the provisions of the Act of Exchange of 1559, it reflects the fact that there had been strenuous opposition to the exchanges, and their legality had been challenged. Evidently this bill met these challenges head on, avoiding the legal difficulties by legislating them away. The Lords, however, decided that the original statute was sound and needed no bolstering. Committed to a large group led by the Archbishops of York and Canterbury, the paper bill was tabled and forgotten.[23]

Anyone familiar with Elizabeth's first Parliament will recognize the name of Sir Francis Jobson on the roll of her next Parliament. Stymied in his earlier attempt to get some manors back from the Bishop of Durham, Jobson tried again in 1563. In mid-February the Lords heard a bill designed to end the long squabble and give him the land. Following the usual custom in such matters the peers appointed a time at which the legal representatives of Jobson and Durham could present 'what could on either syde be saide in furtherance or disallowance' of the claim.[24] The case for disallowance must have been strong, for although the clerk noted the appearance of the lawyers, he never finished the entry, and the bill was never heard of again.[25]

Tackling another problem bequeathed to them by the Parliament of 1559, someone wrote a bill 'for the collacion of bisshops of the Q[ueen's] presentment with suche ceremoneyes as of the tyme of K[ing] E[dward]'.[26] Either by accident or design, Elizabeth's Act of Uniformity had failed to include the Edwardian ordinal. Because of this oversight the Church of England had no legally recognized form for ordaining and consecrating bishops. The 1563 bill would have corrected this and put an end to the confusion the lack of an ordinal had caused. The need for a legal definition of the ceremonies used in making a bishop who had been presented by the Queen instead of the Pope was dramatized by Parker's consecration as Archbishop of

[21] 5 Eliz., I, c. 28.

[22] H.L.R.O., Lords MS. Journals, IV, 75.

[23] Ibid., IV, 81.

[24] Ibid., IV, 92.

[25] Ibid., IV, 96.

[26] H.L.R.O., Commons MS. Journals, I, fol. 236.

Canterbury. When, in the summer of 1559, the order for his consecration was written, its author assumed that the Edwardian ordinal was to be used: 'The order of K[ing] Edwards book is to be observed, for that there is none other Spirituall made in this last session of parliament.' Cecil, however, was not certain that such an assumption was correct, since the Edwardian ordinal had been repealed by a Marian Parliament and had not been reinstated; he wrote a note in the margin which implied his own uncertainty about the order of consecration: 'This booke is not established by Parlement'.[27] In spite of Cecil's qualms, the opinion of the anonymous author of the consecration order carried the day. Although the bill of 1563 was engrossed after its second reading in the Lower House, it then disappeared without a trace.[28] The reason for its death is unknown, but the most likely explanation is that in the opinion of the House it was unnecessary. The Church had been using and would continue to use the 1552 ordinal, even though it did not have Parliament's permission to do so.

The appropriation of the Church's wealth, including that of 1559, and the economic troubles of the age had created a crisis in English education. In an oration made after his confirmation as Speaker of the House, Thomas Williams complained of the dearth of schools and the spread of ignorance in the realm. He blamed both of these evils on the lack of church livings and preferments, caused by impropriators who refused to pay their vicars a living wage and kept the income from the parishes for themselves.[29] At the same time convocation was considering the problems caused by stingy impropriators. One proposal before the clergy suggested that holders of impropriated tithes belonging to poor vicarages in towns be forced to increase the income of their vicars. Another detailed a plan whereby the tithes would be returned to the parish, the impropriator given a yearly pension, and a commission established to ensure the clergy a living sufficient to their needs.[30] There could be no solution to this problem without Parliament's help, and so two bills were introduced which would have aided the poorer vicars. The Lords took the lead in this — almost certainly because the bishops were worried by the problem. The bill introduced on 9 March proposed to give bishops the power to unite parish churches which could not support their incumbents.[31]

[27] P.R.O., SP 12/5,/fol. 97.

[28] H.L.R.O., Commons MS. Journals, I, fol. 239.

[29] Neale, *Elizabeth I and her Parliaments,* I, 99.

[30] Haugaard, *Elizabeth and the English Reformation,* 178-179.

[31] H.L.R.O., Lords MS. Journals, IV, 103. H.L.R.O., Commons MS. Journals, I, fol. 242.

Limited, for obvious reasons of distance and isolation in the rural areas, to churches within cities and corporate towns, these unions could be made as long as the overall value of each combination did not exceed £24. A lengthy proposal — it was given to Justice Southcot to be reduced into two books — the bill passed quickly through its readings in the Upper House.[32] Presented at two afternoon sittings of the Commons, it never received a third reading there, even though ample time remained before the prorogation. At first glance its death comes as a surprise. Undoubtedly important for the well-being of the Church, it could have offended few patrons and it involved very small amounts of money. However, it conflicted with previous precedents and with William Cecil's plans.

The bill for uniting churches was last heard in the Commons on 20 March; on 30 March Cecil introduced its replacement. United in purpose with its predecessor, Cecil's bill (the draft is in his hand) gave the power to the civil authority that the other proposed to give to the bishops. His bill for the augmentation of small livings would have permitted a vicar or stipendiary to appeal to the lord chancellor or lord keeper for financial relief. Upon receiving such an appeal, the official would appoint a commission from the parish or county to investigate the complaint. If, after interviewing the patron and the neighbours, the commissioners found that the living was too small (less than 20 marks a year) they could arrrange to increase its value. This could be done in two ways. In cases where the tithes were adequate but had been impropriated, the impropriator would be required to return enough of them to provide for the living. If the tithes were insufficient, a tax could be imposed on the householders of the parish.[33] This bill, which undoubtedly had the support of the most influential member of the government, was rewritten after it was introduced, with the result that a new bill with the same title was read on 9 April.[34] It died when Parliament was prorogued on 10 April.

Cecil's proposal avoided two problems inherent in the earlier bill for uniting churches. One was that it retained the principle of dealing with each case individually, thus preventing a wholesale rearrangement of the parishes by the bishops. It had been the custom that an Act of Parliament was required to unite churches: Cecil meant to maintain that control and keep power out of the hands of the episcopate. The other was that it made the lord chancellor or lord keeper, not the bishops, protector of the poor clergy. This placed the weight of the secular arm behind the vicars in their attempts to obtain a

[32]H.L.R.O., Lords MS. Journals, IV, 103: 105; 106; 108.
[33]P.R.O., SP 12/28,/fols. 7-11.
[34]H.L.R.O., Commons MS. Journals, I, fol. 248; 251v.

just recompense. Adversely, however, this bill would have assured that little would be done to help those whose livings were insufficient. Many parishes had no curates because the incomes they offered were so small no one could accept them, let alone petition for redress and await the outcome. One is led to suspect that Cecil was not anxious to give the bishops enough authority to correct the problem.

In keeping with their desire for discipline in the Church the members of Convocation made another suggestion that eventually became a bill in Parliament. Both the 'General Notes' and the 'Articles of Government' debated by Convocation had urged that 'all Bisshops in their dioceses' be given authority over 'all exempte places and peculyers'.[35] It was felt that these unruly areas could be reduced to order by the bishops. 'Articles of Government' was the more moderate of the Convocation proposals, suggesting that the bishops' control ought to be extended only to the former monastic exemptions, leaving cathedral chapters in possession of their own peculiars.[36] 'General Notes' went further. It argued for the abolition of all peculiars, while Bishop Alley asked for the right to handle criminal cases and reform disorders within them.[37] To judge by the clerk's description of the bill that grew out of Convocation's deliberations, it followed the 'General Notes', sweeping away all the areas which were exempt from the supervision of episcopal officers. This drastic remedy, however, was not popular in the Lords where it was introduced. Committed to three earls, three bishops, three barons and two chief justices, it was tabled and never given a third reading.[38]

Only one of the many bills designed to improve the effectiveness of the Church machinery was approved by Parliament — and it passed in the final hours of the session. Intended to strengthen the enforcement of sanctions against persons excommunicated by the Church courts, the Act for the Due Execution of the Writ de Excommunicato Capiendo tried to coerce the sheriffs into enforcing the writs by making them returnable in the Kings Bench. The need for this legislation was tellingly described in a proposal submitted to Convocation:

> Foras muche as in these our dayes divers subjects of this realme and other the quenes majesties dominions, are growen into such licience and contempt of the lawes ecclesiasticall . . . that onlesse yt were for feare of the temporall sworde and power they wold altogether despise the neglect the same . . . [which are] often

[35] H.L.R.O., Lords MS. Journals, IV, 110.
[36] C.C.C. 121, 267-269.
[37] Strype, *Annals*, I, i, 476. Haugaard, *Elizabeth and the English Reformation*, 178.
[38] H.L.R.O., Lords MS. Journals, IV, 111.

tymes slowly and negligently executed, by reason that the writte de excommunicato capiendo, beying directed to the sheriff... is either not executed at all, or els so slowly, that thexecution of justice thereby is letted or delayed, and the partie excommunicate therby encouraged to contynewe and persiste in wilfull and obstinate contumacy . . . wherby the corrections and censures of the church do endure in great contempte, and are lyke dayly to growe into more, unlesse some spedy remedy be provided in that behalf.[39]

The proposal went on to petition Parliament for a law requiring that writs of excommunication be sent to all sheriffs, justices and other officials in the sinner's neighbourhood. All of these officials would be empowered to apprehend and imprison the excommunicated person, and to keep him incarcerated without bail until he submitted to the church and paid any fines imposed by the spiritual judge.[40] Acting on this suggestion someone, presumably a bishop, introduced a bill calling for the due execution of the writs.[41] Although dressed in legal niceties, it followed the Convocation proposal to the letter. It passed through the Upper House without a hitch, but when the Commons had heard it they committed it.[42] It appears that the lawyers in the House were not willing to grant such broad enforcement powers without requiring a clear definition of excommunicable offences. Accordingly they added a proviso which named the legal causes of excommunication, and forbade the imprisonment of children, pregnant women and the insane.[43] This attempt to enforce excommunication exposes the growing weakness of the spiritual courts and the devaluation of their penalties. Rarely used before the Reformation, excommunication had come into such frequent use by the 1560s that it was rapidly losing its terror. In an attempt to increase the effectiveness of the censure Parliament had revived the use of writs *de excommunicato capiendo* in the 1550s. The Act of 1563 was a further attempt to restore teeth to the ecclesiastical law, but it had little effect. As the century progressed the writs fell out of use because secular judges seldom treated excommunication as a serious offence.[44]

[39]C.C.C. 121, 280.

[40]*Ibid.*, 380-383.

[41]H.L.R.O., Lords MS. Journals, IV, 110.

[42]H.L.R.O., Lords MS. Journals, IV, 118. H.L.R.O., Commons MS. Journals, I, fol. 250v.

[43]H.L.R.O., Commons MS. Journals, I, fols. 251; 251v. H.L.R.O., Original Acts, 5 Eliz. I, no. 26. The proviso (section 7 of the printed Act) defines the following as excommunicable offences: heresy, refusal of baptism, refusing to take communion 'as nowe ... receyved in the churche of England', error in matters of religion or doctrine now received in the Church of England, incontinence, usury, simony, perjury in the ecclesiastical courts, or idolatry.

[44]Ralph Houlbrooke, 'The Decline of Ecclesiastical Jurisdiction Under the Tudors', *Continuity and Change,* R. O'Day and F. Heal, eds. (Leicester: 1976), 245.

Tightening the enforcement of the penalties for excommunication was one way of improving discipline; another was to increase the penalties imposed on various classes of offenders. Parliament followed this latter course when dealing with sorcery, witchcraft and sodomy. In 1559 the House of Commons had passed a bill which proposed to make these offences felonies, but it had failed in the Lords.[45] In 1563 the need for such a law was still felt, and when Convocation met its members heard suggestions that the 'penal statutes for sodomity, witchcraft, sorcery, and prophesying be revived'.[46] Moved by similar sentiments (and perhaps by the same men) some members of Parliament drafted a bill which revived the statutes against sodomy and witchcraft. Entering the Commons on 18 January, this bill was committed, rewritten, and blended with two other bills.[47] Re-emerging as the 'bill for servaunts robbing their masters, buggery, Invocacion of evill spirits, enchantments, [and] witchcraft', it finished its passage through the Commons in four days.[48] Received by the Lords, this miscellaneous collection was disassembled, turned back into four separate pieces of legislation, passed, and sent back for the approval of the Lower House.[49] In due time the knights and burgesses signified their agreement, the Queen assented, and the 'Act agaynst Conjuracions Inchantmentes and witchcraftes' (5 Eliz. I, c. 16), the 'Act for the punishment of the vyce of Sodomy' (5 Eliz. I, c. 17), and the 'Act agaynst fonde and phantasticall Prophesyes' (5 Eliz. I, c. 15) became law.[50] All these laws seem to be closely connected with the desires expressed by the Convocation, but in at least one instance they were more moderate than the clerics had hoped. William Alley, Bishop of Exeter, had proposed to his episcopal colleagues that 'penal, sharp, yea capital pains' ought to be inflicted upon 'witches, charmers, sorcerers, enchanters and such like'.[51] Parliament did not concur. Instead, the statute was more lenient than its repealed predecessor, 33 Hen. VIII, c. 8, in that sorcery, enchantment, witchcraft and other acts of magic were made punishable by death only when they had caused a human to die. This leniency contrasted

[45]H.L.R.O., Commons MS. Journals, I, fol. 222. Davis, 'Unpublished MS.', 538-539.

[46]C.C.C.C. 121, 337.

[47]H.L.R.O., Commons MS. Journals, I, fols. 218; 219v; 225.

[48]*Ibid.*, fols. 225; 225v; 226.

[49]H.L.R.O., Lords MS. Journals, IV, 88; 102; 106.

[50]H.L.R.O., Commons MS. Journals, I, fols. 242; 242v.

[51]Quoted in Keith Thomas, *Religion and the Decline of Magic* (Harmondsworth: 1973), 306.

sharply with the preferences of English theologians who had been demanding the death penalty for magicians for a long time.[52]

Several suggestions for reforming the Church's courts, customs and clergy were drafted into bills that failed. Foremost among these was a bill that would have required chancellors, commissaries and other officials appointed by bishops to be graduates of Oxford or Cambridge. Liked by the Commons, it met its demise in the Lords because prorogation prevented the completion of its progress.[53] Another bill, decreeing that sanctuary could not be used to protect a man from his creditors, was passed by the Commons, but it too died when the Queen ended the session.[54] Attacking another customary right someone presented 'The bill that all offendors havying clergye shalbe bounde to sue a pardon in the Chauncery'. Read in late January, this one died of neglect.[55] The same disease killed a bill asking that a new office be created to keep the 'churche books for weddyng crystenyng and burying.'[56]

The Parliament of 1563 was little troubled by Protestant radicals: as a political force the genuine Puritan party did not appear until the session of 1566 (if then). That, however, does not mean that religion and the Church were unimportant to the members in 1563. The existence of twenty-three bills affecting various aspects of the Church's relationship with society attest to their concern. Some of these proposals were launched by members who wished to finish business begun in 1559, while others were born out of the immediate troubles facing the Church. Many of them remind us that the Church was deeply entwined with the civil government of the realm: a symbiosis which had to be adjusted as the secular authority gained in power over the spiritual. After scanning the various proposals and noting their fates one impression remains. Some members were sensitive to some of the notes sounded by the Convocation in its attempt to strengthen the Church, but the more radical demands of the Lower House of Convocation were ignored by Parliament. Had the many precisians sitting in the Convocation possessed close political ties with Puritans in the House of Commons, there would have been more bills reflecting their platform. For instance, there was agitation

[52]*Ibid.*, 526. The 'Reformatio Legum' of Edward VI's reign recommended that *poenas gravissimas* be inflicted on magicians. *Ibid.*, 306.

[53]H.L.R.O., Commons MS. Journals, I, fols. 235v; 240; 246. H.L.R.O., Lords MS. Journals, IV, 119.

[54]H.L.R.O., Commons MS. Journals, I, fols. 234; 251.

[55]*Ibid.*, fol. 220v.

[56]*Ibid.*, fol. 237v.

in Convocation for the revival of the committee of thirty-two persons for the reform of the ecclesiastical law. Edmund Sandys even expressed a desire for Parliament to create a committee whose orders would automatically acquire the force of statute.[57] Earnestly though the godly desired it, no one introduced legislation to recreate the committee by Act of Parliament. Instead, members focused on the less radical suggestions of the clergy and legislated (or tried to legislate) matters which were peripheral to the central concerns of the Puritans. The bills which touched the Church in 1563 were moderate and empirical, seeking to solve social problems which were under the purview of the Church.

Although they were hardly radical, few of the bills touching matters ecclesiastical passed both houses. Over half were killed before their third reading, and most of their deaths occurred in the House of Commons. Whether or not members were acting under pressure from the royal government is a mute point; at any rate, they allowed them to expire. In sum, then, we see that a majority of the Commons were not much concerned with the issues of ecclesiastical discipline and administration.

Careless about the technical details of ecclesiastical efficiency, members could be moved to righteous indignation in defence of their religious principles if the right 'signal words' were used to galvanize them into action. One of these emotion-charged terms was 'superstition', which conjured visions of masses, idolatrous statues and ungodly practices, awakening within the Protestant an emotional response. The psychological power of the word appears in an unlikely place in 1563: the debate over the bill 'for encrease of the navye by fysshing'. The trouble began when Admiral Winter asked the Commons to consider some measure for improving the navy. The members promptly put him in charge of a committee to draft such a bill, and two weeks later he introduced it.[58] Designed to enlarge the reserve of ships and sailors available to the fleet, the motion called for a mandatory fish day in each week. The equivalent of a modern subsidy, the fish day created a guaranteed market for fish, ensuring profits to the fishermen and keeping the fishing fleet large. As conceived, the idea of the fish day was purely secular, but someone rose to assert that fish days were superstitious: they smacked of the Catholics' fleshless Fridays and would be misunderstood by the ignorant. The House's reaction was immediate and prolonged. Some members made such an outcry that the bill was committed to Cecil

[57]Wilkins, *Concilia,* IV, 239.
[58]H.L.R.O., Commons MS. Journals, I, fols. 225; 229.

who added a proviso to it and sent it back. However he had qualified it, it still did not suit the members who objected to its superstitious nature. The argument raged on for another three days before the final vote. Forced by the loud confusion to divide the House, the Speaker found one hundred and forty-seven in favour and seventy-seven opposed.[59] The Journal is not clear about what happened next, but it appears that immediately after the vote someone moved to amend the bill by adding a qualification which declared that anyone who maintained that eating fish on the new fish day was required for salvation would be punished as a spreader of false rumours. A majority agreed to this provision, and the bill was sent to the Lords, who passed it.[60]

The difference between the Commons' reaction to 'superstition' and their reaction to administrative reform confirms our earlier impression of the Commons in 1559. In both of these Parliaments a majority of the knights and burgesses were emotionally attached to a vague outline of Protestantism, but, unlike the clergy, they had no clear idea of what political form their allegiance should take. It was enough for them to support their Protestant Queen and resolutely oppose Catholicism. A Puritan party — as distinct from individual Puritans — had not yet emerged in Parliament. A look at 1563 further emphasizes the importance of the bishops in the legislative process. As in 1559, the episcopal bench played a key role in its House. Without their support religious legislation had little chance of passage — unless the government wanted what the bishops opposed. A third lesson taught by the second Parliament of the reign is that the radical clergy had little influence on the legislation introduced by the members. It was difficult to assess the sway they had in 1559, but in 1563, where we can compare their activities in Convocation with what went on in Parliament, it is apparent that they had not yet become the ideological arm of a political party.

---

[59]*Ibid.*, fols. 229v; 233; 237v; 238; 238v.

[60]*Ibid.*, fol. 238v. The qualification is now section 23 of 5 Eliz. I, c. 5.

CONCLUSION

This study began by asking whether the Elizabethan Settlement resulted from a compromise between a Puritan House of Commons and their conservative Queen, or if it was formed in a struggle between the Catholics and Elizabeth. Having sought an answer through the first two Parliaments of the reign, it is time to examine our catch and see what we have found.

The largest fish in our net is the Marian episcopate. The Catholic bishops and the few laymen who supported them played a central role in the creation of the settlement of religion. Reasoning from past experience, Cecil and Elizabeth underestimated the Catholics' unity and determination, resulting in a near disaster for the second bill for supremacy and the attached reform of religion. Only when that bill came out of committee shortly before Easter did Elizabeth realize that the bishops would vote *en bloc* against her proposed alterations. She was reassured, however, by the knowledge that the peers temporal wanted to revive the supremacy, even though a number of them opposed abolishing the mass. After some hesitation, she decided to prorogue Parliament, instead of dissolving it at Easter, and to weaken the opposition in the Lords. Among the moves made along this line were the Westminster disputation, the imprisonment of two bishops, and the preparation of separate bills for supremacy and uniformity. An attempt to defuse opposition in the Lords, these new bills were more moderate than the Protestants liked and the government wished.

There were also militant Catholics in the House of Commons in 1559. Few in number, they seem to have noisily resisted the return to schism and heresy. Led by men like the fiery Doctor Story, who became a Catholic martyr, they probably provoked a large portion of the long debate over the supremacy.

The members against whom the Catholics argued belonged to the Protestant majority. These people were patriotic, anti-Spanish, anti-Catholic and deeply impressed with the horror of the Marian persecution and the courage of its martyrs, but it would be misleading to attach a party label to them. Many were loyal to the Edwardian religious tradition, a few were Henrician or Lutheran, and some were enamoured of the Calvinist model. The more radical of these Protestants are often called 'Puritans,' but there was no Puritan party in 1559. Although they may have agreed on certain issues, it would take ten years of reacting to the Settlement and the royal policy before they could take political action as a group. In the meantime, they and the other Protestants in the Commons were willing to give the Queen what she wanted as long as it was Protestant.

By way of testing the supposed influence of the radical Protestants on the Parliament of 1559, the behaviour of the 1563 Parliament has been examined. Here again no sign was found which would indicate that Puritanism — as distinct from anti-Catholicism, patriotism and non-partisan ecclesiastical concerns — motivated members' activities. As a definite political force standing in opposition to the established Church order, Puritanism did not arrive in Parliament until 1571. In 1559 the radicals certainly voiced their opinions, but they were not leading a resistance to the royal plans.

What was this royal design? Parts of it are clear. From the day she received the crown Elizabeth was intent upon restoring the royal supremacy, reacquiring the revenue Mary had returned to the Church, and reestablishing some variety of Protestant uniformity. The question is, what kind of Protestant uniformity? Henrician? Edwardian? Lutheran? Calvinist? Her preference in this matter is eternally debatable, for we do not have enough evidence to give us an answer proof against appeal. However, it is most probable that Elizabeth intended to reestablish the 1552 prayer book (or a close relative) from the very beginning. The evidence for this first appears in the 'Device for Alteration of Religion' and Goodrich's suggestions. Apparently written in response to a request from the government, both answered specific questions about the best way to reintroduce the supremacy and alter religion. The 'Device' makes it clear that a prayer book would be the vehicle for the new uniformity, and, because it makes no distinction between the 1549 and 1552 prayer books, it is safe to assume that the 1552 book, the one last in force before the Catholic restoration, was to be the one to be reviewed by the committee of divines it called for. When Parliament opened Lord Keeper Bacon asked Lords and Commons to unite the realm under a uniform order of religion, warning them of the dangers of those Roman evils, idolatry and superstition. Complying with his request, someone introduced a bill for a prayer book — a bill which was almost certainly sponsored by the government. No one knows what prayer book this was, but, given the pattern followed by the other religious legislation of 1559, it was probably the one recognized as legal in 1552. This assumption is strengthened by the reaction of Convocation, which condemned it for the same reasons for which the 1552 book had been condemned. As the debate went forward in Parliament Elizabeth gradually altered her chapel service until, by Easter 1559, she was attending a service which closely resembled that of the 1552 book.

On a more abstract level, the political situation into which Elizabeth stepped almost required her to opt for the 1552 book, whatever her personal feelings were. Both the Henrician position and the stance taken by the 1549 prayer book were untenable. The sacramentarian debates of English Protestant theology had carried the nation beyond them, and the heroic martyrs of the Marian persecution had died to deny transubstantiation. Moreover, her firmest political support came from those who were least inclined to turn back the clock. Froude summarized her position when he wrote:

> It was impossible for her to sanction permanently the establishment of a doctrine from which the noblest of her subjects had revolted, or to alienate the loyalty of the party who in her hour of danger had been her most ardent friends.

Uncomfortably caught between the Catholics and the Protestants, Elizabeth gained elbow room by making careful compromises. Clinging tightly to the supremacy and the uniformity, she made some small concessions to her Catholic subjects without antagonizing the Protestants. In order to get the reform she sought through the Lords she had to abandon the harsh laws against Catholics that had been proposed in the beginning, alter the words of institution in the prayer book, and refuse to be called supreme head of the Church. The result was a religious settlement which kept the peace by avoiding precise and divisive definitions.

Religious ideals alone cannot, however, explain the actions of many of the men in Parliament. Votes for the supremacy were recruited from those who might benefit financially from the change. In the Commons some members were primarily concerned with obtaining lands they had lost when Mary restored the Catholic bishops. The wrangling they began filled day after day and seriously disrupted the parliamentary timetable. In the Lords the chance of personal profit seems to have brought conservative votes to the Queen's side. There were also important financial levers moving England toward schism. Queen Mary, in a fit of foolish piety, had, after a protracted parliamentary struggle, diverted the ecclesiastical taxes out of the royal treasury and into the Church's coffers. Although it was logical and even in theory, laudable, Englishmen everywhere had resented this move. The Crown was short enough of money without the voluntary abandonment of thousands of pounds of revenue — revenue which would have to be made up by the nation at large. Hence, in 1559 the bill reviving the royal supremacy was helped to victory by financial considerations.

The creation of the Settlement was not a simple process. It was a difficult political manouevre which might have ended in disaster. The Queen played her role well, handling dissenters and foreign enemies with great care, compromising with all sides, and doing the possible without demanding the impossible. In this she was aided by a kind fate (or the Protestant's God) which disarmed her opponents and covered her mistakes. Perhaps the greatest miracle of the entire episode was that Elizabeth obtained what she sought without either abandoning most of it or causing a civil war. After considering the welter of political problems surrounding the change in religion, one cannot help but admire the political sagacity and sheer luck that brought the reformed faith back to England.

APPENDIX A

MEMBERS OF THE HOUSE OF COMMONS BY COUNTY, 1559

From: P.R.O. E 371/402/fols. 1-7 and *Parliamentary Papers,* 1878, pt. 1,400-402.

Note: Parentheses indicate a deficency in the MS, that has been supplied from elsewhere.

	Counties
Bedfordshire	
Thomas Pygott, esq. John Seynt John, esq.	Bedford Co.
Thomas Leigh, esq. George Gascoigne, esq.	Bedford B'gh.
(Buckinghamshire)	
Henry Lee, miles Paul Darrell, esq.	Bucks Co.
Robert Drurye, esq. William Ryseley, esq.	(Buckingham B'gh.)
Paul Wentworth, esq. Roland Bracebridge, esq.	(Chipping-Wicombe B'gh.)
Arthur Porter, esq. Edward Oldesworth, esq.[1]	Aylesbury B'gh.
(Berkshire)	
William Fitzwilliame, miles Henry Nevell, miles	(Berks. Co.)
Thomas Weldon, esq. Roger Amys, gent.	(New Windsor B'gh.)
Thomas Aldeworth, gent. Thomas Turnor (?), gent.	(Reading B'gh.)
Thomas Wynne, esq. John Fortescue, esq.	(Walingford B'gh.)
Robert Bynge, gent.	(Abingdon B'gh.)

[1]Parl. Papers give Thomas Crawley, gent.

191

(Cornwall)

John Trelawney, esq. [2] Richard Chamond	(Cornwall Co.)
(Richard G)reynfeld, gent. [3] Thomas Hycks, gent.	(Dunheved B'gh.)
?　Moh(une?), esq. Henry Chynton, esq.	(?)
?　Myldmay, esq. John Coyesworth, esq.	(?)
William Sybbes, esq. John Corneshewe, esq.	(Truro B'gh.)
(Hugh Owen) [4] (Stephen Braddon)	(Bossiney B'gh.)
(John Bower or Bowyer) [5] (John Cosworth)	(Penryn B'gh.)
(Peter Edgecombe) [6]	(Lostwithiel B'gh.)
Nicholas Randall, gent. John Fitzwilliam, esq.	Saltashe B'gh.
Richard Raynoldes, esq. [7] Richard Forsett, esq.	Saltashe B'gh.
Nicholas Carmynolde, esq. [8] Digorius Chamond, esq.	Bodman B'gh.
John Tredeneck, gent. [9] Francis Goldsmyth, gent.	Helstone B'gh.
John Smyth, gent. [10] Thomas Chamblayne, miles	Camelford B'gh.
John More, miles [11] William Poley, gent.	Port(hbya) B'gh.
John Ratclyff, miles Ralph Cowche, jr.	(?)

[2]Willis, *Notitia,* III, 62 has Richard Edgecombe, esq.

[3]Willis, *Notitia,* II, 24 has Richard Graynfeld or Grenvelle.

[4]Willis, *Notitia,* II, 121 gives this. These names are not on the other two lists.

[5]*Ibid.,* II, 110.

[6]*Ibid.*

[7]*Ibid.,* III, 63 gives Thomas Carew and Thomas Martin.

[8]*Ibid.,* II, 64 has John Mallet and Francis Brown.

[9]*Ibid.,* II, 73 has William Porter and John Dudley.

[10]*Ibid.,* III, 63, omits Chamblayne.

[11]*Ibid.,* has only John Carminoo.

William Charneshewe, esq.[12]	
John Gayer, esq.	(Liskeard B'gh.)
Peter Osborn, esq.	
Adrian Poynginges, esq.	(?)
Robert Warner, esq.	
Francis Walsingham, esq.	(?)
Christopher Perne, esq.[13]	
Thomas Hussey, esq.	(Grampound B'gh.)
Dr.... Drurye, esq.[14]	
Robert Colshyll, gent.	Mychell B'gh.

Cumberland

Leonard Dacres, esq.[15]	
William Musgrave	Cumberland Co.
? Egleanbye (?), gent.[16]	
Richard Mullcaster, gent.	(Carlisle B'gh.)

Cambridgeshire

Roger Northe, miles	
Francis Hynde, esq.	(Cambridge Co.)
Thomas Ventryes, gent.	
Roger Slegge, gent.	(Cambridge B'gh?)

Chester (Cheshire)

William Brereton, miles	
Ralph Leycester, miles	(Chester Co.)
Laurence Smythe, miles[17]	
William Gerrard, esq.	(Chester City)

Derbyshire

Nicholas Langforde, esq.	
Thomas Kniveton esq.	(Derby Co.)
William Bainbridge, gent.	
Richard Doughtye, gent.	(Derby B'gh.)

[12]*Ibid.*, II, 24 has George Bromlly and Rienold Michamp.

[13]Willis, *Notitia*, II, 98 has John Pollard, miles rather than Hussey.

[14]*Ibid.*, III, 63 has Robert Hopton and Francis Goldsmith.

[15]*Ibid.*, II, 187 has Henry Curwen, not Musgrave.

[16]*Ibid.*, II, 203 has Richard Ashton, not Egleanbye.

[17]*Ibid.*, I, 209 shows Smythe and Gerrard sitting in 4&5 Mary, Thomas Venables and William Assechar in 1559.

Devon[18]

Peter Carewe, miles
John Seyntleger, miles
(Devon Co.?)

John Pollarde, miles
Richard Prestwood, gent.
(?)

Leonard Yoe, gent.
Nicholas Poynes, miles
(Totness B'gh.)

?   Champernon, miles
Nicholas Bla. . . yng, gent.
(?)

Gawain Carewe, miles
Richard Stroode, esq.
(?)

Thomas Wyllyams, esq.
Gerard? Tremayne, gent.
(Exeter City?)

Thomas Southcott, esq.
Edward Yarde, gent.
Dartmouth Clyfton Hardnes

Dorset

Giles Strangeways, miles
John Rogers, miles
Dorset Co.

Walter Haddon, esq.
Humphrey Mychell, gent.
Poole B'gh.

William Holeman, gent.
John Leweston, gent.
Lyme (Regis) B'gh.

John Moynes, gent.
Richard Chave (Shawe?), gent.
(Melcombe Regis B'gh.)

Thomas Fitzwilliams, esq.
John Fowler, esq.
(Weymouth B'gh.)

(Nicholas Throckmorton, miles)[19]
(John Malloke)
(Dorchester B'gh.)

(William Page, gent.)
Robert Mone, gent.
(Bridport B'gh.)

John Zouche, miles
Henry Coker, gent.
(Shaftesburye B'gh.)

John Parrott, miles
John Scryven, gent.
(Wareham B'gh.)

Essex

William Peter, miles
Anthony Cooke, miles
(Essex Co.)

[18]The Exchequer list includes Derby Co. and Borough under Devon.
[19]The History of Parliament Trust supplied me with the information about Dorchester.

Francis Jobson, miles
William Cardynall, esq.   (Colchester B'gh.)

Humphrey Ratclyffe, miles
Henry Goldying, esq.   (Maldon B'gh.)

Gloucestershire

John Seyntlewe, miles[20]
Giles Poole, miles   Gloucester Co.

Herefordshire

Robert Whytney, miles
Humphrey Conyngsbye, esq.   Hereford Co.

John Kerrye, gent.
Thomas Churche, gent.   (Hereford City?)

Thomas Hacluett, gent.
Thomas Conyngsbye, gent.   (Leominster B'gh.)

Hertfordshire

Thomas Parry, miles
Ralph Sadler, miles   Hertford Co.

Christopher Smythe, esq.
John Dodmer, gent.   St. Albans B'gh.

Huntingdonshire

Robert Tyrwhite, miles
Simon Throckmorton, esq.   Huntingdon Co.

Richard Patrycke, esq.
William Simcote (Symons), esq.[21]   Huntingdon B'gh.

Kent

Anthony Seyntleger, miles
Thomas Kempe, miles   Kent Co.

Edward Basshe, esq.
Thomas Broke alias Cobham   Rochester B'gh.

Thomas Fynche, miles[22]
George Maye, gent.   Canterbury B'gh.

[20]Willis, *Notitia,* III, 64 has Arthur Porter, esq. instead of these two.
[21]Willis, *Notitia,* III, 64 spells the name Symons.
[22]Willis, *Notitia,* III, 64 has William Lovelace, esq. in place of these two men.

Lancashire

John Atherton, miles Robert Worseley, miles	Lancaster Co.
Thomas Benger, miles William Fleetwood, esq.	Lancaster B'gh.
Roger Alforthe, gent. Richard Cooke, gent.	Preston B'gh.
Ralph Browne, gent. Thomas Smythe, miles	Liverpool B'gh.
George Howarde, miles Richard Chetwoode, esq.	Newton B'gh.
William Gerrard, esq. Thomas Bromley, esq.	Wigan B'gh.
Thomas Greenacre, esq. Walter Horton, esq.	Clitheroe B'gh.

Leicestershire

Adrian Stokes, esq. Francis Cave, esq.	Leicester Co.
John Hastynge, gent. Robert Breme, gent.	Leicester B'gh.

Lincolnshire

William Cecil, miles Richard Thymbleby, miles	Lincoln Co.
Robert Carre, esq. Leonard Irebye, esq.	Boston B'gh.
Edward Warner, miles John Sellowe, esq.	Great Grymesbye B'gh.
William Cooke John Houghton	Stamford B'gh.
Thomas Randolphe, esq. William More, esq.	Grantham B'gh.

London

Martin Bowes, miles Ranulph Cholmeley, recorder John Marshe, esq. Richard Hilles, gent.	London City

Middlesex

Roger Cholmely, miles Thomas Wrothe, miles	Middlesex Co.

Monmouthshire

William Morgan de Tredegre, esq. Thomas Herbert, esq.	Monmouth Co.
Moritius ap Powell, gent.	Monmouth B'gh.

Norfolk

Robert Dudley, miles, DnΨo Dudley Edward Wyndham, miles	Norfolk Co.
Thomas Hogan, gent. Thomas Waters, gent.	Kings Lynn B'gh.
Thomas Woodhowse, miles William Barker, gent.	Great Yarmouth B'gh.
William Woodhowse, miles Thomas Sotherton, Alderman	Norwich City
Edmund Gascoign, gent. Thomas Pooley, gent.	Thetford B'gh.
Thomas Steynyngs, esq. Nicholas Lestraunge[23]	Castle Rising B'gh.

Northamptonshire

Walter Myldmay, miles Edward Montague, esq.	Northampton Co.
William Fitzwilliams, miles Robert Wyngfeld jr., gent.	Peterborough B'gh.
William Carnell, gent. Edward Kynwelmershe, gent.	Northampton B'gh.
Thomas Knevett, miles Robert Saunders, esq.	Brakely B'gh.
John Purvey, esq.	Higham Ferrers B'gh.

Northumberland

Thomas Braye, miles Cuthbert Horseley, esq.	Northumberland Co.

[23]The writ returned from Castle Rising shows John Ratcliffe, not Lestraunge, to be the elected member.

William Warde, gent. Nicholas Purselowe, gent.	Morpeth B'gh.
? Ms. blank	Berwick B'gh.

Nottinghamshire

John Markeham, gent. John Maners, esq.	Nottingham Co.
Thomas Markham, gent. John Batteman, gent.[24]	Nottingham B'gh.

Oxfordshire

Thomas Bridges, esq. Edward Asshefeld, esq.	Oxford Co.
Thomas Woode Roger Tayller	Oxford B'gh.
Thomas Leighe, esq.[25]	Banbury B'gh.

Rutland

Jacob Harryngton, esq. Kenelme Wigbye, esq.	Rutland Co.

Salop (Shropshire)

Andrew Corbett, miles Arthur Maynewarynge, miles	Salop Co.
George Blunt, miles Richard Prynce, gent.	Bridgnorth B'gh
William Ponghyll, gent. Robert Masone, of Ludlow	Ludlow B'gh
Roland Lacon, esq. George Bromley, esq.	Much Wenlock B'gh
(Nicholas Pursell) (George Lye)	(Shrewsbury B'gh)[26]

[24]Willis, *Notitia*, III, 65 has Humphrey Quarneby, not Batteman.

[25]*Ibid*, III, 66 has Francis Walsingham, esq. in Leighe's Banbury seat.

[26]The ms. gives no names for this borough. These are from Willis, *Notitia*, III, 66.

Somerset

Edward Rogers, miles William Seyntlowe, miles	Somerset Co.
Edward Seyntlowe, esq.[27] William Robinson, esq.	Bath B'gh
? Ms. blank	Taunton B'gh
Thomas Dyer, miles Robert Myllyns, gent.	Bridgwater B'gh
John Ayleworth, esq. John Mawdeley, gent.	Wells B'gh

Southampton

John Mason, miles Thomas White, miles	Southampton Co.
Henry Weston, esq. George Rythe, esq.	Petersfield B'gh
William Wynter, esq. George Cobham, esq.	Portsmouth B'gh
Thomas Bekingham, merchant Edward Willmott, merchant	Southampton B'gh
William Lawrens Robert Bethell	Winchester City

Staffordshire

Ralph Bagnall, miles Simon Harecourte, esq.	Stafford Co.
(Henry?) Pagett, miles Robert Weston, LL.D.	Lichfield City
Edward Stafford, esq. William Bowyer, gent.	Stafford B'gh
Nicholas Bagnall, miles John Skevyngton, gent.	Newcastle-Under-Lyme B'gh

Suffolk

Winns(?) Hopton, esq. William Cavendishe, esq.	Suffolk Co.
Thomas Sakford, esq. Robert Baker, gent.	Gippewit B'gh

[27]*Ibid*. has Edward Ludwell and Thomas Turner, not those given here.

Edward Rowse, miles Gregory Coppyn, esq.	Dunwich B'gh
Richard Wynkfeld, esq.[28] Francis Sone, esq.	Orford B'gh
Clement Throckmorton, esq. Henry Fortescu	Sudbury B'gh

Surrey

Thomas Cawarden, miles Thomas Browne, esq.	Surrey Co.
John Eston, esq. Robert Freman, gent.	Southwark B'gh
John Brace, esq.[29] William Porter, esq.	Bletchingly B'gh
William Howard, esq. John Skynner, esq.	Reigate B'gh
Thomas Palmer, miles Thomas Stoughton, gent.	Guildford B'gh
Thomas Copley, esq. Thomas Farneham, esq.	Gatton B'gh

Sussex

Richard Sakevyle, miles John Carryll, esq.	Sussex Co.
Thomas Sackvile, esq. Humphrey Lloyd, gent.	East Grinstead B'gh
Edmund Wright, esq.[30]	Steyning B'gh
Henry Ratclyff, miles[31] Robert Bowyer, esq.	Chichester B'gh
Richard Straunge, gent.[32] Nicholas Myn, gent.	Horsham B'gh
William Denton, esq. Henry Heyes, gent.	Midhurst B'gh
George Gorying, gent.[33] Thomas Saunders, gent.	Lewes B'gh

[28]Willis, *Notitia,* III, 66 gives Thomas Seckford and William Yaxley the seats.
[29]*Ibid.,* III, 67 shows Robert Keilway and Roger Alford sitting.
[30]*Ibid.,* III, 67 adds Richard Onslow.
[31]*Ibid.,* has Laurence Arderne instead of Ratclyff.
[32]*Ibid.,* and the Parl. Papers have Richard Lestraunge, not Straunge.
[33]Willis, *Notitia,* III, 67 has John Caryl, not Gorying.

Richard Fulinstow, esq.	
John Hussey, esq.	Shoreham B'gh
Henry Gate, miles	
Robert Buxton, gent.	Bramber B'gh
Francis Knolles, miles	
Thomas Hennege, esq.	Arundel B'gh

Warwickshire

Ambrose Cave, miles[34]	
Thomas Lucye, esq.	Warwick Co.
Thomas Throgmorton, esq.[35]	
Thomas Fyssher, esq.	Warwick B'gh

Westmorland

Lancelot Lancaster, esq.	
Thomas Warcopp, esq.	Westmorland Co.
John Eltoftes, esq.	
Christopher Muncketon, gent.	Appleby B'gh

Wiltshire

John Thynne, miles	
John Erneley, esq.	Wiltshire Co.
Francis Newdygate, esq.	
Henry Clifford, esq.	Bedwin B'gh
Andrew Baynton, esq.	
Richard Kingsmylls	Calne B'gh
Edward Bayard, esq.	
Nicholas Snell, esq.	Chippenham B'gh
Walter Dennyce, miles	
John Aysshelye, esq.	Cricklade B'gh
John Yonge, esq.	
Edward Heynes	Devizes B'gh
John Story, LL.D.	
Thomas Gyrdeler, gent.	Downton B'gh
Ralph Hopton, miles	
Richard Palladye	Heytesbury B'gh
William Awbreye, gent.	
Henry Jones, gent.	Hindon B'gh

[34]*Ibid*., shows Cave and Thomas Throckmorton sharing the county honors.

[35]*Ibid*., says John Butler represented the Borough, along with Fyssher.

William Weyghtman, esq. Henry Sharyngton, esq.	Ludgershall B'gh
Lawrence Hyde, gent. David Cerney	Malmesbury B'gh
William Daniell, gent. John Younge, gent.	Marlborough B'gh
John Harryngton, esq. Henry Hart, esq.	Old Sarum B'gh
William Webbe, merchant John Webbe, merchant	Salisbury City[36]
Anthony Carleton, gent. Ralph Skynner, gent.	Westbury B'gh
Henry Bodnam, esq. Thomas Hygate, esq.	Wilton B'gh
Christopher Dysmars, gent. Humphrey Moseley, gent.	Wotton Basset B'gh

Worcester

Thomas Russell, miles Thomas Blounte, of Kidderminster, esq.	Worcester Co.
Francis Newport, gent. Robert Wyethe, gent.	Droitwich B'gh
Richard Bullyngham Guthlac Edwardes	Worcester City

Yorkshire

Thomas Gargrave, miles Henry Savell, esq.	(York Co.)
Laurence Newell, gent. William Syranude (?), gent.	Knaresburgh B'gh
William Strickland Reginald Seseley[37]	Scarsborough B'gh
Francis Kempe, esq. John Sapcote, esq.	Rippon B'gh
John Vaughan, esq. John Salvayne, esq.	(Beverley B'gh)
John Yorke, miles Richard Suney, esq.	(Bor)oughbridge B'gh

[36]Not on the P.R.O. list.

[37]Willis, *Notitia,* III, 64 has Henry Gates in place of Reginald Seseley.

Thomas Gynns, esq. Francis Wylstroppe, esq.	Thirske B'gh
Richard Onslewe, esq. Richard Assheton, esq.	Aldeburgh B'gh

CITIES

William Watson, Alderman Richard Godthorpe (Goldthorpe), alderman	York City
Anthony Thorrold, esq.[38] Robert Farrar, gent.	Lincoln City
John Throckmorton, esq.[39] John Nethermyll, esq.	Coventry City
Thomas Fynche, miles George Maye, gent.	Canterbury City
John Welshe, esq. William Carre, gent.	Bristol City
Nicholas Arnold, miles Richard Pate, esq.	Gloucester City
Richard Hodges, gent.[40] John Beste, gent.	Westminster City
Walter Jobson, gent.[41] John Onsatt, Dr.	Kingston-on-Hull City
Robert Lewen, gent. Cuthbert Blounte, gent.	Newcastle-on-Tyne City
Thomas Beckyngham, gent. Edward Wylmott, gent.	Southampton City

CINQUE PORTS

Thomas Warren John Robyns	Dover
John Franke James Hobson	Hastings
William Baddell[42] Ralph Hasilherst	Hythe

[38]Willis, *Notitia,* III, 64 has Robert Mounson, not Thorrold.
[39]*Ibid.,* III, 67 gives these seats to Thomas Dudley and Richard Grafton.
[40]*Ibid.,* III, 65 has Nicholas Newdigate, not Hodges.
[41]*Ibid.,* III, 64 has John Overall in Jobson's place.
[42]Willis, *Notitia,* III, 68 has Raddell, not Baddell.

Richard Fletcher Robert Marche	Rye
Roger Manwood John Tysarr	Sandwich
Godfrey Whyte Henry Vane	Winchelsea
John Cheseman William Eppes	New Romney

WALES

Anglesey

Roland Meredyth, esq.	Anglesey Co.
William ap Rees ap Howell, esq.	Beaumaris B'gh

Brecon

Roger Vaughan, miles	Brecon Co.
Roland Vaughan, esq.	Brecon B'gh

Cardigan

Harry Johnes, miles	Cardigan Co.
Thomas Phayer, esq.	Cardigan B'gh

Carmarthen

Richard Johns, esq., of the parish of Abergwylly, Co. Carmarthen	Carmarthen Co.
John Parrye, or ap Harry, gent.	Carmarthen B'gh

Carnarvon

Robert ap Hughe, esq.[43]	Carnarvon Co.
Maurice Davyes, gent.[44]	Carnarvon B'gh

[43]Willis, *Notitia,* III, 68 has Maurice Wynn.
[44]*Ibid.* has John Harrington.

Denbigh

John Salesburye de Maghrubed, esq.[45]	Denbigh Co.
Simon Thelwall, esq.	Denbigh B'gh

Flint

John Gruffyth, esq.	Flint Co.
John Hanmer, esq.	Flint B'gh

Glamorgan

William Herbert, esq., of Swansea	Glamorgan Co.
David Evans, esq.	Cardiff B'gh

Merioneth

John Wyn' ap Cadwalader, esq.	Merioneth Co.

Montgomery

Edward Herbert, esq.	Montgomery Co.
John Man, esq.	Montgomery B'gh

Pembroke

William Phyllypes, esq., of Pycton	Pembroke Co.
Henry Doddes, gent.	Pembroke B'gh
Hugh Harris, gent.	Haverfordwest B'gh

Radnor

Thomas Lewis, esq., of Harpton	Radnor Co.
Robert Vaughan	Radnor B'gh

[45]*Ibid.* has Robert ap Hugh.

APPENDIX B

MEMBERS OF PARLIAMENT, 1559

This list should be used in conjunction with the geographical break-down of the membership, where variations and other problems are noted. The orthography followed here is that of the Exchequer roll. Since sixteenth-century spelling was not standardized, the reader is urged to check various spellings for the name he is seeking.

Aldeworth, Thomas, gent. — Reading B'gh, Berks.
Alforthe, Roger-Preston B'gh, Lancs.
Amyce, Robert — New Windsor B'gh, Berks.
Arnold, Nicholas, miles — Gloucester B'gh, Gloucs.
Asshefelde, Edmund, esq. — Oxford Co.
Assheton, Richard, esq. — Aldeburgh B'gh, York.
Atherton, John, miles — Lancaster Co.
Awbreye, William, gent. — Hindon B'gh, Wilts.
Ayleworth, John, esq. — Wells, City, Somerset
Aysshelye, John, esq. — Cricklade B'gh, Wilts.
Baddell, William — Hythe, Cinque Ports
Bagenall, Nicholas, miles — Newcastle-Under-Lyme, B'gh, Staffs.
Bagnall, Ralphe, miles — Stafford Co.
Bainbridge, William, gent. — Derby B'gh, Derby
Baker, Robert, gent. — Ipswich B'gh, Suff.
Barker, William, gent. — Great Yarmouth B'gh, Norfolk.
Basshe, Edward, esq. — Rochester B'gh, Kent.
Batteman, John, gent. — Nottingham B'gh, Notts.
Bayard, Edward, esq. — Chippenham B'gh, Wilts.
Baynton, Andrew, esq. — Calne B'gh, Wilts.
Beckyngham, Thomas, gent. — Southampton B'gh, Southampton.
Benger, Thomas, miles — Lancaster B'gh, Lancs.
Beste, John, gent. — Westminster City
Bethell, Robert — Winchester City, Southampton.
Bla..yng, Nicholas, gent. —
Blounte, Cuthbert — Newcastle-on-Tyne B'gh, N'umberland.
Blounte, Thomas, of Kidderminster, esq. — Worcester Co.
Blunt, George, miles — Bridgnorth B'gh, Salop.
Bodnam, Henry, esq. — Wilton B'gh, Wilts.
Bower, John — Penryn B'gh. Cornwall.
Bowes, Martin, miles — London City.
Bowyer, Robert, esq. — Chichester B'gh, Sussex.
Bowyer, William — Stafford B'gh, Staffordshire.
Brace, John, esq. — Bletchingly B'gh, Surrey.

Bracebridge, Roland, esq. — Chipping Wicombe B'gh, Bucks.
Braddon, Stephen — Bossiney B'gh, Cornwall
Braye, Thomas, miles — Northumberland Co.
Breme, Robert — Leicester B'gh, Leicester.
Brereton, William, miles — Chester Co.
Bridges, Thomas, esq. — Oxford Co.
Broke, Thomas, alias Cobham — Rochester B'gh, Kent.
Bromley, George, esq. — Much Wenlock B'gh, Salop.
Bromley, Thomas, esq. — Wigan B'gh, Lancs.
Browne, Ralph, gent. — Liverpool B'gh, Lancs.
Browne, Thomas, esq. — Surrey Co.
Bullyngham, Richard — Worcester City, Worcs.
Buxton, Robert, gent. — Bramber B'gh, Sussex.
Bynge, Robert, gent. — Abingdon B'gh, Berks.
Cardynall, William, esq. — Colchester B'gh, Essex.
Carewe, Gawain, miles —
Carewe, Peter, miles — Devon Co. (?)
Carleton, Anthony, gent. — Westbury B'gh, Wilts.
Carmynolde, Nicholas, esq. — Bodman B'gh, Cornwall.
Carnell, William, gent. — Northampton B'gh, N'hampton.
Carneshewe, William, esq. — Liskeard B'gh, Cornwall
Carre, Robert, esq. — Boston B'gh, Lincs.
Carre, William, gent. — Bristol City, Essex.
Carryll, John, esq. — Sussex Co.
Cave, Ambrose, miles — Warwick Co.
Cave, Francis, esq. — Leicester Co.
Cavendishe, William, esq. — Suffolk Co.
Cawarden, Thomas, miles — Surrey Co.
Cecil, William, miles — Lincoln Co.
Cerney, David — Malmesbury B'gh, Wilts.
Chamblayne, Thomas, miles — Camelford B'gh, Cornwall
Chamond, Digorius, esq. — Bodman B'gh, Cornwall
Chamond, Richard — Corwall Co.
Champernon, ?, miles —
Chave (Shave?), Richard, gent. — Melcombe Regis, Dors.
Cheseman, John — New Romney, Cinque Ports.
Chetwoode, Richard, esq. — Newton B'gh, Lancs.
Cholmely, Roger, miles — Middlesex Co.
Cholmeley, Ranulph — London City
Churche, Thomas gent. — Hereford City (?)
Chynton, Henry, esq. —
Clifford, Henry, esq. — Bedwin B'gh, Wilts.
Cobham, George, esq. — Portsmouth B'gh, S'hampton.
Coker, Henry, gent. — Shaftesbury B'gh, Dors.

Colshyll, Robert, gent. — Mychell B'gh, Cornwall
Conyngesbye, Humphrey, esq. — Hereford Co.
Conyngesby, Thomas, gent. — Leominster B'gh, Hereford.
Cooke, Anthony, miles — Essex Co.
Cooke, Richard, gent. — Preston B'gh, Lancs.
Cooke, William, — Stamford B'gh, Lincs.
Copley, Thomas, esq. — Gatton B'gh, Surrey
Coppyn, Gregory, esq. — Dunwich B'gh, Suffolk
Corbett, Andrew, miles — Salop Co.
Corneshewe, John, esq. — Truro B'gh, Cornwall
Corbett, Andrew, miles — Salop, Co.
Corneshewe, John, esq. — Truro B'gh, Cornwall
Cosworth, John — Penryn B'gh, Cornwall
Cowche, Ralph Jr.
Coyesworth, John, esq.
Dacres, Leonard, esq. — Cumberland Co.
Daniell, William, gent. — Marlborough B'gh, Wilts.
Darrell, Paul, esq. — Bucks Co.
Davyes, Maurice, gent. — Carnarvon B'gh, Carnarvon
Dennyce, Walter, miles — Cricklade B'gh, Wilts.
Denton, William, esq. — Midhurst B'gh, Sussex.
Digbye, Kenelme, esq. — Rutland Co.
Doddes, Henry, gent. — Pembroke B'gh, Pembs.
Dodmer, John, gent. — St. Albans B'gh, Herts.
Doughtye, Richard, gent. — Derby, B'gh, Derby
Drurye, Dr...?., esq. — Mychell B'gh, Cornwall
Drurye, Robert, esq. — Buckingham B'gh
Dudley Robert, miles 'Dno Dudley' — Norfolk Co.
Dyer, Thomas, miles — Bridgwater B'gh, Somerset
Dysmars, Christopher, gent. — Wotton Basset B'gh, Wilts.
Edgecombe, Peter — Lostwithiel B'gh, Cornwall
Edwardes, Guthlac — Worcester City, Worcs.
Egleanbye, ?., gent. — Carlisle B'gh, Cumberland
Eltoftes, John, esq. — Appleby B'gh, Westmorland.
Eppes, William — New Romney, Cinque Ports.
Erneley, John esq. — Southwark B'gh, Surrey.
Evans, David, gent. — Cardiff B'gh, Cardiff.
Farneham, Thomas, esq. — Gatton B'gh, Surrey.
Farrare, Robert, gent. — Lincoln City
Fitzwilliam, John, esq. —
Fitzwilliams, William, miles — Berkshire Co.
Fitzwilliams, William, miles — Peterborough City, N'hampton.
Fletcher, Richard — Rye, Cinque Ports.
Fletewood, William, gent. — Lancaster B'gh, Lancs.

Forsett, Richard, esq. — Saltashe B'gh, Cornwall
Fortescu, Henry — Sudbury B'gh, Suffolk.
Fortescue, John, — Wallingford B'gh, Berks.
Fowler, John, esq. — Weymouth B'gh, Dorset.
Franke, John — Hastings, Cinque Ports.
Freman, Robert, gent. — Southwark B'gh, Surrey.
Fulinstow, Richard, esq. — Shoreham B'gh, Sussex.
Fynche, Thomas, miles — Canterbury City
Fyssher, Thomas, esq. — Warwick B'gh, Warwick.
Gate, Henry, miles, — Bramber B'gh, Sussex.
Gargrave, Thomas, miles — York Co.
Gascoign, Edward, gent. — Thetford B'gh, Norfolk.
Gascoigne, George, esq. — Bedford B'gh, Bedford.
Gaskeyn, Edmund, gent. — Thetford B'gh, Norfolk.
Gayer, John, esq. — Liskeard B'gh, Cornwall
Gerrard, William, esq. — Chester City, Chester.
Gerrard, William, esq. — Wigan B'gh, Lancs.
Godthorpe, Richard, alderman — York City
Goldsmyth, Fancis, gent. — Helstone B'gh, Cornwall
Goldying, Henry, esq. — Maldon B'gh, Essex.
Gorying, George, gent. — Lewes B'gh, Sussex
Greneacre, Thomas, esq. — Clitheroe B'gh, Lancs
Greynfeld, Richard, gent. — Dunheved B'gh, Cornwall
Gruffyth, John, esq. — Flint Co.
Grydeler, Thomas, gent. — Downton B'gh, Wilts.
Hackluett, Thomas, esq. — Leominster B'gh, Hereford.
Haddon, Walter, esq. — Poole B'gh, Dors.
Hanmer, John, esq. — Fline B'gh, Flint
Harecourt, Simon, esq. — Stafford Co.
Harris, Hugh, gent. — Haverfordwest B'gh, Pembroke.
Harryngton, Jacob, esq. — Rutland Co.
Harryngton, John, esq. — Old Sarum B'gh, Wilts.
Hart, Henry, esq. — Old Sarum B'gh, Wilts.
Hasilherst, Ralph — Hythe, Cinque Ports.
Hastynge, John — Leicester B'gh, Leics.
Hennege, Thomas, esq — Arundel B'gh, Sussex
Herbert, Edward, esq. — Montgomery Co.
Herbert, Thomas, esq. — Monmouth Co.
Herbert, William, esq. — Glamorgan Co.
Heyes, Henry, gent. — Midhurst B'gh, Sussex
Heynes, Edward — Devizes B'gh, Wilts.
Hilles, Richard, gent. — London City
Hobson, James — Hastings, Cinque Ports.
Hodges, Richard, gent. — Westminster City.

Hogan, Thomas, gent. — Kings, Lynn B'gh, Norfolk.
Holeman, William — Dorchester B'gh, Dorset
Hopton, Ralph, miles — Heytesbury B'gh, Wilts.
Hopton, (Winns?), esq. — Suffolk Co.
Horseley, Cuthbert, esq. — Northumberland Co.
Horton, Walter, esq. — Clitheroe B'gh, Lancs.
Houghton, John, gent. — Stamford B'gh, Lincs.
Howarde, George, miles — Newton B'gh, Lancs.
Howard, William, esq. — Reigate B'gh, Surrey.
Hughe, Robert ap, esq. — Carnarvon Co
Hussey, John, esq. — Shoreham B'gh, Sussex.
Hussey, Thomas, esq. — Grampound B'gh, Cornwall
Hycks, Thomas, gent. — Dunheved B'gh, Cornwall.
Hyde, Lawrence, gent. — Malmesbury B'gh, Wilts.
Hygate, Thomas, esq. — Wilton B'gh, Wilts.
Hynde, Francis, esq. — Cambridge Co.
Irebye, Leonard, esq. — Boston B'gh, Lincs.
Jobson, Francis, miles — Colchester B'gh, Essex.
Jobson, Walter, gent. — Kingston-on-Hull City
Johns, Richard, esq. — Carmarthon Co.
Johnes, Harry, miles — Cardigan Co.
Jones, Henry, gent. — Hindon B'gh, Wilts.
Kempe, Francis, esq. — Rippon B'gh, York.
Kempe, Thomas, miles — Kent Co.
Kerrye, John, gent. — Hereford City (?)
Kingsmylls, Richard — Calne B'gh, Wilts.
Knevett, Thomas, miles — Brakley B'gh, N'hampton
Kniveton, Thomas, esq. — Derby Co.
Knolles, Francis, miles — Arundel B'gh, Sussex.
Knyston, Thomas, esq. —
Kynwelmershe, Edmund, gent. — Northampton B'gh, N'hampton.
Lacon, Roland, esq. — Much Wenlock B'gh, Salop.
Lancaster, Lancelot, esq. — Westmorland Co.
Langforde, Nicholas, esq. — Derby Co.
Lawrens, William — Winchester City, S'hampton.
Lee, Henry, miles — Bucks Co.
Leigh, Thomas, esq. — Bedford B'gh, Beds.
Leighe, Thomas, esq. — Banbury B'gh, Oxford.
Lestraunge, Nicholas, — Castle Rising B'gh, Norff.
Lewis, Thomas, esq. — Radnor Co.
Lewen, Robert — Newcastle-on-Tyne City.
Leweston, John, gent. — Lyme (Regis) B'gh, Dorset
Leycester, Ralph, miles — Chester Co.
Lloyd, Humphrey, gent. — East Grinstead B'gh, Sussex.

Lucye, Thomas, esq. — Warwick Co.
Lye, George — Shrewsbury B'gh.
Malloke, John, gent. — Dorchester B'gh, Dors.
Man, John, esq. — Montgomery B'gh, Montgomery
Maners, John, esq. Nottingham Co.
Manwood, Roger — Sandwich, Cinque Ports.
Marche, Robert — Rye, Cinque Ports.
Markham, Thomas, gent. — Nottingham B'gh.
Markeham, John, gent. — Nottingham Co.
Marshe, John, esq. — London City
Mason, John, miles — Southampton Co.
Masone, Robert — Ludlow B'gh, Salop.
Mawdeley, John, gent. — Bridgwater B'gh, Somerset.
Maye, George, gent. — Canterbury City.
Maynewarynge, Arthur, miles — Salop Co.
Meredyth, Roland, esq. — Anglesey Co.
Moh (une?), ?, esq. — ? B'gh, Cornwall.
Mone, Robert, gent. — Bridport B'gh, Dors.
Montague, Edward, esq. — Northampton Co.
Moore, William, esq. — Grantham B'gh, Lincs.
More, John, miles — Porthbya B'gh, Cornwall
Morgan de Tredegre, William, esq. — Monmouth Co.
Moseley, Humphrey, gent. — Wotton Basset B'gh, Wilts.
Moynes, John, gent. — Melcombe Regis B'gh, Dors.
Mullcaster, Richard, gent. — Carlisle, B'gh, Cumberland.
Mullyns, Robert, gent. — Bridgwater B'gh, Somerset.
Muncketon, Christopher, gent. — Appleby B'gh, Westmorland.
Musgrave, William — Cumberland Co.
Mychell, Humphrey, gent. — Poole B'gh, Dors.
Myldmay, ? , esq. — ? B'gh, Cornwall.
Myldmay, Walter, miles — Northampton Co.
Myn, Nicholas, gent. — Horsham B'gh, Sussex.
Nethermyll, John, esq. — Coventry City, Warwick.
Nevell, Henry, miles — Berks Co.
Newdygate, Francis, miles — Bedwin B'gh, Worcs.
Newport, Francis, gent. — Droitwich B'gh, Worcs.
Northe, Roger, miles — Cambridge Co.
Nowell, Laurence, gent. — Knaresborough B'gh, York.
Oldesworth, Edward, esq. — Aylesbury B'gh, Bucks.
Onsatt, John, Dr. — Kingston-on-Hull City.
Onslewe, Richard, esq. — Aldeburgh B'gh, York.
Osborn, Peter, esq. —
Owen, Hugh — Bossiney B'gh, Cornwall.
Page, William, gent. — Bridport B'gh, Dors.

Pagett, (Henry?), miles — Lichfield City, Staffs.
Palladye, Richard — Heytesbury B'gh, Wilts.
Palmer, Thomas, miles — Guildford B'gh, Surrey.
Parrott, John, miles — Wareham B'gh, Dors. (?)
Parry, Thomas, miles — Hertford Co.
Parrye, John, gent. — Carmarthen B'gh, Carmarthen.
Pate, Richard, esq. — Gloucester B'gh, Gloucs.
Patrycke Richard, esq. — Huntingdon B'gh.
Perne, Christopher, esq. — Grampound B'gh, Cornwall.
Peter, William, miles — Essex Co.
Phayer, Thomas, esq. — Cardigan B'gh, Cardigan.
Phyllyppes, William, esq. — Pembroke Co.
Poley, William, gent. — Porthbya B'gh, Cornwall.
Pollarde, John, miles —
Ponghyll, William, gent. — Ludlow B'gh, Salop.
Poole, Giles, miles — Gloucester Co.
Pooley, Thomas, gent. — Thetford B'gh, Norfolk.
Porter, Arthur, esq. — Aylesbury B'gh, Bucks.
Porter, William, miles — Bletchingly B'gh, Surrey.
Powell, Moritius ap — Monmouth B'gh, Monmouth.
Poynes, Nicholas, miles — Totness B'gh, Devon (?)
Poynginges, Adrian, esq. —
Prestwood, Richard, gent. —
Prynce, Richard, gent. — Bridgnorth B'gh, Salop.
Pursell, Nicholas — Shrewsbury, B'gh.
Purselowe, Nicholas, gent. — Morpeth B'gh, N'umberland.
Purvey, John, esq. — Higham Ferrers B'gh, N'hampton.
Pygott, Thomas, esq. — Bedford Co.
Randall, Nicholas, gent. —
Randolphe, Thomas, esq. — Grantham B'gh, Lincs.
Ratclyff, Henry, miles — Chichester B'gh, Sussex.
Ratclyff, John, miles —
Ratclyffe, Humphrey, miles — Maldon B'gh, Essex.
Raynoldes, Richard, esq. — Saltashe B'gh, Cornwall.
Rees ap Howell, William ap, esq. — Beaumaris B'gh, Anglesey.
Rithe, George, esq. — Petersfield B'gh, S'hampton.
Robinson, William, esq. — Bath B'gh, Somerset.
Robyns, John — Dover, Cinque Ports.
Rogers, Edward, miles — Somerset Co.
Rogers, John, miles — Dorset Co.
Rowse, Edward, miles — Dunwich B'gh, Suffolk.
Russell, Thomas, miles — Worcester Co.
Ryseley, William, esq. — Buckingham B'gh, Bucks.
Sackvile, Thomas, esq. — East Grinstead B'gh, Sussex.

Sadler, Ralph, miles — Hertford Co.
Sakevyle, Richard, miles — Sussex Co.
Sakford, Thomas, esq. — Ipswich B'gh, Suff.
Salesburye de Maghrubed, John, esq. — Denbigh Co.
Salvayne, John, esq. — Beverley B'gh, York.
Sapcote, John, esq. — Rippon B'gh, York.
Saunders, Robert, esq. — Brakley B'gh, N'hampton.
Saunders, Thomas, gent. — Lewes B'gh, Sussex.
Savell, Henry, esq. — York Co.
Saynbridge, William, gent. —
Scryven, John, gent. — Wareham B'gh, Dors. (?)
Sellowe, John, esq. — Great Grymsbye B'gh, Lincs.
Seseley, Reginald — Scarsborough B'gh, York.
Seynt John, John, esq. — Bedford Co.
Seyntleger, Anthony, miles — Kent. Co.
Seyntleger, John, miles — Devon Co. (?)
Seyntlewe, John, miles — Gloucester Co.
Seyntlowe, Edward, esq. — Bath B'gh, Somerset.
Seyntlowe, William, miles — Somerset Co.
Sharryngton, Henry, esq. — Ludgershall B'gh, Wilts.
Simcote, William, esq. — Huntingdon B'gh, Hunts.
Skevyngton, John, gent. — Newcastle-under-Lyme B'gh, Staffs.
Skynner, John jr., gent. — Reigate B'gh, Surrey.
Skynner, Ralph, gent. — Westbury B'gh, Wilts.
Slegge, Roger, gent. — Cambridge B'gh, Cambridge.
Smyth, John, gent. — Camelford B'gh, Cornwall.
Smythe, Christopher, esq. — St. Albans B'gh, Herts.
Smythe, Laurence — Chester City, Cheshire.
Smythe, Thomas, miles — Liverpool B'gh, Lancs.
Snell, Nicholas, esq. — Chippenham B'gh, Wilts.
Sone, Francis, esq. — Orford B'gh, Suffolk.
Sotherton, Thomas, alderman — Norwich City, Norff.
Southcott, Thomas, esq. — Dartmouth Clifton Hardness, Devon.
Stafford, Edward, esq. — Stafford B'gh, Staffs.
Steynyngs, Thomas, esq. — Castle Rising B'gh, Norfolk.
Stokes, Adrian, esq. — Leicester Co.
Story, John LL.D. — Downton B'gh, Wilts.
Stoughton, Thomas, esq. — Guildford B'gh, Surrey.
Strangeways, Giles, miles — Dorset Co.
Straunge, Richard, gent. — Horsham B'gh, Sussex.
Strickland, William — Scarsborough B'gh, York.
Stroode, Richard, esq. —
Suney, Richard esq. — Boroughbridge B'gh, York.
Sybbes, William, esq. —

Syranude? William, gent. — Knaresborough B'gh, York.
Tayller, Roger — Oxford B'gh, Oxford.
Thelwall, Simon, esq. — Denbigh B'gh, Denbigh.
Thorrold, Anthony, esq. — Lincoln B'gh, Lincs.
Throckmorton, Clement, esq. — Sudbury B'gh, Suff.
Throckmorton, Nicholas, miles — Dorchester B'gh, Dors.
Throckmorton, John, esq. — Coventry B'gh, Warwick.
Throckmorton, Simon, esq. — Huntingdon Co.
Throgmorton, Thomas, esq. — Warwick B'gh.
Thymblebye, Richard, miles — Lincoln Co.
Thynne, John, miles — Wiltshire Co.
Tredeneck, John, esq. — Helston B'gh, Cornwall.
Trelawney, John, Esq. — Cornwall Co.
Tremayne, (Gerard?), gent. — Exeter City, Devon (?)
Turnor, Thomas, gent. — Reading B'gh, Berks.
Tyrwhite, Robert, miles — Huntingdon Co.
Tysarr, John — Sandwich, Cinque Ports.
Vane, Henry — Winchelsea, Cinque Ports.
Vaughan, John, esq. — Beverley B'gh, York.
Vaughan, Robert — Radnor B'gh, Brecon.
Vaughan, Roger, miles — Brecon Co.
Vaughan, Roland, esq. — Brecon B'gh, Brecon.
Ventryes, Thomas, gent. — Cambridge B'gh, Cambridge.
Walsingham, Francis, esq. —
Warcopp, Thomas, esq. — Westmorland Co.
Warde, William, gent. — Morpeth B'gh, N'umberland.
Warner, Edward, miles — Great Grymsbye, Lincs.
Warner, Robert, esq. —
Warren, Thomas — Dover, Cinque Ports.
Waters, Thomas, gent. — Kings Lynn B'gh, Norfolk.
Watson, William, alderman — York City.
Webbe, John, merchant — Salisbury City, Wilts.
Webbe, William, merchant — Salisbury City, Wilts.
Weldon, Thomas, esq. — New Windsor B'gh, Berks.
Welshe, John, esq. — Bristol City, Gloucs.
Wentworth, Paul, esq. — Chipping Wicombe B'gh, Bucks.
Weston, Henry — Petersfield B'gh, S'hampton.
Weston, Robert, LL.D. — Lichfield City, Staffs.
Weyghtman, William, esq. — Ludgershall B'gh, Wilts.
White, Thomas, miles — Southampton Co.
Whyte, Godfrey — Winchelsea, Cinque Ports.
Whytney, Robert, miles — Hereford Co.
Woode, Thomas — Oxford City, Oxford.
Woodhowse, Thomas, miles — Great Yarmouth, Norfolk.

Woodhowse, William, miles — Norwich City, Norfolk.
Worseley, Robert, miles — Lancaster Co.
Wright, Edmund, esq. — Steyning B'gh, Sussex.
Wrothe, Thomas, miles — Middlesex Co.
Wyethe, Robert, gent. — Droitwich B'gh, Worcs.
Wyllyams, Thomas, esq. — Exeter City, Devon (?)
Wylemott, Edward, m'chant — Southampton B'gh, S'hampton.
Wylstroppe, Francis, esq. — Thirsk B'gh, York.
Wyn' ap Cadwalader, John, esq. — Merioneth Co.
Wyndham, Edward, miles — Norfolk Co.
Wyngfyld, Robert jr., gent. — Peterborough City, N'hampton.
Wynkfeld, Richard, esq. — Orford B'gh, Suff.
Wynne, Thomas, esq. — Walingford B'gh, Berks.
Wynter, William, esq. — Portsmouth City, S'hampton.
Yarde, Edward, gent. — Dartmouth Clifton Hardness, Devon.
Yoe, Leonard, gent. — Totness B'gh, Devon (?)
Yonge, John, esq. — Devizes B'gh, Wilts.
Yorke, John, miles — Boroughbridge B'gh, York.
Younge, John, gent. — Marlborough B'gh, Wilts.
Zouche, John, miles — Shaftesbury B'gh, Dorset.

BIBLIOGRAPHY

1. MANUSCRIPT SOURCES

CAMBRIDGE: University Library, MSS. Ff. v. 14, fols. 81v-84v. and Mm. 1. 29.
Corpus Christi College, MSS 105, 114A, 114B, 118, 119, 121 'Synodalia', 168, 340, 435, 543

CANTERBURY: Cathedral Chapter Library, Reg. U2, 'Sede Vacante'

LONDON: British Library, Add. MSS 13398 vol. 1, 19400, 24196, 26056, 26675, 28173 A, 28178, 28201, 28571, 29196, 29549, 32091, 34729, 35830, 38329, 40061; Cotton MSS Julius F.6, Titus B. 13, Vespasian D. 18 and F. 3, Caligula B. 8 and E. 5; Egerton MS 2836; Harlian MSS 169, 419, 421, 5176; Lansdowne MS 4; Salisbury MS Cecil Papers, M/485
_____ Corporation of London Record Office, Repertories, XIV; Journals, XVII
_____ Guildhall Library, MSS 11588 vol. I, 12071, vol. I, 9531/12
_____ House of Lords Records Office, Historical Collections, Braye MS VI House of Commons Original MS. Journals, I, 'Seimour'. House of Lords Original MS. Journals, III, IV. Original Acts, 1 Eliz. I, 1, 2, 4, 5, 16, 22, 25, 31, 34, 38, 41, 42; Original Acts, 5 Eliz. I, 1, 26, 30, 38, 49
_____ Lambeth Palace Library, MSS 959/28, 1430, 591, 695
_____ Public Record Office, SP 11, SP 12/I-XXVII, SP 30/25, SP 31/3/23, 24, SP 31/9/69, SP 31/10, SP 31/13/I, SP 46/13, SP 63/II, SP 70/I-IV, E 371/402.

ROME: Archivio Segreto Vaticano, Arch. Consist. Acta Miscell fondo 33, III; Arm. LXIV, 28; Lettere di Particulari, I; Lettere di Principi, XI and XXII; Misc. Arm. XII, 91; Fondo Consistoriale, Acta Misc. 33 and 34; Scisma Anglicana: Misc. Arm. I, III and XV. Minutiae Brevia; Arm. LII; Nunziature e Legazioni, Inghilterra, XXXV. Fiandra, CCVII

_____ Venerable English College, Misc. MSS (uncatalogued)

2. PRINTED SOURCES

Allen, William. *A True Defence of English Catholiques that Suffer for Their Faith.* Ingolstadt: 1584.

Arber, Edward, ed. *A Transcript of the Registers of the Company of Stationers of London, 1554-1640 A.D.,* 5 vols. London: 1875-1894.

Ascham, Roger. *The Whole Works, now First Collected and Revised. With a Life of the Author by Dr. Giles,* 3 vols. London: 1865.

Aylmer, John. *An Harborowe for Faithfull and Trewe Subiectes, Agaynst the Late Blowne Blaste, Concerning the Government of Women.* 1559.

Baetson, Mary, ed. 'A Collection of Original Letters from the Bishops to the Privy Council, 1564', *Camden Miscellany IX* (1895).

Booty, John E., ed. *The Book of Common Prayer 1559. The Elizabethan Prayerbook.* Charlottesville: 1976.

Boys, John. *An Exposition of the Dominical, Epistles and Gospels, Used in Our English Liturgie, Throughout the Whole Yeere, Together with A Reason Why the Church did Chuse the Same.* London: 1611.

Calendar of Letters, Despatches, and State Papers Relating to the Negotiations Between England and Spain . . . XIII, Philip and Mary. Royall Tyler, ed. London: 1954.

Calendar of Letters and State Papers Relating to English Affairs, Preserved Principally in the Archives of Simancas, I, Elizabeth, 1558-1567. Martin S. Hume, ed. London: 1892.

Calendar of State Papers, Foreign Series, of the Reign of Elizabeth, Preserved in the Public Record Office. Joseph Stevenson, ed. London: 1863.

Calendar of State Papers, Foreign Series, of the Reign of Mary, 1553-1558. William B. Turnbull, ed. London: 1861.

Calendar of State Papers and Manuscripts, Relating to English Affairs, Existing in the Archives and Collections of Venice. vols. VI and VII. Rawson Brown, ed. London: 1884, 1892.

Calendar of State Papers, Relating to English Affairs, Preserved Principally at Rome, in the Vatican Archives and Library, I, Elizabeth, 1558-1571. J.M. Rigg, ed. London: 1916.

Camden, William, *Annales Rerum Anglicarum et Hibernicarum, Regnante Elizabetha* . . . London: 1615.

_____ *The History of the Most Renowned and Victorious Princess Elizabeth, Late Queen of England.* 4th ed. London: 1688.

Cardwell, Edward, ed. *Documentary Annals of the Reformed Church of England; Being a Collection of Injunctions, Orders, Articles of Inquiry, etc.,* 2 vols. Oxford: 1839.

_____ ed. *The Reformation of the Ecclesiastical Laws as Attempted in the Reigns of King Henry 8, King Edward and Queen Elizabeth.* Oxford: 1850

Christopherson, John. *Exhortation to Beware of Rebellion.* London: 1554.

Clerke, Bartholomew. *Fidelis Servi, subdito infideli responsio, una cum orrorum et calumniarum quarundam examine quae contientur in septimo libro de Visibili Ecclesiae Monarchia a Nicholao Sandero conscripta.* London: 1573.

Coke, Edward. *The Fourth Part of the Institutes of the Laws of England Concerning the Jurisdiction of Courts.* London: 1644.

_____ *The Reports in 13 Parts,* 6 vols. London: 1826.

_____ *The Third Part of the Institutes of the Laws of England Concerning High Treason, and other Pleas of the Crown, and Criminal Causes.* London: 1648.

Dalison, William. *Les Reports de divers special cases adjudge en le Court de Common Bank en les reignes de les tres hault et excellent Princes Hen. VIII. Edw. VI. et les reignes Mar. et Eliz.* London: 1689.

Dasent, John Roche, ed. *The Acts of the Privy Council of England,* new series, vol. VII. London: 1893.

Davies, J. Conway, ed. *Catalogue of Manuscripts in the Library of the Honourable Society of the Inner Temple,* 3 vols. Oxford: 1972.

Davis, E. Jeffries, ed. 'An Unpublished Manuscript of the Lords Journal for April and May, 1559', *English Historical Review* (1913), 531-542.

D'Ewes, Simond. *The Journals of all the Parliaments during the Reign of Queen Elizabeth, both of the House of Lords and House of Commons.* London: 1682.

Dyer, James. *Cy Ensuont Ascuns Novel Cases.* London: 1585.

_____ *Cy Ensuont Novel Cases, collectes per. . . Jasques Dyer. . .* London: 1620.

_____ *La Table al lieur des reports del tresreverend judge Sir James Dyer, iades chiefe justice del Common Banke: per quel facilment cy troveront toutes choses conteinus in icel ore tarde compose per T.A.* London: 1588.

Foley, Henry, ed. *Records of the English Province of the Society of Jesus,* 7 vols. in 8. London: 1877-1883.

Foxe, John. *The Acts and Monuments of John Foxe,* 8 vols. George Townsend, ed. London: 1849.

Frere, Walter Howard, ed. *Visitation Articles and Injunctions of the Period of the Reformation,* vol. III, *1559-1575.* London: 1910.

Gorham, George Cornelius, ed. *Gleanings of A Few Scattered Ears, During the Reformation in England. . . 1533 to A.D. 1588.* London: 1857.

Granvelle, Antoine Perrenot, seigneur de, cardinal. *Papiers d'Etat du Cardinal de Granvelle,* 9 vols. Charles Weiss, ed. Paris: 1841-1852.

Grindal, Edmund. *The Remains of Edmund Grindal.* William Nicholson ed. Cambridge: Parker Society, 1843.

Haynes, Samuel and William Murdin,, ed. *A Collection of State Papers, Relating to Affairs in the Reigns of King Henry VIII, King Edward VI, Queen Mary and Queen Elizabeth. 1542 to 1570. Transcribed from Original Letters and other Authentick Memorials . . . left by William Cecil Lord Burghley . . .* 2 vols. London: 1740-1759.

219

Hayward, John. *Annals of the First Four Years of the Reign of Elizabeth.* John Bruce ed. London: Camden Society VII, 1840.

Hessels, John Henry, ed. *Epistulae et Tractus cum Reformationis tum Ecclesiae Londino-Bataviae Historiam Illustrantes (1544-1622).* Cambridge: 1889.

Hinde, Gladys, ed. *The Registers of Cuthbert Tunstall, Bishop of Durham,* 1530-1559, and James Pilkington, Bishop of Durham, 1561-1576. London: Surtees Society CLXI, 1952.

Holinshed, Raphael. *The Laste Volume of the Chronicles of England, Scotlande and Irelande.* London: 1577.

Hughes, Paul L. and James F. Larkin, ed. *Tudor Royal Proclamations,* vol. II, *The Later Tudors (1553-1587).* New Haven: 1969.

Jewel, John. *An Apology of the Church of England.* J.E. Booty, ed. Ithaca, N.Y.: 1963.

_____ *The True Copies of the Letters betwene John Bisshop of Sarum and D. Cole Upon Occasion of a Sermon.* London: 1560.

Kervyn de Lettenhove, Joseph Bruno M. C., ed. *Relations Politiques des Pays-Bas et de l'Angleterre, sous le Règne de Philippe II,* 11 vols. Bruxelles: 1882-1900.

Knolles, Henry. *Francoforto Anglorum ad Amplissimum Senatum Francofor. Oratio, sive Gratiarum Actio.* Frankfurt: 1559.

Lambert, John James, ed. *Records of the Skinners of London, Edward I to James I.* London: 1933.

Lincoln's Inn. *The Records of the Honourable Society of Lincoln's Inn, The Black Books,* vol. I, *1422-1586.* London: 1897.

Machyn, Henry. *Diary.* J.G. Nichols, ed. London: Camden Society XLII, 1848.

Merson, A.L., ed. *The Third Book of Remembrance of Southampton, 1514-1602.* Southampton: 1955.

Osiander, Lucas. *Epitomes Historiae Ecclesiasticae, Centuriae Decimae Sextae.* Tübingen: 1608.

Parker, Matthew. *Correspondence.* John Bruce, ed. Cambridge: Parker Society, 1853.

───── *Registrum Matthei Parker . . . 1559-1575.* E. Margaret Thompson, ed. and trans. Oxford: Canterbury and York Society, 1928-1933.

Parsloe, Guy, ed. *The Warden's Accounts of the Worshipful Company of Founders of the City of London, 1487-1681.* London: 1964.

Peck, Francis. *Desiderata Curiosa,* 2 vols. London: 1732-1735.

Persons, Robert. 'Memoirs', *Catholic Record Society Miscellany* II (1905), 12-218.

Pole, Reginald, card. *Epistolae Reginaldi Poli . . . et aliorum ad se,* 5 vols. A.M. Quirini, ed. Brescia: 1744-1757.

Ponet, John. *A Shorte Treatise of Politike Power, and of the True Obedience Which Subiectes One to Kyngs and other Civile Governorers . . .* [Strasburg?]: 1556.

Raine, Angelo, ed. *York Civic Records,* vol. V. Yorkshire Archaeological Society, Record Series CX (1946).

Ribadeneira, Peter. *Patris Petri de Ribadeneira Societatis Jesu Sacerdotis Confessiones, Epistolae aliaque Scripta Inedita.* Madrid: Monumenta Historica Societatis Jesu, LVIII-LX, 1920-1923.

Rymer, Thomas. *Foedera, Conventiones, Literae, et cuiscumque Generis Acta Publica, Inter Rigis Angliae. . .* 3rd ed. The Hague: 1741.

Sagittarius, Caspar. *Introductio in Historiam Ecclesiasticam . . .,* 2 vols. Jena: 1718.

Sainty, J.C., ed. 'Further Materials from an Unpublished Manuscript of the Lords Journal for Sessions 1559 and 1597 to 1598', *House of Lords Record Office memorandum,* no. 33. (1965).

Sanders, Nicholas. 'Dr Nicholas Sanders' Report to Cardinal Moroni', *Catholic Record Society Miscellany* I (1905), 1-46.

───── *De Origine ac Progressu Schismatis Anglicani Liber.* Cologne: 1585.

———— *The Rise and Growth of the Anglican Schism . . . with a Continuation of the History, by the Rev. Edward Rishton. . .* David Lewis, ed. and trans. London: 1877.

———— *De Visibili Monarchia.* Louvain: 1571.

Sims, Catherine Strateman, ed. 'Policies in Parliaments' An Early Seventeenth-Century Tractate on the House of Commons Procedure', *Huntingdon Library Quarterly* (1951), 45-58.

Smith, Thomas. *De Republica Anglorum.* London: 1584.

Statutes of the Realm, vol. 4. London: 1819.

Turner, William. *A New Booke of Spirituall Physik for Dyverse Diseases of the Nobilitie and Gentlemen of England.* [Basle?]: 1555.

Whatmore, L.E., ed. *Archdeacon Harpsfield's Visitation, 1557, Together with Visitations of 1556 and 1558,* 2 vols. London: Catholic Record Society, 1950-1951.

Whittingham, William. *A Brief Discourse of the Troubles Begun at Frankfort, in the Year 1554, About the Book of Common Prayer and Ceremonies.* London: 1846.

Wilkins, David, ed. *Concilia Magnae Britanniae et Hiberniae . . . 446-1718,* 4 vols. London: 1737.

Wriothesley, Charles. *A Chronicle of England During the Reigns of the Tudors, from A.D. 1485 to 1559,* 2 vols. William D. Hamilton, ed. London: Camden Society, 1877.

The Zurich Letters, 2 vols. Hastings Robinson, ed. Cambridge: Parker Society, 1842-1845.

3. SECONDARY MATERIALS

(a) Works in Print

Abbott, Lewis M. *Law Reporting in England, 1485-1585.* London: 1973.

Adair, E.R. and F.M. Grier Evans. 'Writs of Assistance, 1558-1700', *English Historical Review* (1921), 356-372.

222

Alvarez, Manuel Fernandez. *Politica Mundial de Carlos V y Felipe II.* Madrid: 1966.

‑‑‑‑‑‑ *Tres Embajadors de Felipe II en Inglaterra.* Madrid: 1951.

Anderson, Andrew H. 'Henry, Lord Stafford (1501-1563) in Local and Central Government,' *English Historical Review* (1963), 225-242.

Anglo, Sidney. *Spectacle Pageantry and Early Tudor Policy.* Oxford: 1969.
Paris: 1927.

Baker, Derek, ed. *Schesm, Heresy and Religious Protest.* Paris: 1972.

Batteli, Giulio, ed. *Bibliografia dell'Archivio Vaticano,* 4 vols. Vatican City: 1962-1966.

Bayne, C.G. *Anglo-Roman Relations, 1558-1565.* Oxford Historical and Literary Studies, II (1913).

‑‑‑‑‑‑ 'The Coronation of Queen Elizabeth', *English Historical Review* (1907), 658-664.

‑‑‑‑‑‑ 'The First House of Commons of Queen Elizabeth', *English Historical Review* (1908), 455-476, 643-682.

‑‑‑‑‑‑ 'Visitation of the Province of Canterbury, 1559', *English Historical Review* (1913), 636-677.

Benett, H.S. *English Books and Readers, 1558 to 1603.* Cambridge: 1965.

Bertrand, Pierre. *Genève et la Grand-Bretagne de John Knox à Oliver Cromwell.* Geneva: 1948.

Bindoff, S.T. 'The Making of the Statute of Artificers', *Elizabethan Government and Society. Essays Presented to Sir John Neale.* S.T. Bindoff et al., ed. London: 1961. Pp. 56-94.

Birt, Henry Norbert. *The Elizabethan Religious Settlement.* London: 1907.

Boyle, Leonard E. *A Survey of the Vatican Archives and of its Medieval Holdings.* Toronto: 1972.

Bradshaw, Paul F. *The Anglican Ordinal, Its History and Development from the Reformation to the Present Day.* London: 1971.

223

Braudel, Fernand. *The Mediterranean and the Mediterranean World in the Age of Philip II,* 2 vols. Sian Reynolds, trans. London: 1973.

Brightman, F.E. *The English Rite. Being a Synopsis of the Sources and Revisions of the Book of Common Prayer,* 2 vols. London: 1915.

Brook, Victor John Knight. *A Life of Archbishop Parker.* Oxford: 1962.

Buechner, Q.A. 'Luther and the English Reformation', *History Today* (1972), 799-805.

Burnet, Bilbert. *The History of the Reformation of the Church of England,* 4 vols. Revised by E. Nares. London: n.d. (1830).

Cam, Helen M., ed. *Selected Historical Essays of F. W. Maitland.* Cambridge: 1957.

Cardwell, Edward. *A History of Conferences and Other Proceedings Connected with the Revision of the Book of Common Prayer.* Oxford: 1849.

Casson, Stephen Hyde. *Lives of the Bishops of Bath and Wells,* 2 vols. London: 1829-1830.

Chadwick, Owen. 'The Sixteenth Century', *The English Church and the Continent.* C.R. Dedwell, ed. London: 1959. Pp. 60-72.

Chambers, E.K. *The Elizabethan Stage,* 4 vols. Oxford: 1923.

Cliffe, J.T. *The Yorkshire Gentry from the Reformation to the Civil War.* London: 1969.

Cockburn, J.S. *A History of English Assizes 1558-1714.* Cambridge: 1972.

Collier, John P. 'On Sir Nicholas Bacon, Lord Keeper, with Extracts from Some of his Unprinted Papers and Speeches', *Archaeologia* (1865), 339-348.

Collins, W.E. 'Queen Elizabeth's Defence of her Proceedings in Church and State', *Church Historical Society* (1899), 42-43.

Collinson, Patrick. *The Elizabethan Puritan Movement.* London: 1967.

Coolidge, John S. *The Pauline Renaissance in England.* Oxford: 1970.

Cowell, Henry J. 'English Protestant Refugees in Strasburg, 1553-1558', *Huguenot Society Proceedings* (1934), 69-120.

_____ 'The Sixteenth-Century English Speaking Refugee Churches at Geneva and Frankfort', *Huguenot Society Proceedings* (1939), 209-230.

_____ 'The Sixteenth-Century English Speaking Refugee Churches at Strasbourg, Basle, Zurich, Aarau, Wesel and Emden', *Huguenot Society Proceedings* (1937), 612-665.

Creighton, Mandell, bp. *Queen Elizabeth.* London: 1899.

Cremeans, Charles D. *The Reception of Calvinistic Thought in England.* Urbana, Ill.: 1949.

Cross, Claire. '"Dens of Loitering Lubbers": Protestant Protest Against Cathedral Foundations, 1540-1640', *Schism, Heresy and Religious Protest.* Derek Baker, ed. Cambridge: 1972.

_____ 'Noble Patronage in the Elizabethan Church', *Historical Journal* (1960), 1-16.

_____ *Royal Supremacy in the Elizabethan Church.* London: 1969.

Crowley, David. 'Thomas Goldwell', *The Venerabile* (1930), 60-65.

Crowson, P.S. *Tudor Foreign Policy.* London: 1973.

Davies, E.T. *Episcopacy and the Royal Supremacy in the Church of England in the XVI Century.* Oxford: 1950.

Davies, Horton. *Worship and Theology in England from Cranmer to Hooker, 1534-1603.* Princeton: 1970.

Davies, R. Trevor. *The Golden Century of Spain 1501-1621.* London: 1964.

Delplace, Louis. 'L'Angleterre et la Compagnie de Jésus avant le Martyre du B. Edmund Campion, 1540-1581', *Précis Historiques* (1890), 219-228, 329-347, 417-435, 492-508.

Dewar, Mary. *Sir Thomas Smith: A Tudor Intellectual in Office.* London: 1964.

Dickens, A.G. *The Marian Reaction in the Diocese of York. The Clergy.* London: 1957.

_____ *The Marian Reaction in the Diocese of York. The Laity.* London: 1957.

Dixon, R.H. *History of the Church of England from the Abolition of the Roman Jurisdiction,* 6 vols. 3rd rev. ed. Oxford: 1895.

Dodd, Charles. *The Church History of England from 1500 to the Year 1688, Chiefly with Regard to Catholicks,* 5 vols. M.A. Tierney, ed. London: 1839-1843.

Dugmore, Clifford W. *The Mass and the English Reformers.* London: 1958.

Ecclesiastical Courts Commission. *Report to the Commissioners Appointed to Inquire into the Constitution and Working of the Ecclesiastical Courts . . .,* 2 vols. London: 1883.

Edwards, Goronwy. 'The Emergence of Majority Rule in the Procedure of the House of Commons,' *Transactions of the Royal Historical Society* (1965), 165-187.

Edwards, Robert Dudley. *Church and State in Tudor Ireland: A History of the Penal Laws Against Irish Catholics, 1534-1603.* London: 1935.

Einstein, Lewis D. *Tudor Ideals.* New York: 1921.

Elton, Geoffrey R. *England Under the Tudors.* 2nd ed. London: 1974.

_____ *Reform and Reformation: England 1509-1558.* London: 1977.

_____ *The Tudor Constitution. Documents and Commentary.* Cambridge: 1960.

Estes, James M. 'Church Order and the Christian Magistrate According to Johannes Brenz', *Archiv für Reformationsgeschichte* (1968), 5-23.

_____ 'The Two Kingdoms and the State Church According to Johannes Brenz and an Anonymous Colleague', *Archiv für Reformationsgeschichte* (1970), 35-49.

Fifoot, C.H.S., ed. *The Letters of Fredrick William Maitland.* Cambridge: 1965.

Foss, Edward. *The Judges of England: With Sketches of Their Lives . . . From the Time of the Conquest.* 9 vols. London: 1848-1864.

Frere, W.H. '*The Elizabethan Religious Settlement . . .* by Henry Norbert Birt, O.S.B., Priest of Downside Abbey (London: George Bell, 1907),' *English Historical Review* (1908), 571-575.

⸻ *The English Church in the Reigns of Elizabeth and James I (1558-1625).* London: 1904.

Froude, James Anthony. *History of England from the Fall of Wolsey to the Defeat of the Armada,* vol. VI. London: 1875.

Garrett, Christina H. 'John Ponet and the Confession of the Banished Ministers', *Church Quarterly Review* (1943), 47-74; (1944), 181-204.

⸻ 'The Legatine Register of Cardinal Pole, 1554-1557', *Journal of Modern History* (1941), 189-194.

⸻ *The Marian Exiles.* 2nd ed. Cambridge: 1969.

Gasquet, Adrian, card. *The History of the Venerable English College, Rome.* London: 1920.

Gee, Henry. *The Elizabethan Clergy and the Settlement of Religion 1558-1564.* Oxford: 1898.

⸻ *The Elizabethan Prayer-Book and Ornaments.* London: 1902.

Gibbs, Vicary, ed. *The Complete Peerage . . . by G.E.C.,* 13 vols. London: 1913.

Gillow, Joseph. *A Literary and Biographical History, or Bibliographical Dictionary, of English Catholics from the Breach with Rome to the Present Time,* 5 vols. London: 1885-1903.

Grieve, Hilda E.P. 'The Deprived Married Clergy in Essex, 1553-1561', *Transactions of the Royal Historical Society* (1940), 141-169.

Haigh, Christopher. *Reformation and Resistance in Tudor Lancashire.* Cambridge: 1975.

Hallam, Henry. *The Constitutional History of England, from the Accession of Henry VII to the Death of George II,* 2 vols. London: 1827.

Haugaard, William. *Elizabeth I and the English Reformation.* Cambridge: 1968.

Head, R.E. *Royal Supremacy and the Trials of Bishops, 1558-1725.* London: 1962.

Heal, Felicity. 'The Bishops and the Act of Exchange of 1559', *Historical Journal* (1974), 227-246.

Hembry, Phyllis M. *The Bishops of Bath and Wells, 1540-1640, Social and Economic Problems.* London: 1967.

Hicks, Leo. 'The Ecclesiastical Supremacy of Queen Elizabeth', *The Month* (1947), 170-177.

_____ 'Elizabethan Royal Supremacy and Contemporary Writers', *The Month* (1947), 216-228.

Hill, J.W.F. *Tudor and Stuart Lincoln.* Cambridge: 1956.

Houlbrooke, Ralph. 'The Decline of Ecclesiastical Jurisdiction Under the Tudors', *Continuity and Change* R. O'Day and F. Heal, ed. Leicester: 1976. Pp. 239-257.

Hughes, Philip E. *The Reformation in England,* 3 vols. in 1. rev. ed. London: 1963.

_____ *Rome and the Counter-Reformation in England.* London: 1942.

_____ *The Theology of the English Reformers.* London: 1965.

Ingram, T. Dunbar. *England and Rome; A History of the Relations Between the Papacy and the English State and Church, from the Norman Conquest to 1688.* London: 1892.

Kennedy, W.M.P. 'Fines Under the Elizabethan Act of Uniformity', *English Historical Review* (1918), 517-528.

Knappen, M.M. *Tudor Puritanism,* Chicago: 1965.

Lee, F.G. *The Church Under Elizabeth,* 2 vols. London: 1880.

228

Lemberg, Stanford E. *Sir Walter Mildmay and Tudor Government.* Austin, Texas: 1964.

Levine, Mortimer. *The Early Elizabethan Succession Question, 1558-1568.* Stanford: 1966.

—— 'A Parliamentary Title to the Crown in Tudor England', *Huntington Library Quarterly* (1962), 121-127.

Linder, Robert D. 'Pierre Viret and the Sixteenth-Century English Protestants', *Archiv für Reformationsgeschichte* (1967). 149-170.

Loades, David M. 'The Enforcement of Reaction, 1553-1558', *Journal of Ecclesiastical History* (1965), 54-66.

—— *The Oxford Martyrs.* London: 1970.

MacCaffrey, Wallace. *The Shaping of the Elizabethan Regime.* London: 1968.

MacColl, Malcolm. *The Reformation Settlement.* London: 1899.

Magee, Brian. 'The First Parliament of Queen Elizabeth', *Dublin Review* (1937), 60-78.

Maitland, Fredrick William. 'Canon MacColl's New Convocation', *Fortnightly Review* (1899), 926-935.

—— *Collected Papers,* 3 vols. H.A.L. Fisher, ed. Cambridge: 1911.

—— 'Defender of the Faith and So On', *English Historical Review* (1900), 120-124.

—— 'Pius IV and the English Church Service', *English Historical Review* (1900), 530-532.

—— 'Queen Elizabeth and Paul IV', *English Historical Review* (1900), 424-430.

—— 'Supremacy and Uniformity — Observations on the Acts of Supremacy and Uniformity, Based upon an Examination of the Actual Parliament Rolls', *English Historical Review* (1903), 517-532.

—— 'Thomas Sackville's Message from Rome', *English Historical Review* (1900), 757-760.

Meyer, Arnold Oskar. *England und die Katholische Kirche unter Elisabeth.* Rome: 1911.

Miller, Amos. *Sir Henry Killegrew.* Leicester: 1963.

Morgan, Irvonwy. *The Godly Preachers of the Elizabethan Church.* London: 1965.

Mullinger, Bass. *The University of Cambridge,* 2 vols. Cambridge: 1884.

Neale, John Ernest. 'The Accession of Elizabeth I', *Essays in Elizabethan History.* New York: 1958. pp. 45-58.

_____ *Elizabeth I and Her Parliaments,* vol. I. London: 1953

_____ "The Elizabethan Acts of Supremacy and Uniformity," *English Historical Review* (1950), 304-332.

_____ *Queen Elizabeth I.* London: 1952.

_____ 'Sir Nicholas Throckmorton's Advice to Queen Elizabeth on Her Accession to the Throne', *English Historical Review* (1950), 91-98.

O'Day, M. Rosemary. 'Thomas Bentham: A Case Study in the Problems of the Early Elizabethan Episcopate', *Journal of Ecclesiastical History* (1972), 137-159.

O'Sullivan, R. *Edmund Plowden, 1518-1585.* Cambridge: 1952.

Owen, Dorothy M. 'Enforcement of the Reformation in Ely Diocese', *Miscellanea Historiae Ecclesiasticae III, Colloque de Cambridge 1968.* Louvain: 1970. Pp. 167-174.

Oxley, James E. *The Reformation in Essex to the Death of Mary.* Manchester: 1965.

Pauck, Wilhelm, ed. *Melanchton and Bucer.* London: 1969.

Peck, G.T. 'John Hales and the Puritans During the Marian Exile', *Church History* (1941), 159-177.

Phillimore, R.J. *The Ecclesiastical Law of the Church of England,* 2 vols. London: 1895.

Pogson, Rex H. 'Reginald Pole and the Priorities of Government in Mary Tudor's Church', *Historical Journal* (1975), 3-20.

Poll, Gerritt Jan van de. *Martin Bucer's Liturgical Ideas: The Strassburg Reformer and His Connection with the Liturgies of the Sixteenth Century.* Assen, Neth.: 1954.

Pollard, Alfred F. *The History of England from the Accession of Edward VI. to the Death of Elizabeth (1547-1603).* London: 1929.

Pollen, J.H. *The English Catholics in the Reign of Queen Elizabeth.* London: 1920.

_____ 'The Passing of Elizabeth's Supremacy Bill', *Dublin Review* (1903), 44-63.

_____ 'The Politics of English Catholics During the Reign of Queen Elizabeth', *The Month* XCIX (1902), 43-60; 131-148; 290-305; 394-411; 600-618; C (1902), 71-87; 176-188.

Porter, Harry C. *Reformation and Reaction in Tudor Cambridge.* Cambridge: 1958.

Primus, John H. *The Vestments Controversy: An Historical Study of the Earliest Tensions Within the Church of England in the Reigns of Edward VI and Elizabeth.* Kampen: 1960.

Procter, Francis and W.H. Frere. *A New History of the Book of Common Prayer.* London: 1902.

Ramsay, G.D. *The City of London in International Politics at the Accession of Elizabeth Tudor.* Manchester: 1975.

Ranke, Leopold von. *A History of England Principally in the Seventeenth Century.* New York: 1966.

Read, Conyers. *Mr Secretary Cecil and Queen Elizabeth.* London: 1955.

_____ *Mr Secretary Walsingham and the Policy of Queen Elizabeth,* vol. I. Oxford: 1925.

Ridley, Jasper. *Thomas Cranmer.* Oxford: 1966.

Romier, Lucien. *Les Origines Politiques des Guerres de Religion, II, La Fin de la Magnificence Extérieure; le Roi Contre les Protestants (1555-1559).* Paris: 1914.

Rose, Elliot. *Cases of Conscience: Alternatives Open to Recusants and Puritans Under Elizabeth I and James I.* Cambridge: 1975.

Ross, G. Lockhart. 'Il Schifanoya's Account of the Coronation of Queen Elizabeth', *English Historical Review* (1908), 533-534.

Ruble, Alphonse de. *Le Traité de Cateau-Cambrésis.* Paris: 1889.

Smith, H. Maynard. 'The Reformation at Home and Abroad', *Church Quarterly Review* (1940), 263-289.

Smith, Lacey Baldwin. *Tudor Prelates and Politics.* Princeton: 1953.

Smithen, F.J. *Continental Protestantism and the English Reformation.* London: 1927.

Smyth, C.H. *Cranmer and the Reformation Under Edward VI.* Cambridge: 1926.

Southgate, W.M. 'The Marian Exiles and the Influence of John Calvin', History (1942), 148-152.

Spalding, James C. 'The Reformatio Legum Ecclesiasticarum of 1552 and the Furthering of Discipline in England', *Church History* (1970), 162-171.

Strype, John. *The Annals of the Reformation and Establishment of Religion and Various Occurrences in the Church of England during Queen Elizabeth's Happy Reign,* 4 vols. Oxford: 1824.

_____ *The History of the Life and Acts of the Right Reverend Father in God, Edmund Grindal . . .* Oxford: 1821.

_____ *The Life and Acts of Matthew Parker, the First Archbishop of Canterbury in the Reign of Queen Elizabeth . . .,* 3 vols. Oxford: 1821.

_____ *The Life of the Learned Sir Thomas Smith . . . Principal Secretary of State to King Edward the Sixth, and Queen Elizabeth.* Oxford: 1820.

Sturge, Charles. *Cuthbert Tunstal Churchman, Scholar, Statesman, Administrator.* London: 1938.

Teulet, Alexandre. *Relations Politiques de la France et l'Espagne avec l'Ecosse au XVIe Siècle.* Paris: 1862.

Thomas, Keith. *Religion and the Decline of Magic.* Harmondsworth: 1973.

232

Trinterud, Leonard J. 'The Origins of Puritanism', *Church History* (1951), 37-58.

Vander Molen, Ronald J. 'Anglican Against Puritan: Ideological Origins during the Marian Exile', *Church History* (1973), 45-57.

Walzer, Michael. 'Revolutionary Ideology: The Case of the Marian Exiles', *American Political Science Review* (1963), 643-654.

Wedgwood, Josiah C. *Staffordshire Parliamentary History,* vol. I. London: William Salt Archaelogical Society, 1919.

Wernham, R.B. *'Elizabeth I and Her Parliaments 1559-1581.* By J.E. Neale', *English Historical Review* (1954), 632-636.

Williams, Glanmor. 'The Elizabethan Settlement of Religion in Wales and the Marches', *Journal of the Historical Society of the Church in Wales* (1950), 61-71.

Willis, Browne. *Notitia Parliamentia or An History of the Counties, Cities, and Boroughs in England and Wales,* 3 vols. 2nd ed. London: 1730.

Wilson, H.A. 'The Coronation of Queen Elizabeth', *English Historical Review* (1908), 87-91.

Yale, D.E.C., ed. 'Maitland to Acton', *Cambridge Law Journal* (1976), 158-164.

Zeefeld, W. Gordon. *The Foundations of Tudor Policy.* Cambridge, Mass.: 1948.

UNPUBLISHED DISSERTATIONS

Beckmann, Kurt-Wilhelm. 'Staatstheorie und Kirchinpolitik im Werke des Englischen Humanisten Thomas Starkey'. Ph.D. dissertation, Hamburg, 1972.

Blackman, G.L. 'The Career and Influence of Richard Cox, Bishop of Ely'. Ph.D. dissertation, Cambridge University, 1953.

Brunk, Gerold R. 'The Bishops in Parliament, 1559-1601'. Ph.D. dissertation, University of Virginia, 1968.

Fisher, Rodney Munro. 'The Inns of Court and the Reformation 1530-1580'. Ph.D. dissertation, Cambridge University, 1974.

Fuidge, Norah M. 'The Personnel of the House of Commons, 1563-1567'. M.A. thesis, University of London: 1950.

Heal, Felicity. 'The Bishops of Ely and their Diocese During the Reformation Period: ca. 1515-1600'. Ph.D. dissertation, Cambridge University, 1971.

Pogson, Rex H. 'Cardinal Pole — Papal Legate to England in Mary Tudor's Reign'. Ph.D. dissertation, Cambridge University, 1973.

Youngs, Fredrick Allen, jr. 'The Proclamations of Elizabeth I.' Ph.D. dissertation, Cambridge University, 1969.

INDEX

Adolphus, Duke of Denmark, 59
Allen, William, 127-8
Alley, William, Bishop of Exeter, 180
'Articles of Government', 180
Arundel, Earl of, 32, 59, 75, 80, 129, 150
Ashley, John, 64
Assonleville, Christopher d', 15
Atkinson, Robert, 173
Augsburg Confession, 6, 15, 57-8, 94-5
Augsburg, Diet of, 1559, 56
Aylmer, John, 87

Babeham, William, 34
Bacon, Sir Nicholas, Lord Keeper, 17, 34, 47-8, 68, 71, 73, 77, 83-5,
    92, 97, 125-7, 150, 157-8, 159
Bateman, John, 64-5
Bayne, Ralph, Bishop of Coventry and Lichfield, 110-12, 152
Bedford, Earl of, see Russell, Francis
Bentham, Thomas, 68, 170
Berwick, 7, 23, 55
Bill, Dr. William, 24, 36, 49, 129
Bills (see also Statutes)
    1559:
        confirming grants and leases by bishops deprived, 89; garbling
        feathers, 89; felt caps, 89; for supremacy, see Supremacy, Act
        of; touching the Bishop of Winchester's lands, 89; for uniformity,
        see Uniformity, Act of; making of ecclesiastical laws by
        committee of 32, 98-9, 155; for toleration of Edwardian
        religion, 103, 115-16; for patentees of Bishop of Winchester's
        land, 105-7; for punishment of the Bishop of Winchester and
        for cancelling records, 106; confirming the now Bishop of
        London, 108; confirming lands of bishopric of London to
        confirming lands of bishopric of London to Darcy etc, 107-8;
        confirming grants and leases made by Bishop Ridley, 108-9;
        guaranteeing title of lands in bishopric of Durham to F.
        Jobson, 110; to discharge a fine levied on T. Fisher by Bishop
        of Coventry, 110-11; to restore deprived bishops, 111;
        confirming grants and leases made by deprived bishops, 111;
        to make lawful the deprivations of bishops of London,
        Winchester, Worcester, and Chichester, 111; that Queen may
        restore spiritual persons deprived, 111, 157; to make deprivations

of spiritual persons pleadable, 111; that Queen shall collate bishops, 115, 130; landing and customing sweet wines, 116; against unlawful assemblies, 116; reviving Act for keeping holy days, 155-6; to restore persons deprived for heresy or marriage, 155, 156-7; to encourage artificers to dwell near the sea in Kent, 157; exempting farmers of benefices from the 10th, 162; touching chantries surrendered to Henry VIII, 162; touching the overplus of chantry lands, 163; chantries granted to Edward VI given to Elizabeth, 163; prohibiting spiritual leases longer than life of incumbent, 167; that sodomy, witchcraft, and sorcery be felonies, 182;

1563:

for assurance of lands assumed by the Queen during the vacation of bishoprics, 177; to give lands of Bishop of Durham to F. Jobson, 177; for collation of bishops, 177-8; to unite parish churches, 178-9; for augmentation of small livings, 179-80; abolishing peculiar jurisdictions, 180; reviving statutes against witchcraft and sodomy, 182; for servants robbing their masters, buggery, witchcraft, enchantments, 182; requiring episcopal officers to be graduates, 183; sanctuary not to protect debtors, 183; offenders having clergy to sue pardon in Chancery, 183; creating office for keeping church books, 183; for increase of the navy by fishing, 184-5;

Blount, Walter, 71, 109-10
Bonner, Edmund, Bishop of London, 31, 34-5, 97, 104, 107-10
Book of Common Prayer, 24, 46, 96-7, 132-4, 135-7, 145-6
    of 1549, 2, 9, 24, 58, 94-5, 96, 132, 136-7
    of 1552, 24-5, 49, 58, 81, 93, 95, 96-8, 122, 133, 136-7, 148, 152, 155
    of 1559, 9, 24, 47, 49, 135-7, 145-6, 147, 148, 152, 176-7
Bourne, Gilbert, Bishop of Bath, 79
Bowyer, Robert, 72
Boxall, Dr., Dean of Peterborough, 151
Brande, Sir John 55
Bromeley, George, Attorney of the Duchy of Lancaster, 71
Browne, Anthony, Viscount Montague, 33, 100, 103, 144, 165, 175
Brown, Rawdon, 46
Bullinger, Henry, 15, 41, 94
Burnet, Gilbert, Bishop, 1

Calais, negotiations concerning, 5, 51-3
Calvin, John, 131
Camden, William, 1, 9, 23, 127-8
Canobio, John Francis, 96, 122

Carewe, Gawain, 64
Carewe, Henry, 14, 64
Carlisle, Bishop of, *see* Ogelthorpe, Owen
Carne, Sir Edward, 54
Carrell, John, Attorney for the Duchy of Lancaster, 69, 85, 86
Cary de Hunsdon, Lord, 79
Cateau Cambrésis, treaty of, 51-3, 56, 119-20
Catholics, Roman
    attitudes to new regime, 10, 11, 16-17
    under Queen Mary, 26-9
    resistance to Elizabeth controlled, 37-42
    in Commons, 1559, 69-70
    in Lords, 1559, 72-81
    in debate over supremacy, 90, 96-103, 140-4
    dispute with Protestants, 123-9
    want reform stopped, 139
    resist uniformity in Lords, 145-52
    as threat to realm, 1563, 171-6
Cave, Sir Ambrose, Chancellor of the Duchy of Lancaster, 33, 93, 127
Cawarden, Sir Thomas, 62
Cecil, Sir William, 17, 20, 24, 31-4, 36, 47-50, 54-6, 57, 61-2, 65, 66, 68, 71, 77-8, 88, 94, 114-15, 117, 130, 132, 136, 140, 150, 151, 166, 171, 172, 178, 179-80, 184-5
Challoner, Thomas, 59
Charles V, Emperor, 58
Chatellerault, Duke of, 56
Chester, Bishop of, *see* Scot, Cuthbert
Chester, Sir William, 71
Chetwood, Agnes, 32, 144
Chetwood, Richard, 32, 63, 144
Cholmely, Randolph, Recorder of London, 71
Cholmely, Sir Roger, 34
Christopherson, John, Bishop of Chichester, 36
clerical marriage, 98, 158
Clerke, Bartholemew, 129
Clinton, Lord Admiral, 19, 32, 63, 81
Clitheroe, 63
Cole, Dr. Henry, 124-5, 128
Commons, House of
    1559:
        composition of, 61-72; sermons heard by, 83, 88; prayers in, 89;
        debates supremacy, 89-96; commital procedure in, 91;
        punishes Bishop of Winchester, 106; censures Dr. Story, 107;

impact of bills concerning church lands in, 112-13; objects to Elizabeth's refusal of *Supremum Caput,* 132; third bill for supremacy in, 140, 144; third bill for uniformity in, 145, 149; resists Act of Exchange, 167-8

1563:
    and Act for Assurance of the Queen's authority, 172-4; relations with convocation, 183-4; reaction to 'superstitious' fish days 184-5

Consensus Tigurinus, 137

Convocation of Province of Canterbury:
    of 1559, 93, 96-7
    of 1563, 169-71, 178, 180-2, 183-4

Cooke, Sir Anthony, 2, 18, 62-8, 89-93

Cooke, Richard, 64-5

Copley, Thomas, 71

Council of Trent, 78

Court of Augmentations, 160

Cox, Richard, Bishop of Ely, 24, 49, 68, 83, 88, 97, 170

Cranmer, Thomas, Archbishop of Canterbury, 102, 152, 166

Crawley, Thomas, 64

Crofte, Sir James, 55

Cumberland, Earl of, 80

Dacre of Gillisland, Lord, 80

Darcy, Lord, 107

Derby, Earl of, 32, 129

'Device for the Alteration of Religion', 16-7, 20, 22-6, 30, 47-9, 54, 69, 92, 135, 159

Dey, William, 125-6

'Distresses of the Commonwealth', 17, 19-20, 166

'Divers Points of Religion Contrary to the Church of Rome' (*see also* Richard Goodrich), 17, 19-22

Dodman, preacher, 41

Dudley, Lord Robert, 59, 66, 75, 107

Dyer, Justice James, 18

Edward VI, King of England, 10, 32-4, 43, 56, 62, 71, 78-9, 98, 101, 104, 106, 109-10, 135, 147, 157, 171, 178

Elizabeth I, Queen of England:
    accession, 5; marriage question, 11, 58-60; Protestant attitude towards, 12; handling of Catholics, 17; Catholics' fear of, 10-11; advice to at beginning of reign, 17-25 royal style, 31-2; new Privy Councillors, 33; prohibits preaching, 38-9; changes her chapel liturgy, 43-4; coronation, 44-6; diplomacy in early 1559, 50-60;

attitude to Augsburg Confession, 57-8; attitude to religious reform, 67-8; licenses Bishop Tunstal's absence, 78-9; creates new peers, 79; attitude towards House of Lords, 81; opens parliament, 83; confirms the Speaker, 85; refuses title of Supreme Head, 101, 130-2; intervenes in dispute over Winchester's lands, 105-6; decides not to dissolve parliament, 114-22; and heresy laws, 115; form of her Easter Communion, 121-2; sets rules of Westminster Disputation, 123-4; bishops wish to excommunicate her, 127-8; makes changes in the prayerbook, 135-7; cautious progress towards reform, 138-9; persuades Lords to support uniformity, 150; urged to veto uniformity, 151-2; reformers fear her moderation, 158-9; desires to return church property to Crown, 160; annexes monasteries, 162-5; assumes right to take temporal possessions from bishoprics, 165-7; plan for reform, 187-9

Ely, Bishop of, *see* Thirlby, Thomas; Cox, Richard
Eric, Prince of Sweden, 6, 59
Eure, Lord, 54, 80

Farrar, Robert, 63
Feckenham, Dr. John, Abbot of Westminster, 8, 107, 127, 146-7, 150, 152
Ferdinand, Archduke, 59
Ferdinand, Emperor, 57
Feria, Count de, Spanish Ambassador, 11, 17, 33, 44, 51, 58, 59-60, 75, 94, 114, 117-9, 121, 123, 124, 126-7, 129, 132, 140, 150, 151-2
first fruits and tenths, 26, 29, 86, 88, 160-2
Fisher, Thomas, 110-11, 112
Fitzwilliams, Sir William, 62, 105
Flanders, *see* Netherlands
Fleetwood, William, 161
Fortescue, Henry, 63
Foxe, John, 1, 82, 170
France, 50-6, 119-20, 176
Fredrick, Count Palatine, 57
Froude, J.A., 1, 188

Gardiner, Stephen, Bishop of Winchester, 27, 87, 104-6
Gargrave, Sir Thomas, Speaker 1559, 85
Gates, Sir Henry, 71
'General Notes', 180
Goldsmith, Francis, 156-7
Goldwell, Thomas, Bishop of St. Asaph, 77-8, 150

Goodman, Christopher, 12
Goodrich, Richard, 17, 20-2, 25, 44, 47, 54, 115
Gower, Thomas, Master of the Ordnance, 54
Granvelle, Cardinal, 10, 52
Graye, Lord John, 14, 24
Gresham, Thomas, 55
Grey, Jane, 65-6, 71
Grindal, Edmund, Bishop of London, 24, 49, 68, 97, 119, 169-70
Guest, Edmund, 49

Haddon, Walter, 72
Hales, John, 11, 87
Harcourt, Robert, 144
Harpsfield, Dr. Nicholas, Archdeacon of Canterbury, 39, 126
Hastings de Loughborough, Lord, 33, 100
Hayward, John, 8
Heath, Nicholas, Archbishop of York, 18, 31, 46, 99, 104, 107, 109,
    123, 127, 129-30, 140, 142
Henry II, King of France, 53, 120
Henry VIII, King of England, 9-10, 33, 56, 62, 78, 85-6, 131, 164
Hilles, Richard, 14-5, 41-2, 91, 94-5
History of Parliament Trust, 61-2, 69
Hoby, Sir Philip, 105
Hogan, Thomas, 63
Holstein, Duke of, 58
Hooper, John, Bishop of Worcester, 104, 109-10
Hopton, Ralph, 66
Hopton, Robert, 66
Horne, Dr. Robert, 125, 128
Horton, Walter, 63
Howard of Effingham, Lord Chamberlain, 33, 52, 62-3, 80, 129
Howard, Sir George, 63
Howard, Thomas, Viscount Howard of Bindon, 79

Ireland, 23, 139

Jewel, Revd Dr. John, Bishop of Salisbury, 10, 15, 36, 67-8, 74, 114,
    123, 125, 127, 131, 137-8, 140, 157, 158-9, 170
Jobson, Sir Francis, 70-1, 109-10, 112, 177
Jugge, Richard, 39, 121
Julius III, Pope, 28

Kelleway, Sir William, 35
Killigrew, Sir Henry, 57

Kingsmill, Richard, 71, 105
Knolles, Henry, 14
Knollys, Sir Francis, 34, 62-5, 89, 91, 93
Knox, John, 12-14, 154

Lainez, Father, 11
Lee, Sir Richard, 55
Lee, Sir Thomas, Lord Mayor of London, 42
Lever, Thomas, 13, 41, 131
Litany, 38-9, 43-4, 89
Lords of the Congregation, 166
Lords, House of
   1559:
      membership of, 72-82; use of proxies in, 81; 2nd bill for
      supremacy in, 96-7, 99-103, 113; 3rd bill for supremacy in,
      140-44; bill for uniformity in, 145-51
   1563:
      and Act of Assurance of the Queen's authority, 175-6
Lutheranism, see Augsburg Confession

Machyn, Henry, 49
Montague, Viscount, see Browne, Anthony
Markham, Thomas, 7
Martyr, Peter, 10, 67, 90, 92, 114, 137, 152
Mary Stuart, Queen of Scotland, 5, 52
Mary, Queen of England, 5, 7, 9, 10-11, 23, 26-9, 31-4, 52, 54, 65-6,
   71, 77, 79, 85-8, 90, 104-6, 110-11, 141, 160, 171, 173-4, 188;
   parliaments of, 26-9, 52, 54; validity of writs calling her parliaments,
   85-8
Mason, Sir John, 32, 105, 119
May, William, 24, 49
Melanchthon, Philip, 117
Mordaunt, Lord, 80
Mountjoy, Lord, 35
Mundt, Christopher, 56
Murren, John, chaplain to Bishop of London, 40

Netherlands, Spanish, 50-1, 55
Neville, Sir Henry, 64-5, 105
Norfolk, Duke of, 19, 63, 150
North, Lord, 107
Northampton, Marquis of, see Parr, William
Northumberland, Earl of, see Percy, Thomas
Nowell, Alexander, 14

Ogelthorpe, Owen, Bishop of Carlisle, 43-4, 46, 99
ornaments rubric, 135-6, 169
Otto Henry, Count Palatine, 57

Paget, Lord William, 27-8, 33, 80
Parker, Matthew, Archbishop of Canterbury, 24, 47-9, 68, 97, 125,
    136, 151-2, 157-8, 170, 177-8
Parkhurst, John, Bishop of Norwich, 170
Parliament, *see also* Commons; Lords
    of Queen Mary, 26-9, 85-8; writs, 1559, 21, 32; preparations for,
    1559, 47; petitions Elizabeth to marry, 1559, 59; membership of,
    1559, 61-82; Elizabeth intended to dissolve before Easter, 114-
    22; reconvenes after Easter, 139; Bacon speaks at closing, 1559,
    159; of 1563, finishes business of 1559, 169; Protestants in, 185-
    7; Catholics in, 186; Puritans in, 186-7;
Parr, Catherine, 8, 33
Parr, William, Marquis of Northampton, 24, 33, 79
Parry, Sir Thomas, 7, 33, 56, 151
Parrys, Thomas, 41
Parsons, Robert, *see* Persons, Robert
Pates, Richard, Bishop of Worcester, 109, 112
Paul IV, Pope, 6, 29, 52-4, 60, 96, 122
Paulet, William, Marquis of Winchester, 32, 34, 37-8, 107, 117, 175
Pembroke, Earl of, 24, 32, 79, 100, 105, 139
Percy, Sir Henry, 56
Percy, Thomas, Earl of Northumberland, 54, 71, 80, 109, 175
Perry, Sir Thomas, 106
Persons, Robert, 127, 150
Petre, William, secretary, 33
Philip II, King of Spain, 5, 9, 11, 27, 29, 50-3, 75, 119, 150-1, 172,
    174
Pickering, Sir William, 59
Pike, Thomas, 37
Pilkington, James, Bishop of Durham, 14, 24, 49, 71
Polantus, Vitus, 57
Pole, David, Bishop of Peterborough, 77-8
Pole, Reginald, Cardinal, 26, 28-9, 75, 77-8, 107, 160
Ponet, John, Bishop of Winchester, 87, 104-6
Privy Council, 18-9, 24, 32-4, 37-42, 47, 54-5, 60, 81, 124, 127,
    128-9, 139, 160
Proclamation:
    accession, 35-6; prohibiting unlicensed preaching, 38-9; captains
    and soldiers to return to the frontier, 55; for receiving communion
    in both kinds, 101-2, 114, 120-2; 'staying interludes', 139

Protestants:
    attitude toward Elizabeth, 12; varying plans for the church in England, 12-16; exiles, 12-14, 63-5; economic incentives for, 16; end of persecution, 34-5; controlled by the Privy Council, 37-42; German Princes, 56-8; in Parliament, 63-9, 72, 75, 102; modify supremacy bill, 98; debate with Catholics, 123-9; impatient for reform, 138-9; prepare declaration of doctrine, 152-5; unresolved concerns of, 158-9; expect further reform in 1563, 169-71; seek harsh penalties against Catholics, 171-6
Pulleyn, preacher, 41
Puritans, 2-4, 98, 169, 170-1, 183, 185
    in House of Commons, 61, 63-72; 'Choir', 66-7; and Act of Exchange, 167-8

Quadra, de, Spanish Ambassador, 172-5

Read, Conyers, 31, 34, 63
'Reformatio Legum Ecclesiasticarum', 98-9
Ribadeniera, Peter de, 11
Riche, Lord Richard, 18, 21, 33, 37, 107-8
Ridley, Nicholas, Bishop of London, 104, 107-8, 152
Rishton, Edward, 131, 150
Rogers, Sir Edward, Comptroller of the Household, 33, 64
Russell, Francis, Earl of Bedford, 17, 19, 24, 33-4, 63, 68, 71, 73, 81, 100, 141
Rutland, Earl of, 63

Sackville, Sir Richard, 33, 105, 127, 161
St. John of Bletso, Lord, 79
Sampson, Thomas, 170
Sampson, Richard, Bishop of Coventry and Lichfield, 110
Saunders, Nicholas, 1, 61, 99, 127-8, 129, 131, 150
Sandys, Dr. Edmund, 36, 68, 97, 131, 136, 151-2, 157, 158, 170, 184
Saunders, Thomas, 69
Saye, William, 34
Schifanoya, Il, 37, 40, 42-4, 46, 88, 96-7, 101, 116, 120-2, 125, 164
Scot, Cuthbert, Bishop of Chester, 100-1, 145-6
Scotland, 23, 50, 52-6
Serjeants Inn, 85-6
Seymour, Edward, Earl of Hertford, 79
Seymour, Sir Henry, 105
'Short Treatise of Politike Power', 87
Shory, John, 37

Shrewsbury, Earl of, 32, 100, 103
Smith, Sir Thomas, 7, 22, 47
Spain, 50-3
Spalding, James C., 99
Stafford, Lord, 107
Starkey, Thomas, 136
Statutes:
    23 Hen. VIII, c. 20, payment of annates, 115
    25 Hen. VIII, c. 20, annates, 115
    26 Hen. VIII, c. 13, treasons, 85
    26 Hen. VIII, c. 17, ecclesiastical leases, 162
    28 Hen. VIII, c. 10, ending pope's authority, 171
    28 Hen. VIII, c. 11, spiritual leases, 167
    33 Hen. VIII, c. 8, against witchcraft and sorcery, 182
    35 Hen. VIII, c. 1, 85
    37 Hen. VIII, c. 4, dissolution of chantries, 163
    1 Ed. VI, c. 1, protecting sacrament of the alter, 130, 133-4
    1 Ed. VI, c. 2, election of bishops, 115
    1 Ed. VI, c. 12, treasons, 171
    5 & 6 Ed. VI, c. 3, for keeping holy days, 155-6
    1 & 2 Phil. & Mary, c. 8, repealing Acts against See of Rome, 28, 86
    1 Eliz. I, c. 1, supremacy, *see* Supremacy, Act of
    1 Eliz. I, c. 2, uniformity, *see* Uniformity, Act of
    1 Eliz. I, c. 3, recognizing Elizabeth's title, 88
    1 Eliz. I, c. 4, first fruits and tenths, 88, 160-2
    1 Eliz. I, c. 5, treasons, 88
    1 Eliz. I, c. 16, unlawful assemblies, 116
    1 Eliz. I, c. 19, Act of exchange, 140, 165-7, 177
    1 Eliz. I, c. 20, tonnage and poundage, 88
    1 Eliz. I, c. 23, restoring Elizabeth in blood, 88
    1 Eliz. I, c. 24, dissolving monasteries, 162-5
    1 Eliz. I, original act #34, assurance of the lands of the bishopric of Winchester to patentees, 105-7
    5 Eliz. I, c. 1, Assurance of the Queen's power, 171-6
    5 Eliz. I, c. 15, against prophecies, 182-3
    5 Eliz. I, c. 16, against witchcraft, 182-3
    5 Eliz. I, c. 17, against sodomy, 182-3
    5 Eliz. I, c. 26, execution of writs de excommunicato capiendo, 180-1
    5 Eliz. I, c. 28, Welsh prayerbook, 176-7
Story, Dr. John, 40, 69, 90, 107, 186
Strickland, William, 66
Strype, John, 23, 49, 108

Sudbury, 63
Supremacy, Act of, 2, 115, 118-19, 157, 163, 171
    first bill for, 89-103; second bill for, 129-34; third bill for, 140-4;
    Irish Act of, 134
Sussex, Earl of, Lord Deputy of Ireland, 139

Thirlby, Thomas, Bishop of Ely, 10, 80, 100
Throckmorton, Clement, 63
Throckmorton, John, 109
Throckmorton, Sir Nicholas, 17-19, 37, 64-5, 76, 109
Thynne, Sir John, 8
Tiepolo, Paulo, Venetian ambassador in Brussels, 132
Tunstal, Cuthbert, Bishop of Durham, 78-9, 110, 150

Uniformity, Act of, 2-3, 74, 84, 117-20, 157, 159, 177
    first bill for, 89, 91-3; second bill (combined with supremacy), 89,
    91-8; third bill for, 134-7; Irish act for, 134

Vergerio, Paul, councillor to Duke of Württemberg, 57
Visitation Injunctions, 1559, 122, 169
Vivaldino, Ottaviano, 101, 121

Waad, Armagill, 17, 19-20, 58, 166
Waldegrave, Sir Edward, 62
Wales, 139, 176-7
Walsingham, Francis, 64-5
Warmington, Robert, 34
Watson, Thomas, Bishop of Lincoln, 74, 126-8, 150
Wentworth, Lord, 80, 107
Westminster, Abbot of, see Feckenham, John
Westminster Disputation, 115, 120, 123-9, 139
Weston, Richard, Solicitor General, 71, 144
Weston, Dr. Robert, Dean of the Court of Arches, 71
White, John, Bishop of Winchester, 11, 36, 74, 77, 89, 105-7, 125-8,
    150
White, Sir Thomas, 93
Whitehead, David, 24, 49, 68, 97
Williams, Thomas, Speaker in 1563, 178
Winchester, Bishop of, see White, John
Winchester, Marquis of, see Paulet, William
Winter, William, Lord Admiral, 184
Wotton, Nicholas, Dean of Canterbury, 18, 32
Wrothe, Sir Thomas, 62, 64-5, 68
Würtemburg, Duke of, 6, 57

Wyatt's Rebellion, 7, 66

Zouche, Sir John, 35
Zwingli, Huldrich, 152

Other volumes in this series

1   The Politics of Stability: A Portrait of the Rulers   *Frank F. Foster*
       in Elizabethan London

2   The Frankish Church and The Carolingian   *Rosamond McKitterick*
       Reforms 789-895

3   John Burns   *Kenneth D. Brown*

4   Revolution and Counter-Revolution in Scotland,   *David Stevenson*
       1644-1651

5   The Queen's Two Bodies: Drama and the   *Marie Axton*
       Elizabethan Succession

6   Great Britain and International Security,   *Anne Orde*
       1920-1926

7   Legal Records and the Historian   *J. H. Baker (ed.)*

8   Church and State in Independent Mexico: *Michael P. Costeloe*
       A Study of the Patronage Debate 1821-1857

9   An Early Welsh Microcosm: Studies in the   *Wendy Davies*
       Llandaff Charters

10   The British in Palestine: The Mandatory   *Bernard Wasserstein*
       Government and the Arab-Jewish Conflict

11   Order and Equipoise: The Peerage and the   *Michael McCahill*
       House of Lords, 1783-1806

12   Preachers, Peasants and Politics in Southeast   *Norman Etherington*
       Africa 1835-1880: African Christian
       Communities in Natal, Pondoland and
       Zululand

13   Linlithgow and India: A Study of British Policy   *S. A. G. Rizvi*
       and the Political Impasse in India 1936-1943

14   Britain and her Buffer State: The Collapse of the   *David McLean*
       Persian Empire, 1890-1914

15   Guns and Government: The Ordnance Office   *Howard Tomlinson*
       under the Later Stuarts

16   Denzil Holles 1598-1680: A Study of his Political   *Patricia Crawford*
       Career

17   The Parliamentary Agents: A History   *D. L. Rydz*

18   The Shadow of the Bomber: The Fear of Air   *Uri Bialer*
       Attack and British Politics 1932-1939

19   La Rochelle and the French Monarchy: *David Parker*
       Conflict and Order in Seventeenth-
       Century France

20 The Purchase System in the British Army   *A. P. C. Bruce*
    1660-1871

21 The Manning of the British Navy during   *Stephen F. Gradish*
    The Seven Years' War

22 Law-Making and Law-Makers in British History   *Alan Harding (ed.)*

23 John Russell, First Earl of Bedford: *Diane Willen*
    One of the King's Men

24 The Political Career of Sir Robert Naunton   *Roy E. Schreiber*
    1589-1635

25 The House of Gibbs and the Peruvian   *W. M. Mathew*
    Guano Monopoly

26 Julian S. Corbett, 1854-1922: Historian of British   *D. M. Schurman*
    Maritime Policy from Drake to Jellicoe

27 The Pilgrimage of Grace in the Lake Counties,   *S. M. Harrison*
    1536-1537

28 Money, Prices and Politics in Fifteenth-   *Angus MacKay*
    Century Castile

29 The Judicial Bench in England 1727-1875:   *Daniel Duman*
    The Reshaping of a Professional Elite

30 Estate Management in Eighteenth-Century England: *J. R. Wordie*
    The Building of the Leveson-Gower Fortune

31 Merchant Shipping and War: A Study of   *Martin Doughty*
    Defence Planning in Twentieth-Century Britain

Copies obtainable on order from
Swift Printers Ltd, 1-7 Albion Place, Britton Street, London EC1M 5RE